DATE DUE

GAYLORD			PRINTED IN U.S.A.

CONTEMPORARY GERMAN FICTION

The profound political and social changes Germany has undergone since 1989 have been reflected in an extraordinarily rich range of contemporary writing. *Contemporary German Fiction* focuses on the debates that have shaped the politics and culture of the new Germany that has emerged from the second half of the 1990s onwards and offers the first comprehensive account of key developments in German literary fiction within their social and historical context. Each chapter begins with an overview of a central theme, such as East German writing, West German writing, writing on the Nazi past, writing by women and writing by ethnic minorities. The authors discussed include Günter Grass, Ingo Schulze, Judith Hermann, Christa Wolf, Christian Kracht and Zafer Şenocak. These informative and accessible readings build up a clear picture of the central themes and stylistic concerns of the best writers working in Germany today.

STUART TABERNER is Professor of Contemporary German Literature, Culture and Society at the University of Leeds. He is the author of *German Literature of the 1990s and Beyond* (2005) and the editor of *German Literature in the Age of Globalisation* (2004).

CAMBRIDGE STUDIES IN GERMAN

General editors
H. B. Nisbet, *University of Cambridge*
Martin Swales, *University of London*

Advisory editor
Theodore J. Ziolkowski, *Princeton University*

Also in the series

J. P. STERN: *The Dear Purchase: A Theme in German Modernism*

SEÁN ALLAN: *The Plays of Heinrich von Kleist: Ideals and Illusions*

W. E. YATES: *Theatre in Vienna: A Critical History, 1776–1995*

MICHAEL MINDEN: *The German 'Bildungsroman' Incest and Inheritance*

TODD KONTJE: *Women, the Novel, and the German Nation 1771–1871 Domestic Fiction in the Fatherland*

STEPHEN BROCKMANN: *Literature and German Reunification*

JUDITH RYAN: *Rilke, Modernism and Poetic Tradition*

GRAHAM FRANKLAND: *Freud's Literary Culture*

RONALD SPIERS: *Brecht's Poetry of Political Exile*

NICHOLAS SAUL: *Philosophy and German Literature, 1700–1990*

STEPHANIE BIRD: *Women Writers and National Identity: Bachmann, Duden, Özdamar*

MATTHEW BELL: *The German Tradition of Psychology in Literature and Thought, 1700–1840*

CONTEMPORARY GERMAN FICTION

Writing in the Berlin Republic

EDITED BY

STUART TABERNER

CAMBRIDGE
UNIVERSITY PRESS

CAMBRIDGE UNIVERSITY PRESS
Cambridge, New York, Melbourne, Madrid, Cape Town, Singapore, São Paulo

Cambridge University Press
The Edinburgh Building, Cambridge CB2 8RU, UK

Published in the United States of America by Cambridge University Press, New York

www.cambridge.org
Information on this title: www.cambridge.org/9780521860789

© Cambridge University Press 2007

First published 2007

Printed in the United Kingdom at the University Press, Cambridge

A catalogue record for this publication is available from the British Library

ISBN 978-0-521-86078-9 hardback

Contents

Contributors

STEPHEN BROCKMANN, Carnegie Mellon University

PAUL COOKE, University of Leeds

INGO CORNILS, University of Leeds

SABINE VON DIRKE, University of Pittsburgh

FRANK FINLAY, University of Leeds

BRIGID HAINES, University of Wales, Swansea

BILL NIVEN, Nottingham Trent University

MARGARET LITTLER, University of Manchester

LYN MARVEN, University of Liverpool

ERIN McGLOTHLIN, Washington University

MORAY McGOWAN, Trinity College, Dublin

HELMUT SCHMITZ, University of Warwick

STUART TABERNER, University of Leeds

Acknowledgments

Without the support of a British Academy Small Research Grant, this volume would have been a less ambitious and far less coherent endeavour. The generosity of the British Academy made it possible for the various people involved in this project to meet to exchange ideas and to work towards the completion of this book.

I am especially grateful, of course, to all the contributors to the volume for their hard work and forbearance with my editing. I would also like to thank my PhD student, Giles Harrington, for his careful indexing and comments on the manuscript. As always, I am indebted to my colleagues at Leeds, and particularly to Professor Frank Finlay for his advice and encouragement throughout.

Note on texts and terminology

Unless otherwise specified, translations from the German are the chapter author's own. Throughout this volume we have followed the convention of using 'East' and 'West' to refer to the pre-1989 German states and 'east' and 'west' to refer to the post-unification regions.

CHAPTER I

Introduction: literary fiction in the Berlin Republic

Stuart Taberner

On 19 April 1999 the parliament of the Federal Republic of Germany (FRG) was convened in the Reichstag (assembly building) in central Berlin as an all-German body for the first time in fifty-eight years during a ceremony to mark the transfer of the capital from the west German city of Bonn. The same occasion also celebrated the conclusion of Sir Norman Foster's dramatic renovation of an edifice which, in 1894, had been inaugurated as the seat for the congress of the first unified German state created in 1870–1, and which had witnessed some of the key moments in the drama of German history during the Wilhelmine period, the First World War, the Weimar Republic and the Nazi dictatorship. Some eight and a half years after the unification of 3 October 1990, the symbolic return to Berlin, marked in a historic structure which had remained derelict since the nation's defeat in 1945, confirmed for many of those watching that the Berlin Republic had finally come into existence.

Norman Foster's innovative redesign for the Reichstag proclaims the values that are to be associated with the 'new' Germany. The glass cupola set upon its nineteenth-century skeleton containing galleries from which the public is able to peer down into the debating chamber thus symbolises a very contemporary commitment to the ideal of democratic transparency. At the same time, the preservation of physical traces of the fighting that had raged around the building during the final days of the Second World War formalises an undertaking to integrate the past, and especially the Nazi period, into the historical consciousness of the present. The Berlin Republic, it seems, is to be characterised by an awareness of the failings of German history, to be sure, but also by the completion of the post-war project for a free, sovereign nation that, in one reading of the history of the 'old' Federal Republic of Germany (FRG, West Germany) and the German Democratic Republic (GDR, East Germany), had been thwarted by division and the Cold War.

The extent to which post-unification Germany has lived up to its promise
to realise democratic rights, tolerance and inclusiveness for all may be
questioned, of course. Indeed, many of the texts discussed in this volume
do precisely that: literary fiction is uniquely suited to probing and subverting a public-political discourse which is itself fashioned out of clever
words, seductive images, convenient metaphors and institutionalised slogans, whether by means of careful deconstruction, an instructive pleasure in
the paradoxical, juxtaposition, subtle irony, mocking parody, biting satire,
or even hyper-imitation. In the age of the internet and digital revolutions
and against the background of the media obsession with the soundbite, it
would be going too far to claim that literature – that is, books – can act
as a fail-safe guarantor of democratic principles, but it can serve to deflate
overblown rhetoric and to undermine official representations of reality.
Or, more modestly, literary texts may explore more subjective processes
often marginalised within dominant constructions of a society's political,
philosophical and cultural self-understanding, such as the relationship of
private memory to public remembrance, the significance of different ethnicities and heritages, or the role of gender and sexuality in shaping personal
identity.

One of the most obvious indicators of the way in which culture remains
at a distance from a mode of characterising social reality which establishes
periods relating to the 'before' and 'after' of key political events or to categories shaped by political and cultural institutions, commerce or the media
is its disregard for the terms employed by these discourses. Politicians, then,
might speak of a new dawn in Germany's relationship to its history or of its
new global role. Or, journalists and social commentators might use labels
such as the Berlin Republic and imagine that these define distinct shifts,
particular moments when individuals began to experience their reality differently. Yet fiction deals first and foremost with those turning points that
are significant for its characters, its plot and its aesthetic coherence; the
issues which exercise its protagonists may well be related to debates seen
as defining for an era, but these debates are inflected in ways that desta-
bilise or even entirely erase their parameters. Literary texts, as the chapters
in this volume demonstrate, may happen to be written *in* something that
scholars choose to call the Berlin Republic – though, more often than
not, fiction anticipates trends that academic observers later distill into
frequently reductive tags, e.g. 'restoration', 'Bonn Republic', 'post-
unification', and so on – but these do not constitute the literature *of* the
Berlin Republic.

INTEGRATION, NORMALISATION AND GLOBALISATION

Certainly, a great many German-language texts written in the first half of the 1990s in anticipation of an entity dubbed the Berlin Republic, or, following the widespread perception that such a thing might now actually exist, from the middle of the decade onwards, *do* engage with three key terms which, arguably, have defined public-political discourse in the period, namely integration, normalisation and globalisation. A number of the chapters in this volume, correspondingly, relate works of fiction to the categories established by these terms. Narratives by writers from the east, for example, are explored with reference to a particular understanding of the challenges of 'incorporating' the former GDR; in a complementary chapter, texts by *west* German authors are read as alluding to ruminations on the legacy of the 'old' FRG. Alternatively, other contributions refer to debates on the question of whether the Nazi era can be 'normalised' or 'historicised', that is, viewed with the same empathetic understanding as any other period in the past – this issue has implications for the Berlin Republic, of course.[1] And finally, several chapters examine the way a range of writers reflect on the manner in which welfare reform and economic liberalisation are presented as inevitable and necessary within a globalised, neo-liberal marketplace.

What German-language literature in the Berlin Republic does most effectively, however, is to reconceive and reposition such terms in a manner which detaches them from the abstractions of public-political discourse and confronts them with the lived experience of the people with whom they purport to be concerned. In a number of texts, then, the rhetoric of integration and social solidarity employed by politicians and social commentators with regard to the former East Germany[2] is both disrupted and nuanced by an insistence on individuals' ability to reimagine and resituate their biographies within changed circumstances. Ingo Schulze's bestseller *Simple Storys* (1998), with its deliberately 'misspelt' title and its series of snapshots of life in the 'east German province', might be taken as illustrative of this trend. Elsewhere, however, a focus on subjectivity, memory and diverse traditions deconstructs the narrow emphasis within the public-political sphere on the ex-GDR. A variety of recent narratives undermine the homogenising aspirations of the integration imperative not in respect of the former East Germany but with regard to ethnic minorities perhaps, or to different groups of immigrants. Here, we might mention *Gefährliche Verwandtschaft* (Perilous Kinship, 1998)[3] or *German Amok* (2002),[4] by

Turkish-German authors Zafer Şenocak and Feridun Zaimoğlu respectively, or the short novel *Esra* (2003) by Maxim Biller,[5] a German-Jewish writer born in the former Czechoslovakia, all of which explore the triangulation of Christians, Jews and Turks within (west) Germany's liberal yet stubbornly non-multicultural 'consensus'. Or, we might draw attention to authors with roots in eastern European countries such as Herta Müller, Richard Wagner, Libuše Moníková, Carmen-Francesca Banciu and Terézia Mora. Once again, a focus on the often tangled interaction of individual life-stories, heritages and cultural contexts blurs the parameters of established discourses.

Similarly, contemporary literary texts may allude to the ongoing discussions in the public-political sphere of the need for a 'normalisation' of Germany's relationship to its past and of its role in world affairs. Thus they often reference the newly elected SPD–Green coalition's decision in early 1999 to join NATO's intervention in Kosovo or, for example, the controversies surrounding the construction of a Holocaust memorial in Berlin, the exhibition 'War of Annihilation: Crimes of the *Wehrmacht* 1941–1944', author Martin Walser's 1998 *Friedenspreisrede* (Peace-Prize speech) attacking the 'instrumentalisation' of Auschwitz 'for present-day political purposes',[6] or the re-emergence of interest in 'German wartime suffering' at the end of the 1990s. F. C. Delius's *Die Flatterzunge* (The Flutter-Tongue, 1999), Ulla Hahn's *Unscharfe Bilder* (Blurred Images, 2003) or Uwe Timm's *Am Beispiel meines Bruders* (In My Brother's Shadow, 2003) might be cited here. Yet, once more, an emphasis on memory and identity explores the significance of the Nazi era for 'real people' rather than simply its function as a foil to the legitimacy of the Berlin Republic. Different questions materialise which engage with more profound issues regarding human nature, the balance between empathy and forgiveness, conscience and the problem of perspective. In other texts, in contrast, alternative 'normalities' emerge. Memories of life in the ex-GDR, as presented in Falko Hennig's *Alles nur Geklaut* (Everything is Stolen, 1999) perhaps, or of a youth spent in the West Germany of the 1980s, as found, for example, in David Wagner's *Meine nachtblaue Hose* (My Night-blue Trousers, 2000), might thus seem more important than the legacy of Nazism.

Finally, relating to the prevailing public-political discourse on globalisation, a substantial corpus of today's German-language writing sabotages the rhetoric of the necessity of a particular form of economic liberalisation by emphasising the durability of memory, once again, and the immediacy of the local. Some contemporary literary texts, then, subvert global capitalism's demand that local populations adapt to its dictates and emphasise their ability to shape their own appropriation of a seemingly homogeneous 'American' culture in a manner which is creative and playful and which preserves a degree of subjective integrity.[7] Schulze's *Simple Storys* might be tendered again, as might Georg Klein's *Libidissi* (1999). In *Libidissi*, the natives of a mysteriously indeterminate metropolis – east Berlin, perhaps – fashion a profitably hybrid culture out of their canny (mis)appropriations of the offerings of global capitalism and their own heritage.[8] Or, we might make mention of writers linked to the so-called 'Trash' and 'Slam' scenes of the early 1990s, or to the 'new' German pop literature of the second half of the decade, such as Karen Duve, Elke Naters, Alexa Hennig von Lange, Tanja Dückers, Sibylle Berg, Christian Kracht or Silvia Szyman-ski. The self-conscious simulation of Anglo-American slang to be found in the work of younger pop authors, hinting, in fact, at the hollowing-out of identity, may paradoxically insinuate a very local, creative response to the self-alienation associated with global consumer culture. In the city and in the province, then, and amongst groups at the margins as much as amongst those who, superficially at least, appear most 'incorporated', different modes of aesthetic, intellectual or cultural resistance or moments of productive hybridity challenge globalisation's supposed erasure of local identities and the individual's sense of rootedness.

MEMORY, POLITICAL CORRECTNESS, GENERATION AND GLOBAL CULTURE

Much of what is most characteristic about German-language literature in the Berlin Republic emerges from what has been detailed above. Above all, contemporary writing in German, almost irrespective of the subject matter of individual texts, explores the lived experience of its protagonists and examines issues of subjectivity, memory and identity in a manner that is only indirectly contingent on a particular political context or an ideolog-ical or philosophical position taken with respect to this context in earlier decades. If large parts of what has become the widely accepted canon of post-war German-language literature had previously explored subjectivity first and foremost in relation to the imperfect democracy of the FRG or the autocracy of the GDR, the circumstances of the Cold War, division, the arms race, the destruction of the environment, or, perennially, the burden of the Nazi past, literary fiction in the Berlin Republic instead emphasises the importance of memory and personal identity as important issues in their own right. We might think here of Ralf Rothmann's *Milch und Kohle* (Milk and Coal, 2000), with its focus on working-class life in the 1950s,

or of Michael Kumpfmüller's *Hampels Fluchten* (The Adventures of a Bed
Salesman, 2000) and its absurdly affectionate image of the opportunism of
its protagonist, Heinrich Hampel, who quits the GDR for West Germany
and becomes a bed salesman before living up to his name as a 'jumping
Jack' (the meaning of 'hampeln') who flees his creditors and the women he
routinely seduces and betrays. Or, we might think of Kathrin Schmidt's *Die
Gunnar-Lennefsen-Expedition* (The Gunnar Lennefsen Expedition, 1998),
which explores both memory and female identity. Emine Sevgi Özdamar's
Seltsame Sterne starren zur Erde (Strange Stars Stare Toward Earth, 2003),
alternatively, exposes the layers of sedimented history both visible and
invisible in Berlin in a narrative that creates an affective bond between
the protagonist's idiosyncratic experience and the reader's own sensibility.
We might also think of the impressive wave of autobiographical works
since 1990, including Ludwig Harig's *Weh dem, der aus der Reihe tanzt*
(Woe Betide He who Dances Out of Step, 1990), Uwe Saeger's *Die Nacht
danach und der Morgen* (The Night After and the Morning, 1991), Ruth
Klüger's *weiter leben* (Still Alive, 1992), Günter de Bruyn's *Zwischenbilanz:
Eine Jugend in Berlin* (Interim Balance: A Youth in Berlin, 1992) and *Vierzig
Jahre: Ein Lebensbericht* (Forty Years: A Life-Report, 1996), Günter Kunert's
Erwachsenenspiele: Erinnerungen (Games for Grown-ups: Memories, 1997),
Christoph Hein's *Von allem Anfang an* (Right from the Beginning, 1997),
Grete Weil's *Leb ich denn, wenn andere leben* (I Live When Others Live,
1998), or Günter Grass's *Mein Jahrhundert* (My Century, 1999), which are
set in the Weimar period (de Bruyn's *Zwischenbilanz*), the Nazi era (de
Bruyn's *Zwischenbilanz*, Harig, Klüger and Weil), the GDR (Saeger, de
Bruyn's *Vierzig Jahre*, Kunert, Hein) or the FRG (Grass) but frequently
also ruminate on a variety of other, more subjective concerns.[9] Indeed,
modern-day German-language writing moves back and forth with greater
facility than ever before between its immediate context and more universal themes such as the texture of individual life-stories or the relationship
between memory, self-knowledge and conscience.

   To an extent, this development may be seen as a continuation of a shift in
the 1980s towards a greater attention to story-telling in both East and West
Germany – once again, the influence of the political caesura of 1989–90
should not be overestimated. Nevertheless, the *Wende* (political turn) in the
GDR in November 1989 and unification just under a year later *did* boost
the credibility of those who had long been complaining of German fiction's
knee-jerk engagement with its immediate social and political context, and
raised hopes of a new start for an all-German literary culture. The 1990
Literaturstreit (Literature Debate), sparked by the condemnation of Christa

Wolf by newspaper critics Ulrich Greiner and Frank Schirrmacher[10] and by Schirrmacher's subsequent 'taking-leave' of the literature of the 'old' FRG[11] and Greiner's dismissal of post-war fiction as *Gesinnungsästhetik* (aesthetics of conviction),[12] thus initiated a discussion of German writers' 'unhealthy' obsession with political themes. Both Greiner and Schirrmacher had been influenced by Karl Heinz Bohrer – 'the most important thinker of the aesthetic' in the German-speaking world according to Jan-Werner Müller[13] – who, from the mid 1980s, had been attacking West German writing's provinciality and lack of ambition. A few years later, commissioning editor Uwe Wittstock's plea for more entertainment and for a literature capable of competing with Anglo-Saxon bestsellers and their emphasis on characterisation and plot prompted reflection on the need for German authors to adapt to an international market.[14] Greiner and Schirrmacher's call for artistic complexity and a focus on the 'big' themes of literary fiction – the individual and society, the conflict between good and evil, or the tortured soul of the sensitive outsider – thus contrasted with Matthias Politycki's call for a *Neue Lesbarkeit* (new readability) to mirror the sounds, sensations and styles of the modern-day consumer universe.

The solutions offered by Greiner and Schirrmacher on the one hand, and by Uwe Wittstock and writers such as Matthias Politycki and Matthias Altenburg on the other, appear to be diametrically opposed: a return to the difficult, aesthetically demanding engagement with individual psychology and society typical of German Romanticism and Modernism or an altogether 'lighter' narrative fiction written for, and in order to ruminate upon, contemporary society. This contrast reflects, in part, different views on what a 'normal', unified Germany should look like. For critics of the supposed superficiality of the present-day FRG, what is needed is a return to the self-confident, 'European' metropolitan culture of the late nineteenth century; for those who bemoan German culture's lack of dynamism, what is required is an embrace of the Anglo-American present. Yet both visions of the future of German literature intersect in their fundamental censure, whether implied or explicit, of the institutionalisation of social engagement and critical thinking as the guiding principles of (West) Germany's intellectual and cultural consensus since the late 1960s.

This brings us to a second significant trend in contemporary German-language writing: a pervasive engagement with so-called political correctness and with the leading role played by the generation of '68 in shaping the intellectual and political conventions of both the 'old' FRG and the present-day Berlin Republic. The 68ers' focus on the Nazi past, their insistence on the lessons to be drawn from German perpetration of the Holocaust, and their claim to have embedded values of transparency, critical engagement and tolerance – all of these were challenged by conservatives (and not just by the intellectual New Right which caused such a furore in the early 1990s),[15] by the 78ers, that is, the generation that had grown up in the shadow of the student movement, and by a younger cohort variously known as the 89ers, the Generation Golf or the Generation Berlin.[16] Above all, the 68ers' tendency to focus on institutions, structures and the normative effect of power relations in both the Nazi period and modern-day society, and on abstract moral and philosophical principles, was subverted. In novels relating to the Nazi past, as already indicated, this often entails an empathetic presentation of 'real' peoples' limited perspective. Martin Walser's 1998 *Ein springender Brunnen* (The Springing Fountain), which relates the story of a young boy growing up between 1934 and 1945 in almost total indifference to the broader context of National Socialism, is a crucial example of this.[17] In present-day pop literature, alternatively, we find a provocative lack of interest in larger ethical issues and an often over-the-top affirmation of a status quo defined by consumerism, life-style, fads and fashions, and self-indulgence.

More important than specific political caesurae, therefore, although clearly influenced by the broader social and cultural impact of such turning points, is the centrality of the dialogue – or conflict – between the generations to today's German-language writing. This is apparent in the pervasiveness of 'intergenerational literature', that is, novels which both enact and reflect upon the 'memory contests' described by Anne Fuchs and Mary Cosgrove as characteristic of contemporary German culture and society.[18] The challenge to the purported dominance of the 68ers emerges, without a doubt, from a uniquely German constellation in which successive cohorts are distinctively and differently moulded by the fact of being born during the Nazi period, in the immediate post-'45 era, in the wake of '68, or perhaps in the years leading up to unification. Yet the desire to unsettle the values institutionalised by one particular generation, to reconnect with the biographies of grandparents about to pass away, or to proclaim the 'modern' values and attitudes of one's own generation, is by no means unique, in the 1990s and into the twenty-first century, to writing in the Berlin Republic. Once again, literary texts in the period examined in this volume frequently face both ways at once. On the one hand, they respond to the concerns of their immediate setting. On the other hand, they also address other, more universal issues to do with family dynamics in the modern-day world, the acceleration of shifts in social mores, sensibilities and fashions, and the apparent absence of shared, broadly accepted understandings of a given society's past or even its present.

A fourth characteristic of recent German-language writing is its incorporation of the ceaseless relativisation, or, put more positively, questioning, typical of western societies today. A number of works might be described as postmodern, if this is taken to mean a scandalous disregard for the boundaries between truth and invention; Thomas Brussig's *Helden wie wir* (Heroes Like Us, 1995) might be cited here. Elsewhere, however, it is possible to discern a more apprehensive, and more consequential, concern with epistemological issues. Younger east German writer Ingo Schramm's *Fitchers Blau* (Fitcher's Blue, 1996) and *Entzweigesperrt* (Trapped in Two, 2002), for example, offer a complex engagement with the philosophical traditions of the Enlightenment after the implosion of utopian thought in the post-communist period.[19] More generally, the frequency with which photographs feature may be indicative of a profound anxiety regarding the desire to reconnect with a twentieth-century history which is more exhaustively documented and visually present than any previous era but which remains largely incomprehensible to us in its arbitrary horror. W. G. Sebald's *Die Ausgewanderten* (The Exiles, 1992) and *Austerlitz* (2001) are prime instances of this phenomenon. Both works feature 'original' images which purport to validate their reconstruction of the biographies of their Jewish (occasionally, non-Jewish) subjects but which appear disconcertingly isolated within the flow of the text.[20] A similar focus on the philosophical and existential uncertainty produced by traumatic memories is typical of texts ranging from Monika Maron's *Pawels Briefe* (Pawel's Letters, 1999), a fictional reconstruction of the life, and death, of the author's grandfather, a Polish Jew murdered by the Nazis, to Herta Müller's account of persecution by the Romanian security services in *Herztier* (Heart Beast, 1994), to Kerstin Hensel's *Tanz am Kanal* (Dance by the Canal, 1994). In *Tanz am Kanal*, as in *Herztier*, traumatic recall, invention and present-day reality all merge, this time in the novel's depiction of Gabriela von Haßlau, a young east German woman who, having been raped and otherwise generally abused in the ex-GDR, ends up sleeping under a bridge after the *Wende* and begins to write her life-story.

Other contemporary novels similarly explore the emotional and intellectual resonances of memories located outside Germany, with the aim of reflecting on the claustrophobia of the Berlin Republic or, alternatively, on the suffocating uniformity of global (read: 'American') consumer culture. This is a fifth characteristic of today's German-language writing: its use of the world beyond Germany as a setting and its engagement with global influences. Examples range from Arnold Stadler's *Feuerland* (Fireland, 1992), in which the narrator travels to Patagonia only to find that things are exactly as at home, to Austrian writer Peter Handke's controversial travelogue *Eine winterliche Reise zu den Flüssen Donau, Save, Morawa und Drina oder Gerechtigkeit für Serbien* (A Winter's Journey to the Rivers Danube, Save, Morawa and Drina, or Justice for Serbia, 1996), which many read as a defence of Slobodan Milošević, to Judith Hermann's short story 'Rote Korallen', from her first collection *Sommerhaus, später* (Summerhouse, Later, 1998), which recreates the Russia of the Tsars in a tale of great passions, vivid colours, homesickness, melancholia and red corals. Stadler's and Hermann's work in particular reflect, in very different ways, on globalisation. In the title narrative of Hermann's second volume, *Nichts als Gespenster* (Nothing But Ghosts, 2003), Ellen and Felix travel across the vistas of the American west in the hope of finding release from the ambivalence of a modern German identity; in other stories, protagonists travel to France, Iceland, Sicily, Holland and the Czech Republic. In Katrin Dorn's *Tangogeschichten* (Tango Stories, 2002), narratives are set in Berlin as well as, unsurprisingly, Buenos Aires.[21] Elke Naters's pop novel *Mau-Mau* (2002), on the other hand, takes five friends on holiday to a paradise island where they compare suntans but are unable to conceal a more profound sense of emptiness.

In many ways, the ambivalence intimated in Hermann's 'Hurrikan (Something farewell)', from *Sommerhaus, später*, summarises the dilemma implicit in much of German language-writing in the Berlin Republic. A longing to escape the confines of German parochialism impels Kaspar, Nora and Cat to travel, once more, to a paradise Caribbean island where they can speak English, indulge in a self-satisfied celebration of ethnic diversity in their unequal flirtations with the local black population, and play a game of 'imagining a life just like this'.[22] Yet their fantasies of what it would be like to remain on the island cannot disguise the fact that Kaspar and Nora were unhappy back in Berlin or that Cat must soon return to Germany. The real story of which they had hoped to have been a part, moreover, has failed to materialise: the storm that threatens the island passes by and, again, nothing of consequence has happened in their lives. Even when Germans imagine that they might embrace the global consumer culture or imitate the unforced self-confidence of Anglo-American culture – as the narrative itself, with its allusions to Hemingway, affects to do – it seems that they nevertheless continue to experience themselves as onlookers.

GERMAN-LANGUAGE LITERATURE IN THE BERLIN REPUBLIC

The chapters in this volume were first presented at a workshop sponsored by the British Academy in London in late 2005. In the course of the debates which followed individual papers, the discussion returned time and again to the always highly mediated relationship between fiction and the labels used to mark a caesura or describe an era. In contrast with previous decades, much of German-language writing in the Berlin Republic is less concerned with the 'state of the nation' than with personal, subjective, local, physical, in a word, intractably specific experience. There are notable exceptions, of course, as the concern of a number of chapters with 'Berlin writing', West German writing, the former GDR, '68 or the Nazi past demonstrates. Just as important, the obsession with specificity examined elsewhere in this volume may in itself say something about the broader historical climate. In addition, two further difficulties were noted, which are of particular relevance to a collaborative project such as this. Most obviously, many of the works considered in one particular contribution might just as easily have featured elsewhere. Hans Ulrich Treichel's *Der Verlorene* (Lost, 1999), for example, is included in Bill Niven's discussion of Germans as perpetrators of Nazi crimes, but might also have appeared in Helmut Schmitz's examination of representations of 'German wartime suffering'. Similarly, Christoph Hein's *Landnahme* (Land Seizure, 2004) or Reinhard Jirgl's *Die Unvollendeten* (The Incomplete Ones, 2003), mentioned in Paul Cooke's chapter dealing with novels which take the ex-GDR as their theme, might have been investigated in terms of their depiction of the fate of Germans expelled from the east after 1945. Christian Kracht's *Faserland* (Frayed-Land, 1995), alternatively, is discussed in my piece on 'west German writing' but might have been explored in Sabine von Dirke's exposition of pop literature. Rafael Seligmann's *Der Musterjude* (The Model Jew, 1997) is cited in Erin McGlothlin's contribution on German-Jewish fiction; again, it would also have been possible to have presented this as a novel by a west German author that engages with debates on political correctness.

A related concern is the status of chapter titles. Thus headings which appear convenient in the preparation of a volume such as this may institutionalise the very categories that a significant proportion of the writers and texts examined seek to undermine. In respect of 'GDR literature' then, the designation 'east German' might unduly discount the universal significance of, say, Christa Wolf's exploration of youthful optimism, adult compromise and eventual melancholia in *Leibhaftig* (In Person, 2002), or predispose the reader of her *Medea. Stimmen* (Medea. Voices, 1996) to interpret her reworking of the Greek legend, featuring the victory of the western city of Corinth over the eastern kingdom of Colchis, exclusively as an idealistic, *post factum* justification of GDR socialism. The term 'west German writing' might similarly underestimate the striving of authors such as Martin Walser or Arnold Stadler to investigate human subjectivity more broadly and not just the parochialism of the (West) German state, or the ruminations of a writer such as Christian Kracht on a *global* consumer culture. Elsewhere in the volume, analogous concerns apply to the titles 'Turkish-German writers'; 'writing from eastern and central Europe', and 'writing by Germany's Jewish minority', which might be taken to imply the narrowness of the themes dealt with by the authors analysed in them or to impose a single identity on writers who frequently challenge ethnic and national descriptors. Just as difficult, the headline 'German wartime suffering' might seem to establish a degree of legitimacy for a concept which many would challenge. The title 'pop literature', alternatively, raises questions about genre, and the notion of 'writing by women' is inherently problematic: Christa Wolf, for example, is self-evidently a woman writer, but she is also an East German author and one who does not always or necessarily write 'like a woman' (even if this could be defined) – or, as discussed, even as an 'East German' – or on 'women's themes' (whatever these might be).

The theoretical considerations described above should be taken as understood throughout the contributions contained in this book. In what follows, I briefly outline the scope, contents and principal arguments of each of its thirteen chapters.

The volume begins with Frank Finlay's presentation of literary debates and changes in the literary market in the post-unification period. The 1990 *Literaturstreit*, the controversies regarding political correctness and the call for a return to German aesthetic traditions versus the plea for greater 'entertainment' and 'readability' on the Anglo-American model are contextualised within the longer trajectory of debates on the role of literature, and of writers, in the German-speaking lands reaching back to Lessing and beyond. Finlay argues that many of the literary *Streite* (controversies) of the post-unification period relate to the relationship between politics and writing, much as the debates of Lessing's epoch, the Romantic age, the nineteenth century, the Weimar Republic and the post-war era often did, but that the 1990s and beyond have brought new challenges for German-language fiction with regard to market share, product differentiation and an ever-more varied readership, and in respect of the viability of literature in the age of the internet, computer games and MTV. The focus of this chapter is on writers' interventions in the media, but many authors, of course, reflect on the same debates in their fiction. F. C. Delius's *Der Königsmacher* (The King-Maker, 2001), to cite but one example, presents an ageing, one-time politically-engaged novelist who finds that he is unable to compete with the stars of the 'pop scene', and especially those in possession of an aristocratic 'von' in their names (e.g. Alexander von Schönburg, Benjamin von Stuckrad-Barre and Alexa Hennig von Lange), with the marketing of a new generation of female writers with stylish photographs and melancholic poses as a *literarisches Fräuleinwunder* (literary girl-miracle), or with the 'East-Nostalgia' of 'the barkingly comic B.' (Thomas Brussig).[23]

Delius's *Der Königsmacher* is also a Berlin novel in so far as its narrator ruminates on the city's retrospective on Frederick the Great during its 'Prussia-Year' of 2001 and includes well-known locations such as the Tiergarten. In our next chapter, Stephen Brockmann starts out from the centrality of Berlin to a wide range of contemporary German-language writing but focuses on Günter Grass's *Ein weites Feld* (Too Far Afield, 1995) – the English translation of the title fails to capture Grass's allusion to nineteenth-century novelist Theodor Fontane's effort to depict in fiction the 'vast subject' of history and society ('ein weites Feld') – Thomas Brussig's *Helden wie wir*, Kerstin Hensel's *Falscher Hase* (False Hare, 2005) and Ulrike Draesner's short story 'Gina Regina' (2004). In spite of significant variations in form, narrative approach and plot, Brockmann contends, a focus on the city of Berlin since the fall of the Wall brings together authors of different generations and provenances in an examination of the success or otherwise of unification and in a more general exploration of the anomie of globalisation and the triumph of a metropolitan lifestyle based in the world's major cities but unique to none.

Paul Cooke's chapter on 'GDR writing in the Berlin Republic' examines the way in which the defunct socialist state features in contemporary German-language writing as a reminder of communitarian values in an altogether less idealistic age, a source of memories for a specifically east German identity, or, just as important, as biographical background for a younger generation. Christa Wolf is examined as an older writer who continues to defend aspects of the ex-GDR's aspirations, if not its reality; authors such as Volker Braun, with *Das Nichtgelebte* (The Unlived, 1995), *Der Wendehals* (The Turncoat, 1995), *Lustgarten Preußen* (Pleasure Garden Prussia, 1996) or *Das unbesetzte Gebiet* (The Unoccupied Region, 2004), or Christoph Hein, with *Das Napoleon-Spiel* (The Napoleon Game, 1993), *Exekution eines Kalbes* (Execution of a Calf, 1994) or *Willenbrock* (2000), might also have been considered. As a contrast to Wolf's idealism, Wolfgang

Hilbig's more sceptical appropriation of GDR values as a means to undermine the present-day Federal Republic is analysed, as are Thomas Brussig's
satires on east German identity after 1989 and the work of younger writers
including Jakob Hein, Falko Hennig and Jana Hensel. Not covered in this
chapter, but another key literary motif in 1990s' German-language fiction,
are those novels by *west* German writers which take the former GDR as
their theme, ranging from F. C. Delius's *Die Birnen von Ribbeck* (The Pears
of Ribbeck, 1991) and *Der Spaziergang von Rostock nach Syrakuse* (The Walk
from Rostock to Syracuse, 1995) to Karen Duve's *Regenroman* (Rain Novel,
1999).

My own chapter on 'west German writing' starts out from the growing
recognition that the 'old' FRG was also dramatically affected by unification and that present-day debates on the history, institutions and values of
the Bonn Republic are just as controversial as post-unification representations of the ex-GDR. I examine conflicting images of the pre-1990 Federal
Republic offered by different generations of writers and by authors with
different political views in order to explore contemporary ruminations on
'political correctness', the purported cultural hegemony of the 68ers, and
on the extent to which the Bonn Republic might serve as a model for the
Berlin Republic. In particular, I am concerned with the fate of a West German tradition of politically-engaged fiction, largely associated with writers
such as Günter Grass and 68ers such as Uwe Timm, F. C. Delius and Peter
Schneider in the context of the attacks launched on it by conservative critics
such as Schirrmacher, Greiner and Bohrer and by younger authors of the
'Generation of '78' and of the so-called Generation Golf. In a postscript
to the chapter, I briefly discuss the impact of Grass's admission, in August
2006, that he had been a member of the *Waffen SS* during the closing
months of the war, and argue that his *Beim Häuten der Zwiebel* (Peeling
the Onion), which appeared shortly after this confession, presents a robust
defence of the continued relevance both of Grass himself and of politically
engaged writing.

Literary reflections on the legacy of '68 are the particular focus of
Ingo Cornils's contribution. Focusing on texts which are almost certain to become canonical representations of this crucial period in West
German history, including Uwe Timm's *Rot* (Red, 2001) and Peter
Schneider's *Skylla* (Scylla, 2005), as well as on perhaps more ephemeral
works largely written in response to specific, very contemporary controversies regarding the meaning of '68 – the question of which texts will endure is
implicit in many chapters in this volume – Cornils once again highlights the
importance of the intergenerational dialogue to German-language writing

in the Berlin Republic. At the same time, he examines the way in which present-day literary portrayals of '68 expose, deconstruct but also reinscribe and expand the mythologisation of that heady era, and of the values linked to it.

Sabine von Dirke's chapter follows on from Cornils's examination of the legacy of '68 in so far as it explores the phenomenon of 'new German pop literature' from the mid 1990s as a reaction, in part at least, to the perceived hegemony of the 68ers. Von Dirke identifies key characteristics of a mode of writing which is at once hostile to the moralising political engagement of much of West German fiction from the late 1960s and yet simultaneously concerned with the alienating realities of the world in which its protagonists live. Popular culture, music, brand names, lifestyle, sex and drugs are central to the texts by, amongst others, Sibylle Berg, Joachim Bessing, Rainald Goetz, Christian Kracht, Thomas Meinecke, Elke Naters, Andreas Neumeister, Eckhart Nickel, Kathrin Röggla, Alexander Schönburg and Benjamin Stuckrad-Barre examined here, but this does not mean that they are necessarily 'trivial' (as implied by the pejorative German term *Trivialliteratur*). This is certainly true of texts such as Karen Duve's *Dies ist kein Liebslied* (This is not a Love Song, 2002), which narrates its protagonist's eating disorder against the background of pop songs from the 1980s, or Alexa Hennig von Lange's début novel *Relax* (1997), which depicts the techno scene of the 1990s whilst also staging an arguably only apparently naive discussion of postfeminism and women's continued (self-)oppression.

Bill Niven's chapter on representations of Germans as Nazi perpetrators and Helmut Schmitz's reflections on depictions of 'Germans as victims' are intended to be read together. The starting point for both is the series of debates on, for example, the Holocaust memorial, the *Crimes of the Wehrmacht* exhibition, Walser's 1998 Peace-Prize speech, or the proposal to build a Centre against Expulsions in Berlin. Once more, these controversies are linked to discussions of the political and cultural impact of the 68ers. Niven notes the absence of 'true' perpetrators in contemporary German-language writing and argues, with close reference to Thor Kunkel's *Endstufe* (Last Phase, 2004), Klaus Modick's *Der kretische Gast* (The Cretan Guest, 2003), Marcel Beyer's *Flughunde* (The Karnau Tapes, 1995), Ulrich Woelk's *Rückspiel* (Return Match, 1993) and Bernhard Schlink's *Der Vorleser* (The Reader, 1995), that novels dealing with German perpetration are more concerned with the question of *how* to depict the Nazi past than they are with the period itself. Helmut Schmitz, similarly, regards the detailed reconstruction of the trauma endured by soldiers on the eastern front or by civilians in the course of Allied airraids, expulsions, mass rapes and arbitrary killings, to be found in novels such as Dieter Forte's *Der Junge mit den blutigen Schuhen* (The Boy with the Bloody Shoes, 1995), Günter Grass's *Im Krebsgang* (Crabwalk, 2002), Ulla Hahn's *Unscharfe Bilder* or Uwe Timm's *Am Beispiel meines Bruders*, as part of what Cosgrove and Fuchs call a parallel 'memory contest' centred on what Harald Welzer has termed a 'family album' of private memories of 'German suffering' and a 'public lexicon' articulating German perpetration.[24]

Media discussion of the wave of 'war texts' from the late 1990s which reflected the contemporary era's more profound interest in individual fates during the Nazi period and its immediate aftermath has focused on works by male authors, such as W. G. Sebald's *Luftkrieg und Literatur* (Aerial Warfare and Literature, published in 1999), Grass's *Im Krebsgang* or Timm's *Am Beispiel meines Bruders*. Novels by women writers are generally overlooked, with the exception, perhaps, of Hahn's *Unscharfe Bilder*. This is the case, for example, with regard to Dagmar Leupold's *Nach den Kriegen* (After the Wars, 2004), a return to the *Väterliteratur* (father literature) of the late 1970s through to the mid 1980s which demonstrates great depth and psychological sophistication, or Tanja Dückers's *Himmelskörper* (Heavenly Bodies, 2003), which deals with the relationship of three generations to the German flight from eastern Europe at the end of the war and, similarly to *Im Krebsgang*, the sinking of the refugee ship *Wilhelm Gustloff*.

Lyn Marven's chapter on women writers begins with a discussion of the problems inherent in any discussion of female authors as a somehow entirely separate category. Above all, she notes the risk that women writers are considered solely *as* women and that their diversity is neglected. These concerns notwithstanding, Marven argues, women writers continue to receive less attention than they may deserve, partly through a lack of recognition and partly through parameters of study which minimise treatment of their work. Thus Marven refers to a range of writers, including Christa Wolf, Irina Liebmann, Monika Maron, Ulrike Kolb, Karen Duve, Tanja Dückers, Katja Lange-Müller, Julia Franck, Terézia Mora, Yadé Kara, Jeanette Lander, Franziska Gerstenberg, Judith Hermann, Emine Sevgi Özdamar, Melanie Arns – the list could be extended, of course, to include authors such as Felicitas Hoppe, Jenny Erpenbeck, Malin Schwerdtfeger, and many others – but focuses on three, Kathrin Schmidt, Kerstin Mlynkec and Ulrike Draesner, and in particular on the physicality of their prose, their use of irony and parody, and their inventive subversions of genre.

Margaret Littler investigates a number of texts that challenge a more or less institutionalised focus on the Nazi period as the primary source of 'cultural memory' in the Berlin Republic by making reference to the Ottoman or other histories of Germany's migrant communities, or the more ancient pasts sedimented in border zones or geological time, or the origins of so many German stories in eastern Europe. Zafer Şenocak's *Der Erottomane* (The Erot(t)omaniac, 1999), Emine Sevgi Özdamar's *Seltsame Sterne starren zur Erde* (Strange Stars Stare Towards Earth, 2003), Jan Böttcher's *Lina oder: Das kalte Moor* (Lina or: The Cold Moor, 2003), Judith Hermann's *Sommerhaus, später*, and Tanja Dückers's *Himmelskörper* are thus examined for the manner in which they deterritorialise memory and produce sensual affinities with other times and other places. (Malin Schwerdtfeger's *Café Saratoga* (2001), which tells of the sexual awakening of Sonia and of Sonia's endeavours to adapt following her family's move from Poland to West Germany just before unification, might offer a further example of the production of such 'affect'.)

Moray McGowan's contribution on Turkish-German fiction may be usefully read alongside Littler's, not least because these two chapters demonstrate how the same texts can be read in different ways and within different contexts. McGowan, then, traces the development of a sophisticated, polyphonic and diverse literature by German-language writers of Turkish origin and looks particularly at the fiction of Feridun Zaimoğlu, Emine Sevgi Özdamar and Zafer Şenocak as examples of a Turkish-German intervention in debates on the relationship between cultural and individual identity, on the interaction of the national and the global, and on the marking – and marketing – of 'ethnic difference'. Of particular interest are McGowan's explorations of Şenocak's *Der Erottomane* and Özdamar's *Seltsame Sterne starren zur Erde*, which, in contrast to Littler's readings, focus less on the deterritorialisation of memory than on the elaboration of alternative masculinities, in *Der Erottomane*, and, in *Seltsame Sterne Starren zur Erde*, on contemporary German-Turkish writing's highly self-reflexive engagement with its own traditions.

In the volume's penultimate chapter, Brigid Haines notes that whilst Turkish-German and German-Jewish writers have attracted a degree of scholarly attention, especially in the UK and the USA, the same is not true of authors from former eastern bloc countries in which, historically, there have existed significant German-speaking communities. Tracing the reception of a range of writers with links, for example, to Romania, the Czech Republic and Hungary, Haines focuses on four key novels: Libuše Moníková's *Verklärte Nacht* (Transfigured Night, 1996), Herta Müller's *Herztier* (Heart Beast, 1994), Zsuzsa Bánk's *Der Schwimmer* (The Swimmer, 2002) and Terézia Mora's *Alle Tage* (Every Day, 2004). In common with east German literature after the *Wende*, she argues, these texts critically assess what has been gained – and lost – since 1989; in common with Turkish-German writing, equally, they also challenge what it is to be German. Above all, however, Haines concludes, they bear witness to the turbulence of twentieth-century European history and to the traces left by the traumas of expulsion and migration on the collective psyche.

The negotiation of trauma is also the subject of the final contribution to the present collection, Erin McGlothlin's examination of writing by Germany's Jewish minority. Starting out from contemporary discussions of the apparent resurrection of the nineteenth-century dream (nurtured almost exclusively by Jews) of a 'German-Jewish symbiosis' in the wake of the flowering of fiction by Jews living in Germany or composing in German, McGlothlin demonstrates how such writing both exposes the contradictions inherent in Jewish life in Germany today and reflects on the very possibility of German-Jewish literature. This she does with particular reference to Barbara Honigmann's *Soharas Reise* (Zohara's Journey, 1996), Rafael Seligmann's *Der Milchmann* (The Milkman, 1999) and Maxim Biller's *Bernsteintage* (Amber Days, 2004). What McGlothlin detects is an emerging tendency to try and move beyond the fixed positions of the twentieth century in order to open up a more genuine dialogue between Jews and non-Jews in Germany, without, however, erasing the fact of the Holocaust for the sake of a spurious 'normalisation' of relations.

CONCLUSION

As the chapters in this volume demonstrate, German-language writing in the Berlin Republic is as diverse, multifaceted and multivocal as modern-day Germany itself. On the one hand, present-day German-language fiction participates in global discourses concerning the fate of 'authentic' identity, memory and subjectivity within an increasingly homogeneous consumer universe and in a world in which migration and the free flow of information and ideas have dissolved national boundaries and any notion of a unitary, 'unadulterated' cultural, philosophical and intellectual tradition. On the other hand, it frequently remains focused on 'German' themes: the Nazi period, the relationship between generations differently shaped by the German past, or precisely the question of what it means to be German in the globalised present. On the level of both form and content, the best of contemporary German-language literature negotiates precisely these tensions – the clash between the universal and the local, the metropolitan and the parochial, the transcendent and the banal, and the claims of an ever-more uniform global society and individual subjectivity. This is the source of its fascination and the reason why it continues to be worthy of our attention.

NOTES

1. See Stuart Taberner and Paul Cooke, eds., *German Culture, Politics and Literature into the Twenty-First Century: Beyond Normalization* (Rochester: Camden House, 2006).
2. See Paul Cooke, *Representing East Germany since Unification: From Colonization to Nostalgia* (Oxford: Berg, 2005) for a comprehensive analysis of discourses on the integration of the ex-GDR.
3. See Katharina Hall, '"Bekanntlich sind Dreiecksbeziehungen am kompliziertesten": Turkish, Jewish and German Identity in Zafer Şenocak's *Gefährliche Verwandschaft*', *German Life and Letters*, 56:1 (2003): 72–88.
4. See Stuart Taberner, *German Literature of the 1990s and Beyond* (Rochester: Camden House, 2005), 96–8.
5. See Stuart Taberner, 'Germans, Jews and Turks in Maxim Biller's Novel *Esra*', *German Quarterly*, 79:2 (2006), 234–48.
6. Martin Walser, *Erfahrungen beim Erfassen einer Sonntagsrede* (Frankfurt: Suhrkamp, 1998), 7–17, here 18.
7. See Stuart Taberner, ed., *German Literature in the Age of Globalisation* (Birmingham: Birmingham University Press, 2004).
8. See Stuart Taberner, 'A New Modernism or "Neue Lesbarkeit"? – Hybridity in Georg Klein's *Libidissi*', *German Life and Letters*, 55:2 (2002): 137–48.
9. See Owen Evans, *Mapping the Contours of Oppression: Subjectivity, Truth and Fiction in Recent German Autobiographical Treatments of Totalitarianism* (Amsterdam: Rodopi, 2006).
10. See Ulrich Greiner, 'Mangel an Feingefühl', *Die Zeit*, 1 June 1990. Collated in Thomas Anz, ed., '*Es geht nicht nur um Christa Wolf*': *Der Literaturstreit im vereinten Deutschland* (Munich: Spangenberg, 1991).
11. Frank Schirrmacher, 'Abschied von der Literatur der Bundesrepublik', *Frankfurter Allgemeine Zeitung*, 2 October 1990, LI, 2.
12. Ulrich Greiner, 'Die deutsche Gesinnungsästhetik', *Die Zeit*, 9 November 1990. In Thomas Anz, '*Es geht nicht nur um Christa Wolf*', 208–16.
13. Jan-Werner Müller, 'Karl Heinz Bohrer on German National Identity: Recovering Romanticism and Aestheticizing the State', *German Studies Review*, 23:2 (2000): 297–316, here 297.
14. Uwe Wittstock, *Leselust: Wie unterhaltsam ist die neue deutsche Literatur? Ein Essay* (Munich: Luchterhand, 1995), 8 and 10. Hereafter *LE*.
15. See Roger Woods, 'Affirmative Past Versus Cultural Pessimism: The New Right Since German Unification', *German Life and Letters*, 58:1 (2005): 93–107.
16. Thus the titles of the *Zeitgeist* publications *Generation Golf* (2000) by Florian Illies and *Generation Berlin* (2001) by Heinz Bude.
17. See Kathrin Schödel, 'Normalising Cultural Memory? The "Walser-Bubis-Debate" and Martin Walser's Novel *Ein springender Brunnen*' in Stuart

Taberner and Frank Finlay, eds., *Recasting German Identity* (Rochester: Camden House, 2002), 69–87.

18. See Anne Fuchs and Mary Cosgrove, eds., *Memory Contests*, special number of *German Life and Letters* (59:2 (2006)). See also Anne Fuchs, Mary Cosgrove and Georg Grote, eds., *German Memory Contests: The Quest for Identity in Literature, Film and Discourse since 1990* (Rochester: Camden House, 2006).

19. See Paul Cooke, 'Escaping the Burden of the Past: Questions of East German Identity in the Work of Ingo Schramm', *Seminar*, 27 (2003): 33–44.

20. See Jonathan Long, 'History, Narrative, and Photography in W. G. Sebald's *Die Ausgewanderten*', *The Modern Language Review*, 98 (2003): 117–37.

21. See Beth Linklater, 'Germany and Background: Global Concerns in Recent Women's Writing in German', in Stuart Taberner, ed., *German Literature in The Age of Globalisation*, 67–88.

22. Judith Hermann, 'Hurrikan (Something farewell)', in *Sommerhaus, später* (Frankfurt: Fischer, 1999), 31–54, here 44.

23. F. C. Delius, *Der Königsmacher* (Berlin: Rowohlt, 2001), 186, 79 and 142.

24. Harald Welzer, Sabine Moller and Caroline Tschuggnall, *Opa war kein Nazi: Nationalsozialismus und Holocaust im Familiengedächtnis* (Frankfurt: Fischer, 2002), 10.

CHAPTER 2

Literary debates and the literary market since unification

Frank Finlay

So musicall a discord, such sweete thunder.

Shakespeare

Kunst geht nach Brot.

Lessing

'Literature isn't a matter of life and death, it is more important than that.' In a discussion of public debates about literature and the literary market place in Germany since the *Wende* (the fall of the Berlin Wall), it is tempting to rework the deliberately ironic view of soccer attributed to a redoubtable manager of Liverpool Football Club. Literature in the Berlin Republic, as this chapter will show, matters very much indeed. Some of the major controversies of the 1990s and beyond have been sparked off by, and coalesced around, arguments about or between writers, their aesthetic *and* political views, as well as the *succès de scandale* of individual works. So piercing has the volume of debate been that it has attracted considerable national and international attention from professional critics and academics. Moreover, as a measure of perceived importance, many of the key texts published in the course of these high-profile literary battles – *Literaturstreite* – and associated, more broadly framed skirmishes, have been swiftly anthologised.

The first of these literary flashpoints ignited around the figure of Christa Wolf. Until unification in 1990, Wolf was acknowledged as one of post-war Germany's most significant authors in both the GDR, where she resided, and the FRG. She was the recipient of a host of literary accolades, including West Germany's prestigious Büchner Prize, and her works enjoyed high recognition abroad, had given rise to an admiring body of scholarship and had entered the canon of literature studied in institutions of higher learning around the world. Within a short period of time following the *Wende*, however, Wolf came to be regarded as representative of all that was wrong in the relationship between East German intellectuals and the state, and as a hapless purveyor of ideologically compromised verbiage. The ostensible trigger for the debate was Wolf's publication in the late spring of 1990 of the slim volume *Was bleibt* (What remains), a semi-autobiographical account of being spied upon by the security services (Stasi) in the aftermath of the GDR's expulsion of songwriter and poet Wolf Biermann in 1976. The considerable temporal remove between the events narrated, in 1979, and the release of the book led to Wolf being widely castigated. The delayed publication smacked of opportunism and, it was alleged, was a pathetic attempt to claim a heroic victim status.

The chorus of disapproval was led by broadsheet critics Ulrich Greiner and Frank Schirrmacher in the review sections of *Die Zeit* and the *Frankfurter Allgemeine Zeitung* (*FAZ*). Acres of newsprint were generated, and no fewer than two separate volumes documenting the furore appeared within a year, a pattern to be repeated in subsequent controversies.[1] There were strong echoes of the initial debate and renewed controversy following, respectively, revelations of Wolf's brief involvement as an irregular informer for the Stasi, the publication of a collection of her essays *Auf dem Weg nach Tabou* (On the Way to Taboo, 1994), and her novel *Medea. Stimmen* (Medea. Voices, 1996).[2] The baleful alliance with the GDR regime on the part of intellectuals such as Wolf, it was argued, had provided a corrupt state with ideological ballast and an underserved reputation abroad. This view was given additional impetus by later revelations regarding the co-operation of other East German writers with the Stasi, which were brought into sharp focus by Biermann's acceptance speech for the Büchner Prize of 1991.[3]

The widespread condemnation of Wolf provoked the perhaps predictable ire of West German leftist writers, including Günter Grass, who raced to her defence only to find himself arraigned on similar charges as the parameters of the dispute expanded rapidly during the summer months to embrace literature in both the ex-GDR and the pre-1990 Federal Republic. While Wolf functioned *pars pro toto* as a representative of allegedly compromised literary intellectuals under 'real existing socialism', writers in West Germany who had shared the formative experience of Nazism and who regarded their literary writing as a form of public-political intervention were also soon to be tarred with the same brush. Two documents, in particular, highlight the way the debate mutated: Frank Schirrmacher's programmatic 'leave-taking' from both the literature of the GDR and of the 'old' Federal Republic, which was published in the *FAZ* on 2 June 1990, the eve of unification (and the Frankfurt Book Fair!), and Ulrich Greiner's dismissal, just over a month later on the first anniversary of the *Wende* on 9 November 1990, of German authors' preoccupation with politics as *Gesinnungsästhetik* (aesthetics of conviction). A generation of writers who had regarded their fiction as a vehicle for influencing political culture, including such internationally recognised figures as Wolf, Nobel laureate Heinrich Böll and Günter Grass, thus had their aesthetic legacy questioned and new works noisily lambasted, as was the case, for instance, with Grass's novels *Unkenrufe* (Call of the Toad, 1992) and, most notably, *Ein weites Feld* (Too Far Afield, 1995).[4]

The debt of Greiner and Schirrmacher to one of Germany's conservative intellectual heavyweights, Karl Heinz Bohrer, the doyen of the influential periodical *Merkur*, has been widely acknowledged.[5] Thus it was Bohrer who, in his study of the conservative writer Ernst Jünger, had modulated the protestant sociologist Max Weber's term *Gesinnungsethik* (ethics of conviction) to produce the term *Gesinnungsästhetik*. It had also been Bohrer's long-held view that, as a mode of experience, the aesthetic realm is incompatible with other modes, such as politics, ethics and morality.[6] For Bohrer, morally committed literature was quite simply an oxymoron. An ideological commitment to the 'project of the Enlightenment', to emancipation, equality and critical reason, he argued, could not be reconciled with the more valid vision of the transcendental power of art as elaborated, for example, by German Romanticism. For Bohrer, Schirrmacher and Greiner, it was time for a 'normal' national literature which would eschew moral posturing and draw a veil over the 'permanent theodicy' which had banished 'zones of the imagination' such as the irrational and evil from literary consciousness.[7]

The unification of two ideologically opposed countries after four decades of division inevitably allowed a plethora of older questions to rise up the agenda. Thus the altercations about literature in the early 1990s may be seen, for example, as a continuation of the *Historikerstreit* (Historians' Controversy) of the mid 1980s when conservative historians such as Ernst Nolte and Michael Stürmer demanded that Nazism should cease to dominate debates about German identity.[8] At the same time, however, the *Literaturstreit* set the tone for what was to prove a disputatious and combative decade. The arts pages of the serious press and a variety of journals remained the battleground for high-profile disagreements which often blurred the boundaries between literary and political discourses. If we were to seek to identify a thread running through these *Streite* (controversies), then it would be the discursive construction by the right in particular, but more generally too, of a left-liberal elite's alleged hegemony in relation to a plethora of political issues, on the one hand, and to readings of German history on the other.

A particularly notable hullabaloo was occasioned in 1993 by the *Symposium* on the state of the nation initiated by *Der Spiegel* and the publication in that magazine of commissioned essays by three leading *literary* figures:

Botho Strauß, Martin Walser and Hans Magnus Enzensberger. It is difficult to imagine a debate of similar import and visibility in the UK or the USA being conducted exclusively by writers. Strauss inveighed in his 'Anschwellender Bockgesang' (A Swelling Goat's Song) against the 'tragic' moral decay and loss of nationalistic values – church, tradition, authority and the soldier – which he saw threatened not least by the presence of foreign nationals. Especially suspect were the overweening and all-pervading 'telecrats' of the electronic media and the left-liberal thinkers who, he claimed, dominated the intellectual landscape of the Federal Republic. These individuals, according to Strauss, had set themselves up as self-appointed arbiters of right and wrong and championed from their 'eyries of darkest Enlightenment' a rationalist modernity which denigrates attachments of emotion and tradition.[9] The essay was reprinted as the centrepiece of a collection edited by Heimo Schwilk and Ulrich Schacht entitled *Die selbstbewußte Nation* (The self-confident Nation, 1994), invariably cited as the manifesto of the intellectual 'New Right' in the early 1990s.[10]

A similar stridency also informs the essays by the older writers Walser and Enzensberger, erstwhile prominent members of the selfsame left-liberal consensus pilloried by Strauss. Walser's polemic 'Deutsche Sorgen' expressed the 'German Concerns' of a writer who had, for well over two decades, been embarked on a journey which had taken him from the centre-left politics of the Social Democrats, via a flirtation with the German Communist Party (DKP), to an espousal, from the late 1970s onwards, of an increasingly ardent German nationalist position. Walser argued that excessive moralising is all too characteristic of German intellectuals, inhibiting any serious engagement with national issues and stifling democratic debate. Against the backdrop of the Gulf War of 1991, Enzensberger's essay 'Ausblicke auf den Bürgerkrieg' (Views of Civil War, 1993), later expanded into a book, similarly attacked politics based on emotionalism and a universal identification with the victim as divorced from pragmatic concerns, although it should be noted that Enzensberger's tone is one of melancholic resignation rather than pleasure in the disintegration of Enlightenment beliefs.[11]

A further critique of (West) Germany's supposed left-liberal intellectual consensus was channelled via the German reception of the Anglo-American debate on 'political correctness'. In Germany, the charge of *politische Korrektheit* was most often deployed to heap scorn on and delegitimise the worldview of the 68er generation.[12] This was certainly the case in a series of heated debates on the public commemoration of the Third Reich, and in particular on the erection of a central Holocaust memorial in Berlin. The most dramatic *literary* scandal, however, was famously sparked in 1998 by Martin Walser when he was honoured with the prestigious 'Peace Prize of the German Book Trade'. Following a laudation by none other than Frank Schirrmacher, Walser used his carefully crafted and expertly delivered oration to castigate the left-liberal insistence on the exceptionality of German wartime crimes and what he saw as the left's instrumentalisation of Auschwitz 'for present-day political purposes'.[13] Walser, whose novel of the same year *Ein springender Brunnen* (The springing Fountain) had challenged the convention that depictions of the Nazi period should focus on the Holocaust, quickly found himself embroiled in a ferocious, public argument with the President of the Central Council of Jews in Germany, Ignatz Bubis, who had been present at the speech in person. Walser pugnaciously countered Bubis's charge of having committed 'intellectual arson' – in effect incitement – with the argument that Germans had a right to reclaim their history as they had 'experienced' it, not in what had become its politically correct version. As the almost mandatory tome documenting the public response to this 'Walser–Bubis Debate' reveals, the fallout was enormous.[14]

Elements of Strauss's attack on the liberal media and of Walser's insistence on subjective experience had already combined in the celebrated Austrian writer Peter Handke's controversial *Eine Winterliche Reise zu den Flüssen Donau, Save, Morana und Drina oder Gerechtigkeit für Serbien* (A Winter's Journey to the Rivers Danube, Save, Morawa and Drina, or Justice for Serbia, 1996). Wrapped in a lyrical account of a recent journey to the region, originally serialised in the *Süddeutsche Zeitung*, Handke had viciously attacked the west's alleged prejudiced and hostile attitudes towards Serbia. The mediated images of the Balkan War of the mid 1990s, Handke claimed, were a travesty, drilling into readers' and viewers' minds a demonic vision of Serbs as the sole aggressors in the conflict. Unsurprisingly, the text generated a *Literaturstreit* of its very own. Most memorably, writer Peter Schneider accused Handke of criminal naivety.[15] Yet Handke's stand against the media was, of course, simultaneously a defence of the primacy of subjective memory in the face of ostensibly objective 'facts'. Similarly to Walser, he championed a focus on the innocence of the 'province' into which the crimes perpetrated in the nearby killing fields – be they in Sbrenica or in German concentration camps – do not intrude.

The suggestion made by Strauss, Walser and Handke to the effect that strident moralising has obscured key aspects of lived experience resurfaced in a series of intertwined debates on a putative neglect in 'official' cultural memory of 'German suffering' during and after the Second World War: why, it was asked, had no 'voice' been given to the victims of the

mass expulsions of Germans from eastern Europe; the systematic rape by
rampaging invading armies, and the conflagration of the Allied Strategic
Bombing Campaign? The role played by writers in this debate is yet again
striking. A number of new works of fiction drew specific attention to such
issues, while the initial trigger for the media focus on the Allied bombing campaign was a set of lectures delivered in 1997 by the writer W. G.
Sebald in Zurich on *Luftkrieg und Literatur* (Aerial Warfare and Literature,
1999), in which he argued that the trauma of the devastation had, with a
few exceptions, never found adequate expression in post-war texts. While
Sebald's thesis has been disputed, subsequent anniversaries, books such as
Der Brand (The Inferno, 2002) by the self-styled independent historian
Jörg Friedrich or Günter Grass's novella *Im Krebsgang* (Crabwalk, 2002),
and debates on the construction of a *Zentrum gegen Vertreibungen* (Centre
against Expulsions) in Berlin or relations with the Czech Republic, have
kept the issue alive.

In what follows, I would like to step back from the immediate contemporary context of the controversies of the 1990s and undertake a necessarily
succinct excursion into the longer literary history of which they are part. In
particular, I hope to offer a reminder that the key issues at stake, notably the
opposition to Enlightenment values and tenets, the role of the intellectual
in society, and the relationship between politics and aesthetics were already
central to discussions of literature in Germany well before unification.

POLITICS AND AESTHETICS IN GERMAN LITERARY HISTORY

It has long been a feature of intellectual life in the German lands that
the condition of literature has been variously contested, and often fiercely
so. This is partly because literature, to a greater extent than, say, in the
United States or the United Kingdom, is frequently linked with questions
of national status, identity or prestige and because writers themselves have
often been concerned to analyse the condition of literature at a given historical moment.[16] Even the most cursory literary-historical *tour d'horizon*
furnishes pertinent examples with some striking and illuminating modern
parallels.

Gotthold Ephraim Lessing's harsh critique in the *Hamburgische
Dramaturgie* (Hamburg Dramaturgy) of 1768–9 and in his *Literaturbriefe*
(Letters on Literature) were decisive factors in curbing the influence of
Gottsched and of his insistence that German art should imitate French
Classicism. It was in the lifetime of these two writers, moreover, that a
complex structural transformation in the private citizen's relationship to

broader society occurred which gave impetus to serious *public* debate on literature. The *Öffentlichkeit* (public sphere) which resulted – the salons, semi-formal meetings to discuss literature and politics and, above all, the cultural journals and magazines – were arguably, as Jürgen Habermas has pointed out, the precursors of what we now read in the review sections of serious newspapers and of today's broadcast media. And Lessing, of course, was one of the first German examples of the freelance journalist embracing a tone of deliberate ferocity and polemic within a *Streitkultur* (culture of public debate) viewed as a prerequisite for Enlightenment and change. This was a stance which, in the twentieth century, was adopted by cultural critics such as Karl Kraus and Kurt Tucholsky.

Leapfrogging for brevity's sake the many poetological debates and controversies that characterised the Age of Goethe, we might alight on the critique of that same age which was published on the Olympian poet's death by Heinrich Heine, his *Romantische Schule* (The Romantic School, 1836). The subsequent *Ästhetische Feldzüge* (Aesthetic Crusades) of some of Heine's contemporaries associated with *Das junge Deutschland* fused a discourse of generational conflict, youth and renewal with a discourse on literature *and* politics. While the artistic works of the 'Young Germans' were generally execrable, they did at least help promote the cause of a critical journalism. In the first half of a new century, the supposed dichotomy between the realm of the intellect and the realm of power, between *Geist und Macht*, was hotly debated, as, for instance, in the famous dispute between Thomas Mann and his brother Heinrich. Only a few years later, however, the Nazi period provided many an example of an unholy alliance between the two, that is, between absolute power and the sphere of art and the imagination.

The post-'45 period offers further examples of controversies relevant to an understanding of the *Literaturstreite* of the 1990s. Thus the years before the founding of two separate states in 1949 were notable for vituperative, *ad hominem* stand-offs between exiles such as Thomas Mann and the so-called inner émigrés, that is, between those who were forced to flee a murderous fascist dictatorship and those who ostensibly 'retreated inwards', remaining in Germany but refusing, or so they maintained, to accommodate themselves with the regime. There are clear and obvious echoes here of the discussion, half a century later, of the relationship between *Geist und Macht* and the role of East German intellectuals such as Christa Wolf who had stayed in the totalitarian GDR.

Alongside returning exiles and those who had 'emigrated inwards' during the Third Reich, there existed a group of writers who would later come to be associated with the *Gruppe 47*. Absolving themselves of any complicity with Nazism by styling themselves as the 'young generation' (despite their actual age and, in many cases, participation in German cultural life during the war years), the initial attempts of the *Gruppe 47* to influence political discourse soon mutated into an aesthetic debate in which a socio-critical yet artistically ambitious 'magic Realism' was set against an apolitical aestheticism. In the 1950s and early 1960s, 'art-for-arts-sake' (*l'art pour l'art*) was set against 'commitment' (*Engagement*), with much of the impetus deriving from Theodor W. Adorno's writings on aesthetics, on the one hand, and the influence of French intellectual Jean-Paul Sartre on the other. Again, there are some uncanny resonances of the controversy surrounding *Gesinnungsäsethetik* in the 1990s. While the early debate was largely an academic discussion, it was given a harder, more overtly political edge when prominent critics such as the literary journalist Friedrich Siegburg intervened to condemn younger writers as unwelcome Jeremiahs at the feast of a newly won prosperity and for their refusal to present a positive portrayal of West German society.[17]

In the early to mid 1960s, an outraged fusillade was aimed against leftist writers for failing to protect vociferously against the erection of the Berlin Wall, for undermining national security during the so-called 'Spiegel Affair', and for their 'pornographic' depictions of human affairs. This culminated in the 'Zurich Literary Debate', during which the distinguished Professor of German at Zurich University, Emil Staiger, on behalf of an embattled conservative elite, railed against contemporary literature's non-affirmative portrayal of society and its abnegation of beauty.[18] With the generational and social turmoil of the mid 1960s, however, this conservative tirade gave way to a left-wing, and even more radical critique of literature, notably in the pages of *Kursbuch* and by writer-intellectuals such as Hans Magnus Enzensberger, the editor of this recently founded journal: imaginative literature, even in its most critical guise, served merely an ideological function in providing the alibi for a repressively tolerant state. This fundamental debate on the social function of literature gave the appearance at the time that 'aesthetics' had been cast out in favour of direct action. When the protest movement lost its momentum, however, and splintered following the programme of social and political reform put through by a social-liberal coalition in the 1970s, critics proclaimed yet another tectonic shift with the emergence of a *Neue Innerlichkeit* (new inwardness) and a return to more seminal, personal concerns. At the same time, however, the 1970s witnessed a series of vitriolic attacks on left-liberal figures, an ominous foretaste perhaps of those which would rage after unification.

One of the most comprehensive assaults came in 1975 from the conservative sociologist Helmut Schelsky in his programmatically titled book *Die Arbeit tun die anderen: Klassenkampf und Priesterherrschaft der Intellektuellen* (The Work is done by Others: Class War and the Priest-Elite of Intellectuals). His primary targets were social-psychologist Alexander Mitscherlich, proponent of the theory that post-war West Germany had been characterised by an 'inability to mourn', that is, to adequately come to terms with the fascist past; critical journalist and editor of *Der Spiegel*, Rudolf Augstein, and the outspoken writer Heinrich Böll. Schelsky's thesis was that with the class struggle all but eliminated a new struggle had emerged between those who create wealth and those who interpret society – journalists, writers and intellectuals concerned not for the welfare of those they claim to represent, but for their own power. Prefiguring the critique of Strauss, Handke and Walser in the 1990s, Schelsky identified a new 'priestly caste' which, he claimed, preached an ethical sermon that devalued the very virtues on which its own position was founded. Many of Schelsky's precepts found their way into Kurt Sontheimer's anti-leftist polemic a year later, *Das Elend unserer Intellektuellen: Linke Theorie in der Bundesrepublik Deutschland* (The Poverty of our Intellectuals: Leftist Theory in the FRG). In the subsequent decade, this critique continued, albeit recast in slightly different terms as an assault on the self-congratulatory moralising at the core of what Cora Stephan termed the *Betroffenheitskult* (cult of moral affectedness).

A brief comparison reveals striking similarities in the rhetorical tropes, patterns and discursive strategies deployed in literary debates through the ages. Specifically, it is noteworthy how grandiose claims to occupy the moral and aesthetic high ground in respect of the future path for literature are often accompanied by attempts by the successful combatants to draw a line under a given historical epoch by attacking its alleged dominant mode. Thus the outcome of the disputes of the early 1990s was the largely successful discursive construction of German unification as a caesura in literary developments. Schirrmacher's 'farewell' to the literature of both East and West Germany is a prime document of this tendency, as is the somewhat later identification by Iris Radisch, influential literary critic for *Die Zeit*, of the fall of the Wall in 1989 as a *zweite Stunde Null*, a second literary 'zero hour' (the first was supposed to have occurred in 1945 after the collapse of the Nazi dictatorship). According to Radisch, the second generation of writers born after the war had been liberated from the burden of duty to write works of 'epochal' significance. For Radisch, what quickly became known as the 'generation of '89' now enjoyed a poetic licence unparalleled in the previous half century – 'a new chapter in literary history' had been

opened.[19] A *Spiegel* cover story published on 11 October 1999, close to the
tenth anniversary of unification, to mark the last Frankfurt Book Fair of
the millennium, may be taken as evidence of the enduring currency of
Radisch's interpretation.[20]

Yet the more or less arbitrary demarcation of periods is, of course, an
inherently problematic tool, which ignores the simple fact that literary
fiction – always and everywhere – is a diverse and elusive cultural phenomenon which stubbornly resists the straitjacket of categorisation. To
cite but two examples: scholars from the 1960s onwards have pointed out
the many continuities – political, biographical, thematic and aesthetic –
between pre- and post-war literature and have demonstrated that the once
popular notion of a *Nullpunkt* (zero hour) in 1945 was a misleading over-
simplification.[21] The attempt to designate 1968 as a cut-off point similarly
ignores the simultaneity of often diametrically opposed trends. Indeed, the
funeral rites for bourgeois literature in '68 did little to wean German readers
off works of imaginative fiction, while the 'new inwardness' in the 1970s
also produced a rather large number of 'political' novels.[22]

We need to be circumspect, therefore, whenever 1989 is offered as *the*
turning point in literary developments in anticipation of what, later in the
decade, would come to be known as the Berlin Republic. The seismic shift
in geopolitical relations of the *Wende* of 1989–90, played out in the glare of
twenty-four-hour news reporting, may have blinded us to continuities with
debates which date back to long before the 1980s. This also holds true for
those more overtly political disputes with which the literary controversies
of the 1990s interconnected. Certainly, it would be timely to question
whether the end of the post-war prosperity in the 1970s, which saw centre-
left governments ejected in a number of western countries, an escalation
in the Cold War, and the reemergence of a self-confident conservatism,
was more important as a watershed. Though it clearly lacked the drama
of 1989, Helmut Kohl's proclamation of a 'spiritual-moral turning-point'
(*geistig-moralische Wende*) in March 1983, when he succeeded the SDP's
Helmut Schmidt as Chancellor, might emerge as the more pertinent point
of departure for a changed agenda. Indeed, the fostering of a new national
pride, the attempt to normalise Germany's attitudes to its past, and the
focus on the experience of ordinary Germans during the Second World
War, all have their beginnings in the early to mid 1980s. In the literary
sphere, to cite but one example, the death of Heinrich Böll in 1985 was
widely seen as drawing an exemplary veil over the broadly accepted notion
of the socially engaged writer as 'conscience of the Nation'.[23] With him, the
supposedly second-rate 'Literature of the Federal Republic' could be laid

to rest. The hostility of the reception meted out to Grass's eco-apocalyptic novel *Die Rättin* (*The Rat*, 1986) serves merely to underscore this point.

Thus far, I have argued that a number of often-dormant themes running through German cultural history resurfaced in the literary debates of the 1990s, and in particular the debate on the relationship between political engagement and aesthetics. I have also argued that the *Literaturstreit* of 1990 was not so much the clear-cut caesura that it appears to be in contemporary accounts in the cultural pages of the serious press or in subsequent literary historical accounts; rather, it is another marker in a nationalist-conservative project traceable at the very least to the early 1980s. If I am correct, however, even allowing for the generalisations inevitable in a study of this brevity, we need to ask whether the literary debates of the 1990s contributed anything fundamentally new. Our attention, then, now turns to the transformation of the literary market in recent years and to the redefinition of literature, and of the role of writers, within the public sphere.

GERMAN LITERATURE AND THE LITERARY MARKET

In tandem with the debate on the relationship between social engagement and literary fiction, fundamental doubts were raised in the 1990s as to the viability and sustainability *per se* of German literature in the competitive global marketplace which emerged following the end of the Cold War. Writers, agents, publishers, book producers and critics thus turned their attention to the economic context within which literature is produced and sold. Concern was expressed first for the fate of the literary institutions of the former GDR and later, in relation to a series of sometimes hostile mergers and acquisitions in the book trade which consolidated the position of German-based multi-nationals, such as the Holzbrinck or Bertelsmann groups, at the expense of small, independent publishers. The mood of gloom deepened when the Red–Green coalition elected in 1998 briefly considered abolishing the net book agreement and removing tax breaks, both of which were essential to the survival of the smaller houses. Economic factors, therefore, were to preoccupy writers and critics as never before. Moreover, with independence compromised by cross-ownership, the predicted popularity of a given work within a particular market might determine to a greater degree what was published.[24] Anxieties also surfaced about the objectivity of book reviewing when many of the opinion-shaping newspapers were in the same stable of ownership as publishers.

These external economic and political developments in what sociologist Pierre Bourdieu has termed the 'literary field' combined with fears that literature *qua* literature was being displaced as a mediator of human experience by de-regulated, multi-channel, terrestrial and satellite broadcasting, the internet, email and other forms of downloadable communication. The new media have a number of features that were perceived as a threat to literary fiction. Live broadcasts, for example, offer real-time encoding and decoding; as a result, distances shrink, and accelerate and serial visual images alter our relation to time and space and the tempo of our perception, perhaps disempowering us in the process and undermining 'authentic' experience. Indeed, the media philosopher Nobert Bolz claimed in 1992 that the book is no longer adequate to our complicated social systems[25] and declared a new shift to the world of hypermedia, which would render obsolete the traditional reading public and the notion of a public space for literature.

This was the backdrop for a further *Literaturstreit*. Inevitably, it too had a normative dimension, with each of the two opposing camps claiming to 'know' the 'right' course for literature. Thus the Bohrer-Greiner-Schirrmacher triumvirate, along with like-minded allies, restated their advocacy of a literature which would hark back to German traditions but also embrace the lode stars of an urbane, decadent European 'high modernism', for example, Baudelaire, Wilde and Joris Karl Huysmans. Pitted against them were a number of writers and, above all, proselytising publishers and influential commissioning editors, such as Martin Hielscher, Uwe Wittstock and Michael Krüger, who pleaded for the adoption of 'international' norms which privileged 'entertainment', 'enjoyment' and 'a literature of every day life'. What the two camps shared, however, was their belief that current literary standards were woeful, that the future of the domestic product was severely endangered, and a rejection of the moralising literature of the 'old' FRG.[26] A cursory look at the best-seller lists, dominated by foreign imports, served merely to emphasise in their minds German writers' lack of import.

German literature, Uwe Wittstock argued, had a reputation at home and abroad for being difficult, austere and navel-gazing. This state of affairs, he claimed, had been compounded by a tendency among German critics to regard popular and entertaining writing as not 'serious' literature at all. Wittstock quickly produced two volumes as a rallying call for works of fiction with a broader-based appeal, *Roman oder Leben: Postmoderne in der deutschen Literatur* (The Novel or Life: Postmodernism in German Literature, 1994) and *Leselust* (Reading Pleasure, 1995). Later he was even to campaign for a major rethinking of the role that literary prizes might play in bringing middlebrow literature to a wider public, based on his appreciation of the boost given to shortlisted authors of the Booker Prize and the Prix Goncourt, with the former securing sales of between 60,000 and 80,000.[27] What was required, his professional soul mate, Martin Hielscher, averred, was a return to, or a rebirth, of the narrative.[28] While Wittstock looked to the reception of international postmodern styles in the 1980s by German-language authors such as Patrick Süskind, Sten Nadolny and Christoph Ransmayer, with their delight in highly allusive texts and disregard for the distinction between 'high' and 'low' art, Hielscher offered his stable of writers at Kiepenheuer & Witsch – and anyone else who cared to listen – a list of Anglo-American role models, including Nick Hornby, Brett Easton Ellis, Raymond Carver and William Geddis.[29] Around the same time, practising authors weighed into the debate. Thus Maxim Biller pithily accused some of his colleagues of producing works of fiction that possessed 'as much sensuality as a city map of Kiel', the northern seaport hideously rebuilt in lines of serried concrete after the Second World War,[30] while his colleague Matthias Altenburg argued for a return to a greater realism in the place of the introspection and stylistic pomposity which he associated with literary *flâneurs* such as Peter Handke.[31] The aesthetic concept which emerged from this debate is now often described as a *Neue Lesbarkeit* (new readability), a term coined by writer Matthias Politycki.

The debate on the need to adopt Anglo-American models and their emphasis on entertainment, 'reading pleasure', characterisation, plot and sensuality was, to a greater extent than any of its precursors, both constitutive of, and constituted by, major changes in the literary market. Above all, this related to the way in which literature – and authors – came to be 'staged' as media events. While literature was regarded as in unequal competition with the new media, publishers were not slow to exploit the changed landscape to their advantage. And, of course, the very different mode of the visual media imposed its own format on the presentation of writers and their texts, producing enticing or, just as often, salacious portraits of the author as 'media star' which were, in effect, 'teasers' with scant attention paid to the literary merits of the work of fiction. This trend was described by critic Sigrid Löffler, a member of the vaunted *Literarisches Quartett* – for most of the decade *the* prime-time TV book show – as 'Vertrailerung' (trailering).[32] For Ulrich Greiner, it was tantamount to 'literary consumer advice' and evidence of a 'thumbs-up-thumbs-down' culture which was of no intellectual value.[33]

In retrospect, the second half of the 1990s appears to have witnessed a boom in new writing. For a brief period, writers seemed to have more in common with rock stars or sporting celebrities: their public images were carefully nurtured and their media presence skilfully managed via, for example, exclusive interviews, glossy photo-portraits, celebrity talk-show appearances on terrestrial and satellite TV, performance-style public readings, or 'events' in unconventional venues. And in the networked world of globalised communications, of course, no self-respecting authors were without their own personal website. More than ever before, young writers became branded products and could command inflated advances from publishers keen to market indigenous writers in the face of the spiralling costs of securing rights to the works of foreign authors. Thus it was widely rumoured that the precocious Benjamin Lebert, author of the hit novel *Crazy* (1999), had received an advance of 540,000 euros.[34] From the mid 1990s onwards, there was a bull market in the novels of so-called *Debütanten* (debutants). Here, the *literarische Fräuleinwunder* (literary girl-miracle), which catapulted young female authors such as the photogenic Judith Hermann to commercial and critical success, is one of the most obvious examples.[35] Yet the overemphasis on personality and appearance – with good looks regarded as essential – all too often grouped together disparate literary works at the expense of any serious engagement with their aesthetic complexities. A similar fate befell a range of aesthetically 'ethnic' writers. The phenomenon was perhaps most pronounced in the intense discussion of the so-called *Neue deutsche Popliteratur*, or New German Pop Literature, with Christian Kracht as its figurehead. This was not a literary movement in the conventional sense but a marketing umbrella term for writers united by a focus on quasi-autobiographical writing, a celebration of the ephemeral and superficial delights of the *Spaßkultur* (fun culture), as described in Florian Illies's *Generation Golf* (2002), the title of which entered an ever-expanding lexicon of cultural slogans.[36]

The sudden ubiquitousness of pop texts by previously unknown authors prompted fears that literary success was largely attributable to marketing techniques. In 1998, writer Norbert Niemann described his own experiences of the literary market and concluded that fiction had been debased by the 'event culture' and colonised by a neo-liberal capitalism.[37] A year later, the success of Austrian author Robert Schneider's novel *Die Luftgängerin* (The Air-Walker, 1998), the follow-up to his best-selling *Schlafes Bruder* (The Brother of Sleep, 1992), in spite of its overwhelmingly negative reception in over two hundred newspaper reviews sparked a lengthy discussion of the triumph of marketing over serious literary debate.[38] By the beginning of the new millennium, however, there were clear indications that the literary market had been transformed once again. The South Sea bubble of 'emerging writers' had been pricked by a complex combination of literary, economic and wider political developments. These included market saturation; the concerns of authors such as Matthias Politycki that *Neue Lesbarkeit* encouraged cultural homogeneity with German novelists, in his term, barking up a 'hollow American tree';[39] the end of the dot-com boom, which had resulted in reduced marketing budgets; and a re-orientation towards older writers. Indeed, several publishers had suffered a poor return on their investments in the 'debutants': Zoe Jenny and Michael Kumpfmüller were only two notable examples of recently fêted authors whose second novels proved abject failures. Following the attacks of 9/11, moreover, a consensus emerged that the 'fun culture' was as redundant as it was tasteless. At the same time, older figures from the generation of '68, such as Uwe Timm and Peter Schneider, enjoyed a rehabilitation, although their work continued to engage with the social and political context, albeit now in a less partisan way. This was most strikingly the case in relation to Günter Grass, for many the quintessential 'politically engaged' author. Critical reassessment in the wake of his Nobel Prize of 1999 thus combined with rapturous praise for his treatment of 'German wartime suffering' in *Im Krebsgang* (*Crabwalk*, 2002). This contrasted, of course, with the oppro-brium heaped on *Ein weites Feld* in 1995.

CONCLUSION

As the latter part of this chapter was being researched in the summer of 2005, the reverberations of a new *Literaturstreit* were making themselves felt. To coincide with the Klagenfurt literary festival and following the end of the Red–Green government amid economic gloom and inertia, four writers, Martin R. Dean, Thomas Hettche, Matthias Politycki and Michael Schindheim, published their thoughts on the purpose of the novel – tra-ditionally the genre which most engages with social issues – and declared a 'manifesto for a Relevant Realism' by which their generation, the 79ers, would steer a middle way between neo-conservative self-referentiality and pop self-indulgence, and place itself at the heart of public debate.[40] In response, however, and in the same issue of *Die Zeit*, the voice of an oppos-ing camp also made itself heard. Thus Uwe Tellkamp, in an article written with his fellow authors Andreas Maier and Hans-Ulrich Treichel, replied somewhat pithily and to the point: 'What we ought to do is write good books and avoid bad ones. *The rest is irrelevant*' (italics denote English in the original).[41]

With its obvious echoes of previous battles and skirmishes, this latest controversy is a timely illustration that German *Literaturstreite* possess an abiding vigour and capacity to capture public attention. Although these controversies may occur at particular, conceptually problematic 'turning points' in history and possess their own peculiar terms of reference, for the most part they have returned time and again to the tensions between opposing notions of what is 'art'; between 'aesthetic literature' and 'political writing'; between the subjective and the objective. What the future holds is open to speculation, of course, but, as later chapters in this volume reveal, it seems that, at a time when the Berlin Republic appears to have become more or less established, and following German literature's frenzied attempts to become more 'international' in the mid to late 1990s, writers are beginning to engage once again with contemporary German society, with its pre-history and its present-day identity, much as they have done throughout the post-war period in both the 'old' FRG and the former GDR.

NOTES

1. Ulrich Greiner and Frank Schirrmacher's articles are to be found in Thomas Anz, ed., '*Es geht nicht um Christa Wolf'*: *Der Literaturstreit im vereinten Deutschland* (Munich: Spangenberg, 1991), 208–16 and 77–89.
2. See Stefan Neuhaus, 'The Power of the Media and the Four Christa Wolf "Affairs"' in Arthur Williams, Stuart Parkes and Julian Preece, eds., *Literature, Markets and Media in Germany and Austria Today* (Bern: Peter Lang, 2000), 159–77.
3. See Paul Cooke and Andrew Plowman, eds., *German Writers and the Politics of Culture: Dealing with the Stasi* (Palgrave Macmillan: Basingstoke, 2003).
4. See Oskar Negt, ed., *Der Fall Fonty: 'Ein weites Feld' von Günter Grass im Spiegel der Kritik* (Göttingen: Steidl, 1996).
5. See Stephen Brockmann, *Literature and German Reunification* (Cambridge: Cambridge University Press, 1999), particularly chapter 3.
6. See Jan-Werner Müller, 'Karl Heinz Bohrer on German National Identity: Recovering Romanticism and Aestheticizing the State', *German Studies Review*, 23:2 (2000): 297–316.
7. Karl Heinz Bohrer, 'Die permanente Theodizee: Über das verfehlte Böse im deutschen Bewußtsein', in *Nach der Natur: Über Politik und Ästhetik* (Munich: Carl Hanser, 1988), 131–61, here 154–5.
8. See H. J. Hahn, '"Es geht nicht um Literatur": Some Observations on the 1990 *Literaturstreit* and its recent anti-intellectual implications', *German Life and Letters* 50:1 (1997): 65–80. Hahn's insightful analysis informs some of the arguments of the second section of the present chapter.
9. Botho Strauß, 'Anschwellender Bocksgesang', *Der Spiegel* (8 February 1993), 202–7.

10. See Roger Woods, 'Affirmative Past versus Cultural Pessimism: The New Right Since Unification', *German Life and Letters*, 58:1 (2005): 94–107.
11. See Gerhard Fischer, ed., *Debating Enzensberger: Great Migration and Civil War* (Tübingen: Stauffenberg, 1996) and Stuart Parkes, *Understanding Contemporary Germany* (London and New York: Routledge, 1997), 198–201.
12. See Sally Johnson and Stephanie Suhr, 'From "Political Correctness" to *Politische Korrektheit*: Discourses of "PC" in the German Newspaper *Die Welt*', *Discourse and Society*, 14:1 (2002): 49–68.
13. Martin Walser, *Erfahrungen beim Erfassen einer Sonntagsrede* (Frankfurt: Suhrkamp, 1998), 18.
14. Frank Schirrmacher, ed., *Die Walser–Bubis-Debatte: Eine Dokumentation* (Frankfurt: Suhrkamp, 1999). See Kathrin Schödel's 'Normalising Cultural Memory? The "Walser–Bubis Debate" and Martin Walser's novel *Ein springender Brunnen*' in Stuart Taberner and Frank Finlay, eds., *Recasting German Identity* (Rochester: Camden House, 2002), 67–84.
15. See Hubert Lengauer, 'Pitting Narration against Image: Peter Handke's Literary Protest Against the Staging of Reality by the Media' in Arthur Williams, Stuart Parkes and Julian Preece, eds., *Whose Story? – Continuities in Contemporary German-language Literature* (Bern: Peter Lang, 1998), 353–70.
16. See Stuart Parkes, 'Drowning or Waving: German Literature Today' in Taberner and Finlay, eds., *Recasting German Identity*, 257–72, here 263.
17. See Franz Schonauer, 'Siegburg & Co: Rückblick auf eine sogenannte konservative Literaturkritik', *Literaturmagazin*, 7 (1977): 237–51.
18. See issues 25 and 27 (1967) of *Sprache im technischen Zeitalter*.
19. Iris Radisch, 'Die zweite Stunde Null', *Die Zeit*, 7 October 1994.
20. See Volker Hage's 'Die Enkel kommen', *Der Spiegel*, 41 (1999), 244–50.
21. See Hans Dieter Schäfer, 'Zur Periodiserung der deutschen Literatur seit 1930', in his *Das gespaltene Bewußtsein* (Munich and Vienna: Hanser, 1981), 55–71 and Keith Bullivant, 'The Periodisation of the Literature of the Federal Republic' in his *The Future of German Literature* (Oxford/Providence: Berg, 1994), 32–46.
22. See Keith Bullivant's *After the 'Death of Literature': West German Writing of the 1970s* (Oxford and New York: Berg, 1989).
23. See my *Heinrich Böll's Aesthetic Thinking* (Amsterdam: Rudopi, 1996), 4–11.
24. Hubert Winkels, 'Einleitung', in Volker Hage, Rainer Moritz and Hubert Winkels, eds., *Zur deutschen Literatur 1998* (Stuttgart: Philip Reclam, 1999), 5–39, here 6.
25. Nobert Bolz, *Die Welt als Chaos und als Simulation* (Munich: Fink, 1992), 128.
26. See Stuart Taberner's introduction to *German Literature in the Age of Globalisation* (Birmingham: Birmingham University Press, 2004), 1–24.
27. Uwe Wittstock, *Die Welt*, 8 November 2000.
28. See, for example, Martin Hielscher's 'Literaturbetrieb im Wandel', *Neue Gesellschaft*, 47:11 (2000): 679–81, and 'The Return to Narrative and to History: Some Thoughts on Contemporary German-Language Literature', in Williams,

Parkes and Preece, eds., *Literature, Markets and Media in Germany and Austria Today*, 295–309.

29. See Martin Hielscher, *Wenn der Kater kommt: Neues Erzählen – 38 deutschsprachige Autorinnen und Autoren* (Cologne: Kiepenheuer and Witsch, 1996).

30. Maxim Biller, 'Soviel Sinnlichkeit wie der Stadtplan von Kiel'. Originally in *Die Weltwoche*, 25 July 1991. In Andreas Köhler and Rainer Moritz, eds., *Maulhelden und Königskinder: Zur Debatte über die deutschsprachige Gegenwartsliteratur* (Leipzig: Reclam Verlag, 1998), 62–71, here 62.

31. Matthias Altenburg, 'Kampf den Flaneuren: Über Deutschlands junge, lahme Dichter'. Originally in *Der Spiegel*, 12 October 1992. In Köhler and Moritz, eds., *Maulhelden*, 72–85.

32. See Stefan Weidner, 'Vertrailert und verkauft: Literaturkritik in einer sich wandelnden Medienlandschaft', *Neue Zürcher Zeitung*, 169 (24/25 July 1999): 33.

33. See Ulrich Greiner, 'Der Betrieb tanzt: Über Literatur und Öffentlichkeit', *Neue Deutsche Literatur*, 46:520 (1998): 162.

34. See Stuart Parkes, 'Contemporary German-Language Literature: The Changing Agenda', in Arthur Williams, Stuart Parkes and Julian Preece, eds., *German-Language Literature Today: International and Popular?* (Bern: Peter Lang, 2000), 1–18, 2, and the introduction to Thomas Kraft, ed., *aufgerissen: Zur Literatur der 90er Jahre* (Munich: Piper, 2000), particularly 11–12.

35. See Peter Graves, 'Karen Duve, Kathrin Schmidt, Judith Hermann: "Ein literarisches Fräuleinwunder"?' *German Life and Letters*, 55:2 (2002): 196–207.

36. See Andrew Plowman, '"Was will ich denn als Westdeutscher erzählen?": The "old" West and Globalisation in Recent German Prose', and Frank Finlay, '"Dann wäre Deutschland wie das Wort Neckarrauen": Surface, Superficiality and Globalisation in Christian Kracht's *Faserland*', both in Taberner, ed., *German Literature in the Age of Globalisation*, 47–66 and 189–208. See also Horst Spittler, 'Die Dichter der Generation Golf', *Literatur und Leser*, 25:3 (2002): 189–96.

37. Norbert Niemann, 'Vom Feind umzingelt: Literatur und Literaturkritik in der Zwickmühle von Medien und Ökonomie', *Die Zeit*, 22 (20 May 1998).

38. See the special edition of *Sprache im technischen Zeitalter*, 'Positionen der Literaturkritik' (2002), edited by Norbert Miller and Dieter Stolz, documenting a symposium attended in 2000 by many of Germany's leading critics.

39. See Stuart Taberner, 'New Modernism or "Neue Lesbarkeit"? Hybridity in Georg Klein's *Libidissi*', *German Life and Letters*, 55:2 (2002): 137–48, here 140.

40. Martin R. Dean, Thomas Hettche, Matthias Politycki and Michael Schindheim, 'Was soll der Roman?', *Die Zeit* (23 June 2005).

41. Andreas Maier, Hans-Ulrich Treichel and Uwe Tellkamp, 'Der Roman schaut in fremde Zimmer hinein', *Die Zeit* (23 June 2005).

CHAPTER 3

Berlin as the literary capital of German unification

Stephen Brockmann

The years since German unification have witnessed a remarkable boom in literature about Berlin. If Frank Schirrmacher, a cultural editor for the *Frankfurter Allgemeine Zeitung*, had complained in 1989 that since the 1920s German literature had remained essentially provincial,[1] a decade later it was clear that German authors had relocated Berlin as a capital of the German literary imagination and were struggling to condense and communicate the experience of living in a major metropolis undergoing rapid and frequently painful social transformation.

The much-publicised search for the great novel of German unification has in essence also been a search for the great Berlin novel, since it is in Berlin that the tensions of economic and political change in Germany are at their most obvious. It is here, in the formerly divided city, that east meets west most intimately, and that the German history of the twentieth century most prominently intrudes on the present. As a character in Uwe Timm's Berlin novel *Rot* (Red, 2001) ruminates, 'Here you have the catastrophies of German history gathered together iconographically: the wars, the founding of the Reich . . . revolution, the Weimar Republic, the Nazi period.'[2] It was to Berlin that the government ultimately moved in 1999, eight years after a contentious debate and parliamentary vote in 1991. The new-old capital even gave the larger, post-unification Federal Republic its unofficial name: the 'Berlin Republic', a contrast to the sleepier pre-1989 'Bonn Republic'. At least in one sociologist's view, Berlin also gave the new generation of German youth a collective identity as the 'Berlin generation'.[3]

The list of authors who have contributed to the growth and development of Berlin literature in the last decade and a half is long and includes some of the most prominent, internationally respected German writers. The list starts, appropriately enough, with Christa Wolf's controversial *Was bleibt* (What Remains, 1990), the subject of the first major post-unification literary debate about the politics of German literature; among other things, Wolf's novella was also a contribution to Berlin literature.[4] The text prefigured much of subsequent metropolitan literature by depicting the threatened existence of a lonely individual more or less trapped inside her own apartment while thematising the specific freedom of language and literature as modes of resistance to social oppression. The novella's semi-autobiographical female narrator invokes a language that 'is in my ear but not yet on my tongue' in which she will one day be able to speak and write, 'easily and freely', thus overcoming the oppressive language of the Stasi operatives who spy on her.[5] This liberated language will carry out literature's traditional function of defining 'was bleibt' (what remains): it will provide to both current and later generations a human compass in the midst of change; and it will reveal 'what is at the root of my city and what is rotting it from within', that is, an unfree language that interferes with rather than enhances life.[6] The city is hence the epitome and crucible of society itself, just as Berlin becomes the epitome and crucible of German unification. This is a unification not just between two formerly separate halves of the country but also between isolated urban individuals and the newly unleashed urban society that surrounds and sometimes threatens to engulf them.

The list of Berlin literature in the first fifteen years after German unifi-cation includes challenging modernist works such as Ulrich Peltzer's *Stefan Martinez* (1995), *Alle oder keiner* (Everyone or No One, 1999), and *Bryant Park* (2001 – also a New York novel in the wake of the 9/11 terrorist attack), all of which explore the consciousness of a male protagonist and his inter-actions with the urban environment around him. Christian Jäger has called Peltzer's fiction a post-unification version of Alfred Döblin's famous mod-ernist novel *Berlin Alexanderplatz* (1929), undoubtedly the prime example of the classic Berlin novel; Jäger argues that with Peltzer's work, which is 'simultaneously of its time and beyond its time', the wait for the great Berlin novel of the post-1989 period has come to an end.[7] At a high level of lin-guistic and literary innovation, Peltzer examines the intersection between language, consciousness and the metropolis as a lived and humanly con-structed reality; Peltzer is also politically committed to economic and social justice, and the title of his novel *Alle oder keiner* comes from the famous poem by Bertolt Brecht from *Die Tage der Kommune* (The Days of the Commune, 1949) demanding the basics of life for all human beings, not just a privileged elite.[8] In Peltzer's fiction the city as the intersection between society and the individual, and the city novel as the literary invocation of the individual's confrontation with society, demand an open exploration of dif-ferent, and more liberating political possibilities; and literature, especially at a high level of complexity, is an embodiment and prefiguration of social freedom.

Most contemporary Berlin novels are not as demanding as Peltzer's work, however, since one of the most noticeable developments in German literature over the last decade has been the emergence – after prominent criticisms of contemporary German literature in the early 1990s as too difficult and demanding – of a more easily readable literature that seeks to imitate American models of light popular literature.[9] Thomas Brussig's *Helden wie wir* (Heroes Like Us, 1995) was perhaps the first major example of such literature dealing with Berlin, and Brussig has followed that success with two further Berlin novels, *Am kürzeren Ende der Sonnenallee* (On the Shorter End of Sun Alley, 1999) and *Wie es leuchtet* (How Bright It Is, 2004). Brussig sets out in the latter work to provide the definitive novel of German unification. In addition to Brussig, who writes from a distinctly male perspective, the last decade has witnessed the development of a so-called *literarisches Fräuleinwunder* (literary girl-miracle) characterised by popular Berlin literature – often short stories – by young women.[10] Prominent examples of this development are Judith Hermann's collections *Sommerhaus, später* (Summer House, Later, 1998) and *Nichts als Gespenster* (Nothing But Ghosts, 2003), as well as Tanja Dückers's *Spielzone* (Play Zone, 1999) and Julia Franck's *Bauchlandung: Geschichten zum Anfassen* (Belly Flop: Stories You Can Touch, 2000).

The post-unification period has also seen a number of significant Berlin novels from authors already well established prior to 1989 – most prominently Günter Grass's *Ein weites Feld* (Too Far Afield, 1995). In addition, three well-known West German writers born in the 1940s – the generation referred to as 68ers because of their association with the progressive social ferment of the late 1960s – have written Berlin novels. Peter Schneider published *Eduards Heimkehr* (Eduard's Homecoming) in 1999, a novel about a West German returning from the United States to reunified Berlin in the 1990s and rediscovering his united homeland and its capital city.[11] Uwe Timm published *Johannisnacht* (Midsummer's Night, 1996) and the aforementioned *Rot*; the former relates a summer night in Berlin during the time of Christo and Jeanne-Claude's famous art project *Wrapped* Reichstag in 1995 – a project which seemed to prepare the way for the building's redesign by Sir Norman Foster and reemergence in the late 1990s as the seat of the reunified German parliament – while the latter tells the story of Timm's own 68er generation, with its dashed hopes for a fairer world. Finally, F. C. Delius published *Die Flatterzunge* (The Flutter-Tongue) in

1999, among other things an exploration of German identity and the transformation of Berlin during the 1990s.[12]

One major trend in recent Berlin literature has been the sometimes nostalgic exploration of particular local neighbourhoods. Sven Regener's entertaining *Herr Lehmann* (2001), for instance, provides an affectionate account of West Berlin's countercultural Kreuzberg neighbourhood during the 1980s, when no one was thinking about unification; while Brussig's *Am kürzeren Ende der Sonnenallee* offers a nostalgic invocation of East Berlin and the former German Democratic Republic (GDR). Less nostalgic but equally devoted to an exploration of East Berlin's past is Klaus Schlesinger's *Die Sache mit Randow* (The Randow Affair, 1996), which recounts the politically problematic developments in the GDR generally, and in the Prenzlauer Berg neighbourhood specifically, during the post-war period, especially the 1950s. Irina Liebmann's novel *Die freien Frauen* (The Free Women, 2004) is also a powerful exploration of an east Berlin neighbourhood, Mitte (Middle), in the present and the past; and Norman Ohler's programatically titled novel *Mitte* (2001) explores both the transformation of Berlin's centre in the aftermath of German unification and the haunting of Berlin's present by Berlin's past. Meanwhile a great number of novels have explored the city not only in the past and present but also in a vaguely imagined and rather terrifying future. Georg Klein's *Libidissi* (1999) and *Barbar Rosa* (2001) appear as innovative detective and suspense novels set in a somewhat threatening German future,[13] while Tim Staffel's *Terrordrom* (1998) exposes Berlin as a potential site for chaos and destruction. Pieke Biermann's clever feminist detective novels *Herzrasen* (Racing Heart, 1993) and *Vier, Fünf, Sechs* (Four, Five, Six, 1997 – a play on Billy Wilder's 1961 film comedy *One, Two, Three*) portray the city as a site not only of crime but of social, sexual and political conflicts that contain both positive and negative potential for change.[14]

This is only a partial list of Berlin literature in the first fifteen years after unification, and it could easily be expanded. The point is that a great many German authors have accepted the challenge to depict Berlin and its transformations. It is true that much contemporary Berlin literature explores Berlin precisely in its local neighbourhoods – in a sense, such works explore Berlin's provinciality – and hence might fall foul of critics such as Karl Heinz Bohrer, the *eminence grise* who edits *Merkur* and who prominently complained about Germany's purported provincialism in 1990.[15] However, such criticisms overlook a crucial fact about major metropolises; part of the delight of cities like Berlin, New York or London is, paradoxically, precisely their provincialism, which enables residents to experience simultaneously the larger world of global capitalism and the protective confinement of a local neighbourhood. It is this simultaneous experience of openness and protectedness that leads to what Walter Benjamin once called the 'incomparably reassuring and uplifting power' of large cities.[16] In contemporary urban-theoretical parlance, a major city like Berlin is 'glocal', combining both the powerful historical thrust of globalisation and the stubborn resistance of the local. Such cities therefore capture two of the primary forces of our time.

Contemporary authors writing about Berlin come from all generations, and from both east and west. Authors of Berlin fiction write in a variety of styles, from Peltzer's challenging postmodern works to Schneider's or Hermann's comparatively undemanding and easy-to-read fiction. Particularly for many younger German writers, Berlin seems to exert an almost irresistible magnetic pull. For Bodo Morshäuser, whose novella *Berliner Simulation* (1983) was itself a significant contribution to Berlin literature in the 1980s, Berlin today is 'the only true [German] city, because it isn't silent about anything', including especially the problematic German past.[17] Berlin is of course also attractive to non-German writers. The American writer Ward Just, who spent three months at the American Academy in Berlin in the winter of 1999, thus had the protagonist of his novel *The Weather in Berlin* (2002) invoke Berlin as 'a narrator's utopia, the story of the world, ruin and rebirth', a story that 'belonged to whoever could tell it best'.[18] For one of Just's characters, 'Berlin will be the capital of the twenty-first century as Paris was the capital of the nineteenth and New York the capital of the twentieth'.[19]

At times the search for the great novel of unification and of Berlin during the last fifteen years has taken on an almost obsessive, even farcical quality. Thomas Brussig, for instance, argues more or less without irony that the great German novel of today should include all aspects of 1989–90 and the emotions that went along with it: 'this acceleration of events, the roller coaster ride of emotions, the excitement, the insecurities, the fears and hopes, and this condition in which the cards were being reshuffled – all of that has to be included. Yes: HAS TO!'[20] Brussig's *Wie es leuchtet* is an overly self-conscious attempt to do precisely this, and that is no doubt one reason why the novel fails aesthetically; it is essentially a laundry list of German unification. Some writers have satirised prescriptive attitudes such as Brussig's. Matthias Zschokke, a writer born in Switzerland who has been living in Berlin for more than two decades, published his satire *Der dicke Dichter* (The Fat Writer) in 1995, about a writer desperately trying but failing to create the new city novel. In the ruminations of his protagonist,

Zschokke makes fun of critics' expectations for the new Berlin novel: 'It will only take a few weeks, I promise you, maybe just days or even a few more hours until the knot inside me comes untied and the new big-city novel pours out of me in glowing prose.'[21] Needless to say, Zschokke's fat writer never manages to publish his great Berlin novel. The novel's title is a play on words, since the German word 'Dichter' also means 'thicker' or 'person who thickens/condenses', and at their best German 'Dichter' are able to condense experience into poetry and/or prose. However Zschokke's protagonist is responding not to an inner poetic urge but rather to public expectations. Hence the novel's hero is suffering from literary constipation or writer's block; that is the sum of his condensation. Zschokke's satire is a gentle rebuke to the expectations of literary critics and a plea for the autonomy of literature. Joachim Lottmann, one of the creators of the new German 'pop literature' of the 1990s, similarly parodied expectations for the great Berlin novel in a work that bore the title *Deutsche Einheit* (German Unity, 1999). Lottmann's writer-protagonist has no experience with east Germans or with the eastern part of the country in general; thus the idea that he could write a meaningful novel about the unification of the German east with the German west, and about Berlin as the crucible of that unification, is absurd.

Meanwhile, in 1999 a group of five young German pop writers including Benjamin von Stuckrad-Barre and Christian Kracht – the writers stylised themselves as a 'pop-cultural quintet' – closeted themselves in a Berlin hotel to produce a kind of manifesto for the new pop literature, *Tristesse Royale*, which purported to describe the jaded cultural situation of the new Berlin Republic and of the wealthy, bored younger generation of Germans living in that republic after the end of all utopian dreams and even all idealism. The manifesto's title was a play on both a popular 1980s television show about urban paparazzi directed by Helmut Dietl and written by Patrick Süskind and an alcoholic drink – made with champagne and crème de cassis and usually spelled with an extra 'e' at the end – named *Kir Royal*; this title demonstrated the young pop authors' easy familiarity with television, film, pop music and alcohol, and also their air of world-weary fatalism. Lottmann's and the 'pop-cultural quintet's' stylisations of themselves were of course partly satirical and partly serious, as much satire often is.

Satirical depictions of German writers and the expectations placed on them to create the great Berlin novel raise important questions about the role of literature in general and in the public sphere in particular. Must literature, as Brussig argues, include all of the thoughts and feelings that accompanied Germany's national transformation? Why is such an encyclopedic account needed, especially given the fact that German unification was widely reported in other media, such as television, radio, newspapers, magazines and subsequent historical accounts? Is it the role of literature to compete with such media on their own turf, or should literature instead seek to provide something that these media cannot? Such questions, although vital, are difficult to answer without recourse to history, since literature has served different purposes at different times. However, given the widespread media saturation of the postmodern world and also the existence of a relatively large number of high-quality Berlin movies over the past decade – feature films such as Tom Tykwer's *Lola rennt* (Run, Lola, Run, 1998), Andreas Dresen's *Nachtgestalten* (Night Shapes, 1999), Wolfgang Becker's *Das Leben ist eine Baustelle* (Life is a Construction Site, 1997) and *Goodbye, Lenin!* (2002), Leander Haußmann's *Sonnenallee* (2000 – a companion piece to Brussig's novel *Am kürzeren Ende der Sonnenallee*) and Hannes Stöhr's *Berlin is in Germany* (2001), as well as documentaries such as Hubertus Siegert's *Berlin Babylon* (2001) and Thomas Schadt's *Berlin: Sinfonie einer Großstadt* (Berlin, Symphony of a Great City, 2002, a homage to Walter Ruttmann's classic 1927 silent film) – they have become more pressing. Hence the most successful authors have sought to provide what film and other competing media cannot: close attention to language itself as a source of aesthetic pleasure and as a primary medium of human consciousness, and to the narrative perspective that literary language can communicate so masterfully. It may be a platitude that a picture is worth a thousand words, but the best contemporary Berlin literature denies this platitude and claims that words are often more valuable than any number of conventional, conformist pictures manipulated by media conglomerates or government agencies.

A story that captures literature's often agonised relationship to other contemporary media such as film and television is Jochen Langer's 1991 'Reichstag', which recounts a West German's experiences in Berlin on the night of 2–3 October 1990, when Germany was officially reunited and there was a major celebration at the Reichstag building in Berlin. Instead of going to the Reichstag and taking part in the event, Langer's lonely protagonist, who has just been jilted by a girlfriend in West Germany, goes to his hotel room, turns on the television, and proceeds to masturbate on its images of national unification: 'the flood of sperm covers the faces as the mouths open up to sing the German hymn. The thick fluid warms up on the television screen and runs in two rivulets into the mouth of the Chancellor and the mouth of the President.'[22] Undoubtedly Langer is aiming at shock value in this narrative, which prefigures other sexually explicit and even perverse renderings of Berlin in post-1990 fiction, such as

Thomas Hettche's *Nox* (1995) – a sadomasochistic account of 9 November 1989 – and Brussig's *Helden wie wir*. But what is significant is not so much the desecration of a solemn national ceremony as the disrespect for television and its images, the very images that were so widely broadcast at the moment of unification. Langer is perhaps suggesting that literature provides more meaningful access to the sometimes uncomfortable and depressing realities of human consciousness than the television screen.

In what follows I explore four very different Berlin texts, each successful in its own right, that illustrate the broad range of contemporary Berlin fiction since unification, as well as those aspects of Berlin literature that give it an advantage over other media, such as film and television. Two of these texts are already well known, and therefore I treat them only briefly: Grass's *Ein weites Feld* and Brussig's *Helden wie wir*. Two others are much less well known, partly because they are more recent: Kerstin Hensel's *Falscher Hase* (False Hare, 2005) and Ulrike Draesner's short story 'Gina Regina' (2004). This list of authors is representative in several ways. It includes two women and two men, two East Germans (Brussig and Hensel) and two former citizens of the 'old' Federal Republic (Grass and Draesner). The list includes one internationally famous author (Grass, who won the Nobel Prize for literature in 1999) and three authors now in their forties who have established or emerging reputations (Hensel was born in 1961, Draesner in 1962, and Brussig in 1965). Moreover, this list includes different approaches to literature and modes of writing. Whereas Grass writes challenging prose in the modernist tradition and is respectful of literary precedent, Brussig writes easy-to-read pop literature. Hensel and Draesner are somewhere in between, neither at the high level of complexity achieved by Grass nor at the relatively easy-to-read level of Brussig. Three of the works I discuss are novels, and this reflects the novel's continuing status as Germany's most important literary genre. One of the works, however, is a short story; its presence in my account reflects the growing significance of shorter fiction in contemporary German-language literature. Finally, three of my authors (Hensel, Draesner and Brussig) are demographically clustered around the year 1964, which saw the highest number of births ever recorded in Germany.[23] It is quite likely that writers of this generation will influence and perhaps even dominate German literature in the future. This generation grew up in a still-divided Germany, but its adulthood has been dominated by unification and its consequences. It is this generation that, because of its life experiences, can be expected to give a particularly compelling account of Germany's, and Berlin's, coming-together.

EIN WEITES FELD

Günter Grass's *Ein weites Feld* takes place in Berlin in the months following the collapse of the Berlin Wall. Its major character, Theo Wuttke (Fonty), is a late-twentieth-century reincarnation of the great nineteenth-century Berlin writer Theodor Fontane. Fonty is thus a living embodiment of German literary traditions and sensitivity to them. For Fonty the collapse of the Wall presents an opportunity for him to reacquaint himself with sections of Berlin that have been closed to him for decades, such as the great city park known as Tiergarten or the centre of West Berlin near the zoo train station: 'Fonty liked such walks, especially now that the Tiergarten's paths in the West gave him room to roam.'[24] Fonty goes about reunifying West and East Berlin mentally in his walks around town, and at the same time he unifies Berlin's present with its past, since he is always aware of the history of the spaces that he occupies. Fonty registers the Americanisation of Berlin in a McDonald's near the zoo, but at the same time, 'with the burden of time upon him', he connects the fast-food restaurant to a longer Scottish history about 'the historical MacDonalds and their mortal enemies, the Campbells'.[25] Probably the most important interior space in Grass's novel is the building where Fonty works, the former East German House of the Ministries (Haus der Ministerien), which had housed Hermann Göring's Aviation Ministry (Luftfahrtministerium) during the Nazi period, which witnessed some of the most significant events of the 1953 uprising in East Berlin, and which, in the novel's narrative present, is the headquarters of the Treuhandanstalt (trustee agency) responsible for dealing with East Germany's former state-owned properties. (The building currently houses Germany's Finance Ministry and is called the Detlev-Rohwedder-Haus in memory of the first leader of the Treuhandanstalt, who was assassinated in 1991.)

Fonty's reflections on this history-laden building are typical of his sense of the historicity of Berlin in general: whenever he goes into it he reminds himself 'that Otto-Grotewohl-Straße, which ran past the building's long side, had been known as Wilhelmstrasse during the years of the empire, during the Weimar Republic, and as long as the Reich Aviation Ministry remained in operation'.[26] Fonty's travels through this building, and through Berlin generally, remind readers that cities are not just architectural but also mental constructions, and that the literary city is far more capable of capturing the various pasts of Berlin than any physical building or monument. Fonty's Berlin is what Sigmund Freud calls a 'psychic city' constructed of memories; it is a palimpsest in which the creation of new buildings and city parts – unlike the process of city planning and architectural construction that transformed the physical city in the years after unification – does not destroy old ones.[27] In Fonty's Berlin the present can coincide with multiple pasts. Perhaps more than any other contemporary Berlin novel, Grass's *Ein weites Feld* also re-establishes Berlin as the capital not just of Germany but of Brandenburg, the state surrounding Berlin that Theodor Fontane had explored in his famous *Wanderungen durch die Mark Brandenburg* (Travels Through the Brandenburg March, 1860s–1880s). Fonty connects the newly emerging international capital Berlin with its immediate surroundings in contemporary Brandenburg, and with its past as the capital of Prussia. This rediscovery of Prussia, and of Berlin as Prussia's capital, has been an important part of the rediscovery of the five new German *Länder*.

HELDEN WIE WIR

Brussig's *Helden wie wir* is by now the most famous and popular novel about the opening of the Berlin Wall. The most important innovation of Brussig's novel is its outrageous, provocative humour. *Helden wie wir* tells a funny story about a serious occurrence. At the same time it makes the opening of the Berlin Wall an intimate personal event, mapping the political onto the sexual; as Klaus Uhltzscht, the novel's narrator, asserts, 'the history of the Wall's fall is the history of my dick'.[28] Uhltzscht, of course, is a completely unreliable narrator. He is a former Stasi operative who has kidnapped a woman and donated blood to the ailing East German leader Erich Honecker, a procedure that has, according to his own account, made his formerly diminutive penis sufficiently large to force the opening of the Berlin Wall when revealed to awed East German border guards on the evening of 9 November. In a comic way, Brussig recounts the momentous events in Berlin in late 1989 that led to German unification: the protests against the SED dictatorship, the Stasi's persecution of demonstrators, the involvement of East German writers like Christa Wolf in calls for a democratic socialism, and finally the opening of the Wall. Brussig treats all of these events, which are depicted in media culture as serious and heroic, as humorous and rather pathetic – indeed buffoonish. Uhltzscht's narrative is addressed to a reporter from the *New York Times*, and is specifically intended as a counterpoint to conventional media representations of the events of 1989. If Christoph Hein had referred to Leipzig, the urban origin of the demonstrations that culminated in unification, as a 'Heldenstadt' (city of heroes), Brussig shows that many of East Germany's self-proclaimed heroes were dismal and perhaps even perverse conformists. However, whereas other accounts of the GDR dictatorship emphasise its horrific sides, Brussig emphasises the ridiculous. In fact, the novel becomes less successful in its final passages, when the previously idiotic and cruel Uhltzscht is suddenly transformed into a purportedly legitimate critic of writers like Christa Wolf; this hardly credible turn to seriousness is a narrative flaw in an otherwise consistently frivolous literary construction. Brussig's *Helden wie wir* was transformed into a film by Sebastian Peterson in 1999, but that film's artistic failure demonstrated that at least in this instance the linguistic and narrative freedom of literature are preferable to the conformist constraints of so much contemporary film and television production.

FALSCHER HASE

Kerstin Hensel's novel *Falscher Hase*, which appeared ten years after Brussig's *Helden wie wir*, demonstrates the way that individual memory and urban geography frequently overlap. Paffrath, the novel's protagonist, was born in Berlin in the middle of a bombing raid in 1941. His father, a fireman, is away at work, and his pregnant mother, alone in a small apartment near the Tiergarten, can hear the camels from the zoo screaming as her contractions begin.[29] The apartment catches fire, and Martha Paffrath begins to give birth to her child in the burning building. Suddenly her husband, Heinrich arrives and extinguishes the fire with his own fire-extinguishing invention, which he calls VENUS. Heini is thus born in the midst of near-catastrophe and loud noise. This traumatic birth, and Heini's equally traumatic childhood affect him for the rest of his life. As a child, he cannot stand loud noises, and his mother creates special ear muffs to protect him. Heini believes that he can never be quite the man that his father is, and even his diminutive name seems to signal his lack of adult male power. This weakness is further underscored by Heini's early experiences in occupied Berlin. While trying to buy food on the black market, Heini probably – although this is never made explicit – becomes the target of a pederast American soldier whom he thinks of as 'Sartschend Ben' (Sergeant Ben, *FH*, 59). In adolescence, Heini is never popular with other children, and even his father and mother consider him strange.

In essence, Heini remains an infantile being and never makes the transition to adulthood. He is fixated on authority and neatness. Later on in life, Heini, like his father, is fascinated by uniforms. Indeed, both are examples of what Theodor W. Adorno called the 'authoritarian personality'.[30] Every day Heini does the same things, even eating precisely the same dish, the 'falscher Hase' of the novel's title, at his local restaurant. Unable to make friendships or romantic relationships in the real world, he makes them in his head. Because he is constantly eating sweets in order to console himself, his teeth are ruined, and he has to go to the dentist, where he ultimately gets a complete set of dentures. At the dentist's office he meets a pretty young dental assistant with whom he becomes infatuated; but when the Berlin Wall is built in August of 1961 – Heini is twenty – Maschula remains on the other side of the Wall. Without thinking a great deal about it, Heini decides to follow her. He then goes in the opposite direction to the way so many of his fellow Berliners are going: rather than escaping East Berlin to the West, he escapes West Berlin to the East. In the GDR Heini winds up as a policeman in Pankow.

In a way, the GDR is ideal for Heini, completing his escape from freedom (Eric Fromm).[31] It provides him with precisely the security and order that he needs. When Heini's parents die in a traffic accident in 1983, Heini declines to go to the funeral, because to do so would mean crossing back over the border and physically returning to his childhood. For Heini the Wall becomes not just a physical but also a mental barrier protecting him from the reality and the pain associated with his childhood: 'He was not tempted to cross over the border. The border was his protective wall, his security, and he had begun to love it. No one could take it away from him' (*FH*, 125). By associating himself with the police, Heini becomes a part of the authoritarian power structure, and its Wall, in a sense, is his Wall. The political, the geographical and the psychological are all mapped onto each other.

Ultimately Heini becomes a murderer when he kills a husband and wife in his apartment building who have rejected his friendship and love. He had first become infatuated with the wife and then the husband, who, as it turns out, works for the Stasi. He imagines himself married to the two of them. When they fail to show up for a dinner he has invited them to – 'falscher Hase' from his favourite restaurant, of course – he sneaks into their apartment at night, turns on the gas and leaves. Everyone in the neighbourhood believes that the deaths are a double suicide, and Heini not only gets away with the murder, but he is actually able to move into the dead couple's apartment and sleep in their still intact bed. He leaves their name on his door and imagines himself living with the two of them; he even holds conversations with them out loud in his apartment and in his sleep.

When the GDR collapses, Heini is in a coma, because he has had an accident coming home from a police training camp. Although he now has the chance to rise in the police force by going to training in the west, Heini declines, since he has promised himself he will never go back over the Wall – which, of course, no longer exists. In essence, Heini refuses to acknowledge reality. He remains in Pankow, his small sector of Berlin, in which he feels safe and comfortable.

The inevitable implosion of Heini's world comes with his retirement from the police force at the age of sixty-two in May of 2003. This event confronts Heini with the absolute loneliness of his life, and with freedom, which terrifies him. It is at this point that Heini makes the S-Bahn trip back to the Tiergarten and into the landscape of his youth:

> The train he gets onto is going toward the Zoologischer Garten train station. The stations that he rode through thirty years ago are taking Paffrath back to something whose memories he had erased. Into a blotted-out world that he wasn't willing to visit until today, because he believes it to be dead and buried: the Vineta of his biography. (*FH*, 183–4)

A great deal has changed in west Berlin, but not everything; and the house in which Heini was born in December of 1941 is still standing. The world of Heini's past is not as dead as he had hoped. In west Berlin Heini's adult world collapses. In order to protect himself, he purchases a new uniform, that of a successful western businessman, and he proceeds to go to an expensive cigar bar, where he orders a Havana cigar, winds up hiding out in the bathroom after closing time, and then sets the entire place on fire during the night. At the end of his life Heini embraces the chaos and destruction of fire that his father had dedicated his life to fighting: the chaos and destruction out of which he was born. The novel ends as Heini returns to the Pankow police station to turn himself in to the young west German policeman who used to be his superior officer. Heini is a German and a Berliner who is incapable of living in freedom. For him there are only two alternatives: rigid control on the one hand or chaos and anarchy on the other.

In its emphasis on individual loneliness and alienation, and on Berlin as a city of memories, *Falscher Hase* resembles several other Berlin novels and stories. However, because it deals with a west–east German life, it is able to bridge the gap between east and west more effectively than most other literary fiction. Hensel's narrative gives readers a genuine sense of place in Pankow, Tiergarten and Charlottenburg; but it also shows the profound connections between geography and history. Hensel is also able to provide a psychological explanation for citizens' willingness to put up with the Wall – i.e. the division of their city – that is unusual and much needed in Berlin fiction.

'GINA REGINA'

At its most crass level, Ulrike Draesner's 'Gina Regina' is a short story about a young woman who, unbeknownst to her sexual partners, collects their sperm and sells it to female American customers on the World Wide Web who are eager to be impregnated with the semen of attractive, intelligent German males. Gina literally combines business with pleasure – 'a simple business procedure that was also fun', as Gina puts it in the interior monologue of which the story consists.[32] Gina is a hip young resident of Berlin-Mitte, the coolest part of contemporary Berlin. She is sexy, smart and irreverent, moving smoothly from Ludwig Wittgenstein's *Tractatus Logico-Philosophicus* to collecting sperm in the space of a single series of thoughts. Draesner's portrait of a jaded 'Berlin generation' is quite similar to Judith Hermann's pictures of contemporary urban youth, particularly young women, in Germany. Gina believes that she is above and beyond 'Retrovalues', i.e. a belief in morality, sentiment, order and authority. Her only problem is that she has made the mistake of falling in love with one of her lovers, a student named Gordian, who makes her pulse beat faster while she imagines kitschy 'beating red hearts in front of her, like a Piemont cherry dipped into Mon Chéri!' (*GR*, 12). This description neatly sums up Gina's problem: she cannot conceive of romantic love as anything other than a cliché or a consumer advertisement, something thought up by an older, unironic, boring generation. Love is precisely part of the 'Retrovalues' that Gina rejects: a remnant from an older, stick-in-the-mud culture; or else it is simply an enticement to buy.

Gina is caught on the horns of a terrible dilemma. The hip, urban, cool culture of which she likes to consider herself part is a culture that denies the possibility of real intimacy and fulfilment. And Gordian, whose name is of course also a reference to the impossible-to-untie Gordian knot of Greek antiquity, is himself a member of this hip, cool culture; he is not receptive to Gina's emotional 'authenticity number' (*GR*, 18). In the end Gina saves a vial of Gordian's sperm for her own possible future use, withdrawing it from the capitalist circulation that she otherwise cheerfully serves, while reassuring herself that the lacquer covering her breasts is 'unharmed' ('unverletzt') by her unruly emotions. Like the female narrator of Christoph Hein's powerful GDR novel *Der fremde Freund* (The Distant Lover, 1982), Gina has shielded herself from involvement and intimacy. The lacquer represents the dragon's blood in which she, like Siegfried – and Hein's character – has bathed in order to make herself invulnerable. She has transformed one of the softest and most intimate parts of her body into a hard, glitzy shield meant both to display and to hide itself. The irony is that Gina's very invulnerability is also slowly suffocating her. Draesner provides access to her character's thoughts and feelings in a way that Judith Hermann, in her short stories, does not. Both women describe a similar world, but Draesner allows her readers, paradoxically, to get emotionally close to emotional distance. Draesner achieves this while painting a realistic and lively picture of contemporary Berlin and its urban youth subculture.

CONCLUSION

In spite of the differences between the four works I have discussed, all four display certain characteristic similarities. They all depict lonely and frequently neurotic individuals in a modern or postmodern urban land-scape. In all four the city is open to the currents of history, but it is also a cocoon in which the main characters sometimes seek to resist change and avoid vulnerability. All four authors show a distinctive approach to nar-rative language. Grass's novel features a hidden narrator highly cognisant of literary and geographical precedent, while Brussig's novel features an unreliable narrator who is completely ignorant of literature (even if Brussig is not). Grass's layered language harks back to the language of Theodor Fontane's Berlin and Brandenburg, while Brussig's language looks forward to a flatter, more American, and perhaps less German, Berlin. Hensel's and Draesner's language, while embedded in third-person narratives, remains largely focused on and limited to one protagonist's perspective. Both Hensel and Draesner give their readers interior monologues that provide access to their protagonists' thoughts – and, by implication, to what is absent or repressed from those thoughts.

In their sometimes detailed attention to Berlin as a place, these works are profoundly German. Grass's and, paradoxically, Brussig's attention to German literary tradition also mark their works as specifically German. Hensel's focus on a traumatic wartime childhood that began during the bombing of Berlin responds to recent discussions about the trauma of specifically German wartime suffering and the permissibility of discussions about that suffering (see Helmut Schmitz's chapter in this volume). On the surface, Draesner's story is the least German of the four narratives, since it focuses on a self-consciously *global* youth culture. However the specific power of Gina's rejection of traditionalism, and of her openness to global levelling, implies a refusal of the kind of authority, literary and otherwise, for which Grass's Fonty stands. This rejection is in itself very German. As Gina notes, her work combines 'the national and the international, the generally German with the individual' (*GR*, 15). Gina is a personification of the young German who no longer wishes to be really German, or to accept German traditions.

These narratives about individual loneliness and social anomie simultaneously reflect international trends, such as Bret Easton Ellis's or Michel Houellebecq's novels of urban social despair, in which, as the narrator of Houellebecq's novel *The Elementary Particles* notes, 'feelings such as love, tenderness and human fellowship' have, 'for the most part, disappeared'.[33] They suggest that throughout the world the explosion of globalisation that was to a large extent unleashed by the opening of the Berlin Wall, German unification, and the subsequent collapse of the eastern bloc have placed extraordinary pressures on subjectivity and language, as well as on literature itself. Literature responds to those pressures precisely through subjectivity and language. Faced with the flux of a contemporary metropolis that threatens to overwhelm, literature builds a metropolis of words that represent, and recreate, subjectivity.

NOTES

1. Hajo Steinert, '"Döblin, dringend gesucht!" Berlin-Romane der neunziger Jahre' in Christian Döring, ed., *Deutschsprachige Gegenwartsliteratur: Wider ihre Verächter* (Frankfurt: Suhrkamp, 1995), 234–45; here 234.

2. Uwe Timm, *Rot* (Cologne: Kiepenheuer & Witsch, 2001), 306–7.

3. Heinz Bude, *Generation Berlin* (Berlin: Merve, 2001).

4. See Stephen Brockmann, *Literature and German Reunification* (Cambridge: Cambridge University Press, 1999), 64–79.

5. Christa Wolf, *Was bleibt* (Berlin: Aufbau, 1990), 5, 76.

6. Wolf, *Was bleibt*, 76.

7. Christian Jäger, 'Berlin Heinrichplatz: The Novels of Ulrich Peltzer', trans. Stephen Brockmann, *Studies in 20th & 21st Century Literature*, 28:1 (2004): 183–210, here 208.

8. Bertolt Brecht, 'Keiner oder Alle', from *Die Tage der Kommune*, in Werner Hecht et al., ed., *Werke: Große kommentierte Berliner und Frankfurter Ausgabe*, vol. 8 (Berlin, Weimar and Frankfurt: Aufbau and Suhrkamp, 1992), 243–317, here, 307–8.

9. See Stuart Taberner, *German Literature of the 1990s and Beyond: Normalization and the Berlin Republic* (Rochester: Camden House, 2005), 6–8.

10. Volker Hage, 'Ganz schön abgedreht', *Der Spiegel* (22 March 1999), 244–6, here 245.

11. See Stephen Brockmann, 'Divided and Reunited Berlin in Peter Schneider's Fiction' in Carol Anne Costabile-Heming, Rachel J. Halverson and Kristie A. Foell, eds., *Berlin: The Symphony Continues – Orchestrating Architectural, Social,*

and *Artistic Change in Germany's New Capital* (Berlin: Walter de Gruyter, 2004), 223–43.

12. See Carol Anne Costabile-Heming, 'The Presence and Absence of the Past: Sites of Memory and Forgetting in F. C. Delius's *Die Flatterzunge*', *Studies in 20th & 21st Century Literature*, 28:1 (2004): 240–57.

13. See Taberner, *German Literature of the 1990s and Beyond*, 221–5.

14. See Katrin Sieg, 'Post-colonial Berlin? Pieke Biermann's Crime Novels as Globalization Critique', *Studies in 20th & 21st Century Literature*, 28:1 (2004): 152–82.

15. Karl Heinz Bohrer, 'Provinzialismus', *Merkur* 501 (December 1990), 1096–1102.

16. Cited in Erhard Schütz, 'Benjamins Berlin: Wiedergewinnung des Entfernten' in Detlev Schöttker, ed., *Schrift Bilder Denken: Walter Benjamin und die Künste* (Frankfurt: Suhrkamp, 2004), 32–47, here 38.

17. Bodo Morshäuser, *Liebeserklärung an eine häßliche Stadt* (Frankfurt: Suhrkamp, 1998), 138.

18. Ward Just, *The Weather in Berlin* (Boston and New York: Houghton Mifflin, 2002), 304.

19. Just, *The Weather in Berlin*, 104.

20. "Ich bin die Wenderoman-Polizei", interview with Thomas Brussig, *Sonntag* (20 September 2004), S1.

21. Matthias Zschokke, *Der dicke Dichter* (Cologne: Bruckner & Thünker, 1995), 127–8.

22. Jochen Langer, 'Reichstag', in *Die Zeit danach: Neue deutsche Literatur* (Cologne: Kiepenheuer & Witsch, 1991), 92–101, here, 100–1.

23. Thomas Tuma, 'Generation XY ungelöst', *Der Spiegel* (29 March 2004), 66–72.

24. Günter Grass, *Too Far Afield*, trans. Krishna Winston (New York: Harcourt, 2000), 7.

25. Grass, *Too Far Afield*, 23.

26. Grass, *Too Far Afield*, 54.

27. Sigmund Freud, *Civilization and its Discontents*, trans. James Strachey (New York: Norton, 1989), 16.

28. Thomas Brussig, *Helden wie wir* (Berlin: Volk & Welt, 1995), 7.

29. Kerstin Hensel, *Falscher Hase* (Munich: Luchterhand, 2005), 37–8. Hereafter *FH*.

30. Theodor W. Adorno et al., *The Authoritarian Personality* (New York: Harper, 1950).

31. Erich Fromm, *Escape from Freedom* (New York: Farrar & Rinehart, 1941).

32. Ulrike Draesner, 'Gina Regina', in Draesner, *Hot Dogs* (Munich: Luchterhand, 2004), 7–20, here 9. Hereafter *GR*.

33. Michel Houellebecq, *The Elementary Particles*, trans. Frank Wynne (New York: Knopf, 2000), 3.

CHAPTER 4

'GDR literature' in the Berlin Republic

Paul Cooke

'How can you call this book "GDR Literature" . . . The GDR no longer exists!'[1] This was the indignant retort of Thomas Brussig, one of the more successful writers from the former East Germany, to a question about the status of his bestselling novel *Helden wie wir* (Heroes Like Us, 1995). For Brussig, clearly, 'GDR literature', along with the state itself, had passed into history with unification on 3 October 1990. Yet, if this is truly the case, how are we to understand the title of the volume *DDR-Literatur der neunziger Jahre* (GDR Literature of the Nineties), published in 2000 in Heinz Ludwig Arnold's Text+Kritik series, or, indeed, of the 1996 edition of Wolfgang Emmerich's seminal *Kleine Literaturgeschichte der DDR* (A Short Literary History of the GDR), which similarly refers to texts from the 1990s?[2]

In this chapter I examine this tension and explore competing definitions of 'GDR literature since unification'. I focus on a range of authors, from those who first came to public attention in the GDR itself to those who were not yet adults at the time of the *Wende* (the fall of the Berlin Wall). I look at how the political and aesthetic stances adopted by established GDR writers continue to impact upon the literature of the Berlin Republic and at a form of post-1990 'GDR literature' with a less ideological, more visceral relationship to the now defunct state. Here, we find authors attempting to protect a specific sense of an east German identity which is contingent upon their pre-1990 experience and which they often feel is ignored in the present. Much of this fiction has been viewed as a form of *Ostalgie*, the term applied to a range of cultural phenomena and political attitudes that seem to evoke nostalgia for aspects of East Germany. As we shall see, however, writing by east Germans does not universally present an impression of discontent with united Germany. For some authors, moreover, the GDR seems to be losing its appeal as a literary topic. This suggests that Brussig's declaration of the death of GDR literature might have been premature but was perhaps not entirely mistaken.

IDEALISM AND SOCIALIST VALUES

That the end of the GDR would mean the end of GDR writing – and, indeed, of West German fiction – was certainly the supposition of a number of West Germany's most influential literary critics during the so-called *Literaturstreit* (Literature Debate) of 1990 sparked by the delayed publication of Christa Wolf's story *Was bleibt* (What remains). Based on her victimisation by the East German security services (Stasi) and largely written in 1979, its appearance in 1990 saw the author, previously praised for bravely challenging GDR autocracy, now condemned by Ulrich Greiner in *Die Zeit* as a lackey of the state who had helped prolong the life of a dictatorial regime. For Greiner, the publication of *Was bleibt* in 1990 was at best an act of cowardice and at worst a cynical attempt by the author to paint herself as a dissident.[3] The *Was bleibt* controversy subsequently provoked a broader debate on the validity of GDR literature *per se*, a debate which was then reignited as information began to surface about the extent to which other authors previously considered to be dissidents had actively co-operated with the Stasi.[4] Greiner's condemnation appeared to have been validated, such that it now seemed impossible that Wolf and her fellow GDR writers might have any role to play in the cultural life of the newly unified state. However, throughout the 1990s and beyond, many of the GDR's most important writers continued to examine the GDR's failings as well as their own complicity with these failings. Indeed, such writers were determined to reassert the legitimacy both of socialist values and of the writer's role as social critic.

Wolf's 2002 novel, *Leibhaftig* (In Person), for example, revisits the debate about the author's 'complicity' via the story of a writer confined to hospital following an appendix operation just as the GDR was about to collapse. Under heavy sedation the narrator goes on a hallucinatory journey into her past, a surreal descent 'into Hades' accompanied by 'a female Cicerone', her anaesthetist Kora,[5] in order to examine her continued faith in socialism in the face of its corruption by the state's ruling elite. From the very outset of the work, when she remembers the suppression of the Prague Spring by the Warsaw Pact in 1968, the moment that shattered the socialist beliefs of so many of her generation, this faith is challenged. At this stage, however, she accepts her mother's view that 'there are worse things' (*L*, 7). And it is not long before we are given a glimpse of what these 'things' might be: she travels further back in time, to the persecution of the Jews and the destruction unleashed by the Nazi regime (*L*, 113). Yet, as we subsequently move forward into the GDR period and learn of the narrator's relationship with Urban, a one-time friend from whom she became estranged as he moved up the party hierarchy, her defence of the GDR appears ever more strained. For the narrator, Urban is typical of those 'ambitious, talentless' individuals (*L*, 47) who came to run the GDR, a further incarnation of the unimaginative 'Hop-Hop people' identified in *Nachdenken über Christa T.* (The Quest for Christa T., 1968) that had corrupted the state's founding ideals.[6] The narrator of *Leibhaftig*, however, admits her collusion with such people. Thus she recounts the story of Paul, a good-natured young man whom Urban uses as a scapegoat when a youth policy which she had helped to write fails. She had known at the time that this was likely to happen but had continued to work with the party functionary (*L*, 134).

By the end of the novel, we learn that Urban has taken his own life, having been dismissed from his job and finally rejected by the state as it rushes towards self-destruction (*L*, 153). As for the narrator, it is clear that her illness is psychological rather than physical. Indeed, her miserable state of mind is exacerbated once her imaginary journey into Hades takes her into the future, into the post-communist Berlin of the 1990s.[7] This is a dystopian prospect: 'the city, a once holy place, has been desecrated . . . And there is no turning back from this new wilderness' (*L*, 146). Yet the narrator does succeed in turning back. She returns with Kora from her vision of hell, rejects the nihilism that caused Urban to commit suicide and attempts to reinvigorate her hope for a future that would finally make good on the GDR's failed promise (*L*, 183). In the last lines of the text, moreover, the message of Wolf's 1990 *Was bleibt* is restated, as implied, most specifically, in the invocation of Hölderlin's poem 'Remembrance' in the title of the earlier story. Overcome by the view from her hospital window and by her returning health, the narrator reflects on the power of poetry both to encapsulate the beauty of the world and, more importantly, to give guidance on how to respond to this world (*L*, 184). At a moment when so much else has been lost, it would seem that, in Hölderlin's words, 'poets establish what remains'.[8] In uncertain times, one can still rely on literature as a source of truth. Although discredited in the wake of *Wende*, the author Christa Wolf clearly still believes in her role as a writer and in the socialist standpoint inscribed into her fiction.

The characters of Wolfgang Hilbig, an east German writer publishing since the 1970s, also often inhabit grotesque, subterranean fantasy worlds.[9] We might think, for example, of *Eine Übertragung* (A Translation, 1989) and its narrator's descent into the underworld, or of Hilbig's post-unification meditation on the role of the Stasi in the artistic life of the GDR, '*Ich*'

('I', 1993), the informant-protagonist of which dwells in the same cellars through which Wolf's narrator moves. In Hilbig's work, however, there is no endorsement of Wolf's belief in an idealised GDR socialist project. Instead, Hilbig, a self-educated former manual worker, exposes the lie at the heart of the so-called 'Worker and Farmers' State'. Working in the modernist tradition of Kafka and Beckett, his multi-layered, semi-autobiographical texts explore the destructive effects of authoritarianism on those for whom the state was ostensibly founded. Indeed, his third full-length novel, *Das Provisorium* (The Temporary Solution, 2000), which is discussed here, includes a particularly damning indictment of the cultural intelligentsia to which Wolf belonged. Overcome with anger, the narrator suggests that those who had legitimised the GDR, be it 'through poetry, cultural politics or as part of the police force', should simply be 'pushed . . . into a corner and mown down with a machine gun'.[10]

Hilbig's protagonist, a reincarnation of the writer-worker 'C.' featured in many of his earlier texts, is as venomous as ever in his attack on the GDR. In *Das Provisorium*, however, there is some development in respect of the author's previous work: the novel depicts a GDR writer in exile coming to terms with living in *West* Germany prior to unification. Having struggled in vain to gain recognition as a writer in the East, C. is finally given a visa to travel to West Germany for a year in the mid 1980s. He finds it impossible to settle, however, and suffers writer's block. The freedom that he longed for has been bought at the cost of an overwhelming sense of homelessness (*P*, 16). Rather than helping him to recover, however, his subsequent, obsessively regular trips back to the GDR simply underscore the debilitating liminality of his situation and, as implied in the title of the novel, the *provisorisch* (provisional) nature of his life.

Although set in the 1980s, the novel predicts the sense of homelessness of which many east Germans complained after unification as they struggled to come to terms with the new capitalist system. C.'s *Wende* effectively takes place four years before the events of 1989 – rather than finding a Promised Land in the Federal Republic, he is shocked by what he sees as the vapidity of western consumer culture. Indeed, the hegemony of consumerism is seen by C. as a new form of fascism. Recalling in one of his drunken rants the sign above the gates to Auschwitz concentration camp – 'Through work to freedom' – Hilbig's protagonist provocatively declares that in this new state a similar sign might read 'through *Shopping* to freedom' (*P*, 263). In this post-unification novel, then, and in contrast with his earlier work, it appears that Hilbig wishes, implicitly at least, to recuperate the declared socialist values of the ex-GDR, coming closer to the position of Wolf than he ever could in his pre-unification writing. As the author himself suggests in his 1996 'Kamenzer Rede' ('Kamenz speech') 'Perhaps one day we'll realise that it was by joining the FRG that we became the GDR citizens that we never were before, at least not as long as we were forced to be.'[11] What is particularly lamentable for C. is that literature has no value in the West. In Hilbig's earlier fiction, his writer-workers at least feel that they have a purpose, writing being a means by which they can attempt to imbue the banality of their life as a worker with meaning. In *Das Provisorium*, C. is trapped inside a world that is just as banal, but now he cannot even write. While Hilbig, in a similar way to Wolf, might continue to believe in fiction as a means of expressing dissent and social critique, the protagonist of *Das Provisorium* has no faith that this kind of literature will be able to play a central role in the new Germany.

If Hilbig has moved closer to Wolf since unification, becoming the 'GDR writer' he could never be while the state existed, his worldview nonetheless remains far bleaker than hers. As such, he has more in common with GDR writers not endorsed by the state, such as Gert Neumann, a highly influential figure on Hilbig's early career. He might also be compared with members of the alternative Prenzlauer Berg cultural scene such as Uwe Kolbe, or with other younger writers including Kurt Drawert. These artists began to come to public attention in the final years of East Germany's existence and were viewed by western commentators as an important new departure for GDR literature; post-unification, however, they have tended to remain on the margins of literary life.[12] The novels of Reinhard Jirgl, a writer who has only managed to find a publisher since unification, also recall Hilbig in their similarly modernist-inspired apocalyptic vision of a post-Cold War world, most notably in *Abschied von den Feinden* (Farewell to the Enemies, 1995), *Hundsnächte* (Dog Nights, 1997) and *Die Atlantische Mauer* (The Atlantic Wall, 2000).[13] In addition, we might mention here the work of Kerstin Hensel and Ingo Schramm; in his first novel, *Fitchers Blau* (Fitcher's Blue, 1996), Schramm in fact cites Hilbig, reflecting on the latter's complex literary critique of socialism and its aftermath: 'language of this kind is dissipated in the storm of a world epoch consisting of nothing but noise'.[14] Schramm's text then explores the destructive effects of Germany's violent history, from National Socialism, through the perverted socialist experiment that was the GDR, to what the narrator perceives as the amorality of contemporary capitalist society, employing, as Helmut Schmitz suggests, 'modernist forms' in order to signal a 'desire to withdraw from the grip of aesthetic standardisation by the market'.[15]

INGO SCHULZE'S 'SIMPLE STORYS' FROM THE FORMER GDR

The allusion to the modernist literary tradition as a means of critiquing post-unification society also informs Ingo Schulze's *Simple Storys: Ein Roman aus der ostdeutschen Provinz* (Simple Storys: A Novel from the East German Province, 1998), one of the most successful east German novels of the 1990s. Here, however, the emphasis is almost entirely on east Germans' difficulties in the present in adjusting to the realities of the new capitalist system. Schulze brings the everyday experience of east Germans, whom he presents as living on the periphery of united Germany, into the foreground.[16] In a series of twenty-nine short stories, told from a variety of narrative perspectives, the novel plots the lives of a diverse group of individuals from Altenburg, a small town in the former GDR, from early in 1990 to 1997 as they try to deal with the rapid pace of change after the *Wende*. We meet, for example, the Meurer family, at the head of which is Ernst Meurer, a retired head teacher and ex-party official who is struggling with social exclusion after the collapse of the old regime, a struggle which eventually leads to the failure of both his health and his marriage. His stepson, Martin, is a redundant academic whose life also falls apart after he loses his job, an event which leads indirectly to the death of his wife in a road accident and to rejection by his son. The death of Ernst's wife brings Barbara Holitzschek into the narrative, a doctor and politician's wife, who is responsible for the accident and, although not prosecuted for it, is gradually consumed by guilt. Elsewhere in Altenburg, we meet Christian Beyer, a middle-aged business-man struggling to maintain a local advertising newspaper, and Raffael, the boss of a failing taxi company. Then, from the younger generation, we are introduced to Jenny, a student nurse, who we learn has been prostituting herself to an older married man. This man is Dieter Schubert, one-time colleague of Ernst Meurer, who still bears the scars of his denunciation by Meurer before the GDR's collapse.

The further we progress through these 'simple stories', the more we realise that each of the characters is linked through a highly involved net-work of interconnections. Individual figures appear again and again in the stories, often in different constellations and in different settings. Each story constitutes a momentary snapshot in the changing lives of the people of Altenburg, as we see them move from relationship to relationship and from job to job. As a result of the reader's engagement, the interstices between these moments are filled. These are far from singular 'simple stories', then, but are – as is made clear in the novel's table of contents – chapters in an intricately structured depiction of a social and historical reality. At the heart of this narrative – although never directly discussed – lies the act of German unification. This appears to the inhabitants of Schulze's society as the beginning of a devastating process of 'colonisation'. A petrol station owned by a western company that appears in the darkness in front of a driving couple is thus described as an 'Ufo', that is, as an alien invading the landscape (S, 67). But is not only the territory of the GDR that has been colonised – the language of its population has also been permeated by the vocabulary of western capitalism. In the final chapter of the novel, for instance, we see Martin Meurer, a man whose life we have followed through-out the book, reduced to working in the west German city of Stuttgart as a live advertisement for a fish restaurant. When he calls the piece of paper that he has to hand out to potential customers a 'Zettel' (leaflet), his boss insists that he use the word 'Flyer' (S, 296). The indigenous German word is replaced by the Americanised language of marketing.

That the 'colonisation' of the east is seen as synonymous with American-isation is demonstrated not only at the level of content, but also of form. Central to the success of *Simple Storys* was undoubtedly Schulze's use of the American short-story tradition. Peter Michalzik notes, for example, the importance of Hemingway, Anderson and Raymond Carver to Schulze's text. In addition, he, like many other critics, sees Robert Altman's filmic reworking of Carver, *Short Cuts* (1993), as a precursor to the novel.[17] At the same time, the inappropriateness of the Americanised model to local condi-tions is insinuated in the very title of the novel: *Simple Storys* is, the author insists, to be pronounced as German, the (in English) incorrect spelling of 'Storys' being the correct German plural as it appears in *Duden*.[18] Further-more, the critical focus on the use of American literary antecedents ignores the fact that Schulze also draws on a tradition of GDR modernist litera-ture. As Holger Briel notes, Schulze's Altenburg recalls, for example, the provincial world of Johannes Bobrowski or Uwe Johnson.[19] Indeed, one might even suggest Brecht as an influence on the intriguing plot summaries that precede each story and which often deliberately obfuscate, rather than clarify, the content of the subsequent narrative.

THOMAS BRUSSIG AND GERMAN UNIFICATION

Schulze's exploration of east German experience post-unification may be viewed as a further development of a GDR modernist tradition, albeit one which also draws on western literary forms. It also hints at the melan-cholic worldview to be found in the post-1990 writing of Wolf, Hilbig and Schramm and described by critic Iris Radisch as the dominant characteristic of contemporary east German fiction: 'the east is tragic, the west funny'.[20] This characterisation, however, ignores the wealth of satirical texts penned by east German writers since unification, ranging from Matthias Biskupek's *Der Quotensachse* (The Token Saxon, 1996), a satire on the rediscovery of a pride in Saxon regional identity after 1989,[21] to Jens Sparschuh's *Eins zu Eins* (One to One, 2003), which lampoons *Ostalgie* and the western transformation of East Germany into a heritage park.[22] In these and other works, including Bernd Schirmer's *Schlehweins Giraffe* (Schlehwein's Giraffe, 1992) and Sparschuh's earlier *Der Zimmerspringbrunnen* (The Living Room Fountain, 1995), we find neither the continuation of a GDR modernist tradition, nor a consistently melancholic view of the world, but rather a development of East Germany's vibrant cabaret culture.[23] This is most obviously true of Biskupek, who was an active member in the *Fettnäppchen* Cabaret in Gera during the GDR era.

The best known of these satirists, Thomas Brussig (born 1965), also acknowledges his debt to this tradition in his working relationship with the Dresden cabarettist Uwe Steimel, with whom he has collaborated on several projects.[24] Brussig's literary breakthrough came with the 1995 publication of *Helden wie wir*, a novel that tells the story of a Forest Gump-like Stasi officer, Klaus Uhltzscht, who stumbles through the history of the GDR, affecting it at key moments. This is most notably the case on the night of 9 November 1989 when, Uhltzscht claims, it was he who caused the first breach in the Wall on the Bornholmer Straße by exposing himself to the border guards. Shocked by the size of his member, the guards simply moved aside, he boasts, to allow the waiting crowds to pass through.[25] On the one hand, by caricaturing the history of the GDR as a state dominated by its Security Service, even suggesting that the Stasi was responsible for the population's final 'liberation', the text satirises the media frenzy for accounts of Stasi scandals that filled the German press in the early 1990s. On the other hand, *Helden wie wir* viciously attacks the fantasy that a GDR citizenry which had been so overwhelmingly conformist for forty years could ever have brought about its own emancipation through the power of its 'we are the people' declaration on the streets of Leipzig and Berlin in 1989. 'Look at the east Germans before and after the fall of the Wall', Klaus declares, 'they were passive before and they're still passive' (*H*, 320).[26] Indeed, Brussig's satire is not only directed against the masses. The novel's final chapter, entitled 'Der geheilte Pimmel' ('The Healed Willy') – a satirical reference to Wolf's canonical text *Der geteilte Himmel* (The Divided Heaven, 1963) – contains a sustained diatribe against Christa Wolf. Klaus witnesses the author's famous speech on 4 November 1989 at Berlin's Alexanderplatz, in which she rejected unification in favour of socialism 'with a human face' (reproduced in full, *H*, 283–5), although he comically confuses Wolf with Jutta Müller, the trainer of the ice skater Katarina Witt, an icon of GDR sport. Klaus is disgusted by what he sees as Wolf's defence of the GDR's socialist project:' it would be laughable', the narrator suggests, 'if only it wasn't so bloody tragic' (*H*, 287).

The facetious conflation of Wolf with Müller mocks the ideals of Wolf's generation of writers. In his subsequent work, including *Wie es leuchtet* (How Bright It Is, 2004), however, Brussig strikes a more conciliatory tone. In this highly ambitious project, the author delivers a panoramic account of events between the summers of 1989 and 1990.[27] Reminiscent of the structure of *Simple Storys*, if not of its gloomy tone, the novel presents a range of entertaining characters who come to the fore at various moments in the narrative. Thus we glimpse the human story behind the iconic pictures by which this now historical period is remembered. We are introduced to Paulchen, one of the many who escaped across the Hungarian border in the summer of 1989, as well as to a number of state functionaries including the high-ranking minister Valentin Eich, a literary incarnation of the GDR's state money launderer Alexander Schalk-Golodkowski, who tries to disappear when it becomes clear that the SED regime's days are numbered. Elsewhere we meet Alfred Bunzuweit, the manager of the elite GDR Palasthotel, who, desperate to curry favour with his West German guests, falls for the nineteen-year old confidence trickster Werner Schiedel, a young man posing as the son of a Volkswagen director sent to the East to enter into negotiations with the GDR car industry. Other characters include the Stasi informant turned PDS politician Gisela Blank, who quickly burns her State Security file in order to prevent the truth of her past coming to light, only to be photographed by a journalist in the act (*W*, 185). We follow these and numerous other figures from the mass euphoria of 9 November to the first free elections in March and monetary union in July 1990, as the population attempts to deal with the economic, legal and moral confusion the East German dictatorship left in its wake.

Initially, *Wie es leuchtet* appears to take up where *Helden wie wir* left off, with the east German population being held to account for their complicity with the communist state. We meet, for example, an 'unshaven little poet', a star of the cultural scene during GDR times, who descends into blind panic when he realises that unification is on the way; this character, it is soon apparent, is a thinly veiled version of the author Volker Braun. While Brussig remains critical of the GDR intelligentsia, however, his tone has clearly softened. By the time we get to read Braun's poem 'Das Eigentum'

(Property), reprinted in full in the novel (*W*, 584), we have begun to see the disillusion that would follow the euphoria of those early post-*Wende* days as the population tried to come to terms with a society in which shared socialist values had been replaced by the pursuit of individual wealth. Somewhat surprisingly, given the viciousness of the attack in *Helden wie wir* on GDR intellectuals and their often naive defence of the East German state's concept of anti-fascism, furthermore, we are reminded of the trauma endured by the poet during the Allied bombing of Dresden in early 1945 (*W*, 583). Through such allusions, we are encouraged to sympathise with a man who, having been left stranded by history, finds a moment of satisfaction in his work as an artist and in the creation of a good poem with some social relevance: 'I've still got it, he rejoiced, I've still got it' (*W*, 584).

In reviews of his work following *Helden wie wir*, Brussig has often been charged with promoting *Ostalgie*, a charge which has certainly not hurt sales of his novels. Indeed, in recent years nostalgia for the GDR has become big business, as demonstrated by the growing market for re-launched East German consumer goods.[28] Certainly, the author defends the right of east Germans to remember fondly aspects of everyday life in the East German dictatorship.[29] Far from indulging in a kind of unreflected wistfulness, however, he explores the impulses behind *Ostalgie* itself. In *Am kürzeren Ende der Sonnenallee* (On the Shorter End of Sun Alley, 1999), for example, a novel based on Leander Haußmann's hit comedy about a group of East German teenagers living in the shadow of the Berlin Wall, *Sonnenallee* (Sun Alley, 1999), Brussig explores contemporary manifestations of *Ostalgie* as a response to western misrepresentations of the GDR as a 'Stasi state' that allowed no space for 'normal' human experience. For Brussig, growing up in the East was not necessarily any less 'normal' than an adolescence lived out in the West.[30] The nostalgic recollection of this experience, consequently, need not be taken as a worrying sign of Germany's continued disunity. In *Wie es leuchtet* too, nostalgia is presented as a 'normal' human emotion. The East German Palasthotel, for example, has a 'nostalgia bar'; this suggests that a sentimentalised longing for the past already existed in the GDR prior to 1989 (*W*, 138), albeit differently inflected. We are also transported back to the early 1990s in the west, during which the reader is allowed to indulge in a parallel and equally harmless form of nostalgia, this time for America rather than for East Germany. Thus Lena travels to New York in the summer of 1990, during which she visits the roof of the World Trade Centre (*W*, 576). Since 11 September 2001, of course, the world represented by the Twin Towers has been changed for ever. The New York of 1990, like East Germany, no longer exists. Nonetheless, the reader can enjoy a moment of nostalgic recollection for this world which does not erase the changed reality of the present, just as a citizen of the ex-GDR might enjoy drinking a glass of East German *Sekt* without wishing to see the Berlin Wall rebuilt.

In *Wie es leuchtet*, Brussig expresses the sense of frustration felt by many in the east who are unable to identify with the values of a corrupt socialist regime but equally unable to come to terms with the realities of capitalist society. At the end of the text, however, there is a sense that while this history must be remembered, those directly affected will eventually pass on, leaving a generation of post-unification Germans for whom the East German state will be less significant (*W*, 600–7). This notwithstanding, it is clear that the legacy of the GDR, as well as the difficulty of adjusting to life in the now unified state, continues to impact upon the generation of writers who were only children at the time of the state's collapse. In a recent spate of autobiographical texts by writers born in the decade after Brussig, including Claudia Rusch's *Meine freie deutsche Jugend* (My Free German Youth, 2003), Jana Simon's *Denn wir sind anders* (For we are Different, 2003) and Jana Hensel's *Zonenkinder* (Children of the Zone, 2002), we find a continuation of the melancholic tone we see in Schulze and Schramm. Hensel's *Zonenkinder*, for example, examines both the experience of a childhood spent in the GDR and its protagonist's post-unification alienation.[31] Born in 1977, Hensel was thirteen at the time of the *Wende*. In this autobiographical essay, the events of 1989 are portrayed as the moment when the author lost her innocence (*Z*, 11), as the moment at which she was cut off from her childhood. Through writing, Hensel attempts to reconnect with this past life. She digs deep into her memory in a nostalgic recollection of life as a young girl and reconstructs her 'East German experience' in minute detail, often through the inclusion of pictures of everyday GDR products, many of which were being marketed as *Ostalgie* at the time of the novel's publication. However, it becomes obvious that an authentic reconstruction of the past is impossible, since her perception has necessarily been shaped by her experience of living in a capitalist society: 'We are the first *Wessies* from east Germany, and no one can tell where we come from' (*Z*, 166). The only way that her generation can construct an identity for itself is by highlighting its feeling of not belonging: 'we grew up in neither the GDR nor the Federal Republic. We are the children of the Zone' (*Z*, 159). Hensel views east Germans of her age as members of a lost community, a 'we' caught in limbo. As Owen Evans suggests: 'If the generation immediately before the "Zonenkinder" were seen as "hineingeboren" [the ones born into it] in the GDR, to use Uwe Kolbe's famous phrase . . . then they themselves might be seen as "herausgerutscht" [the ones that slipped out]'.[32] This is a fragile generation with no fixed points of orientation.

Yet the recollection of the GDR by this younger generation is not always as fraught. In the work of writers such as Jochen Schmidt, Jakob Hein and Falko Hennig – artists associated with east Berlin's lively literary performance scene – we discover an exploration of a childhood in the GDR contrasted with life in the unified state.[33] To an extent, works such as Schmidt's *Müller haut uns raus* (Müller Kicks us Out, 2002), Hein's *Mein erstes T-Shirt* (My First T-Shirt, 2001) and Hennig's *Alles nur geklaut* (Everything is Stolen, 1999), replicate the emphasis on the everyday experience of growing up in the GDR to be found in Brussig's *Am kürzeren Ende der Sonnenallee*. In *Mein erstes T-Shirt*, for example, we read of the narrator's attempts to impress his friends with his musical prowess at parties and of his difficulties in negotiating puberty and dealing with girls.[34] Yet, whereas Brussig defiantly insists on an 'east German normality' as a form of resistance to what he sees as western marginalisation, for Hein such normality is a given; this makes possible a far more matter-of-fact portrayal of life in the GDR. Moreover, he has little time for those who excuse the GDR's failings. He may have been 'normal', but the GDR was not. In answer to the question 'do you miss anything about the GDR?', asked by one interviewer, the author responded: 'no, because you can't have part of it without the whole of it. The GDR was a package deal and I'm glad to be rid of it.'[35]

At the same time, Hein is clearly grateful for the healthy sense of cynicism his experience of the GDR helped him nurture, a cynicism that is invaluable in relation to life in the west. This does not imply a melancholic image of east Germans as the 'losers' of unification. Rather, we are presented with an image of a wily survivor, dealing with whatever life throws at him. Indeed, it would appear that his biography makes him *better* able to deal with life under capitalism than those who have never experienced the duplicities of the GDR. As Wladimir Kaminer puts it in his introduction to *Mein erstes T-Shirt*, Hein writes 'with an ironic countenance, western money in his left-hand pocket and eastern money in his right. A citizen of the world, made in the GDR.'[36] The moment of dislocation generated by the collapse of the GDR has, it seems, given him a broader perspective than that available to many of his peers in the west. Hein and other east German writers of his age have travelled between different societies, between east and west and between communism and capitalism, and this has equipped them well, it seems, to negotiate this new world.

In the work of Hein and Hennig there is very little of the trauma to be found in Hensel and Schramm, or the anger that we find in Brussig with regard to the GDR past. The east German state is simply a location for their stories. Indeed, in Hennig's *Trabanten* (Satellites, 2002) and Hein's *Vielleicht ist es sogar schön* (Perhaps it's Even Nice, 2004), it is not the GDR that is the primary focus but the legacy of National Socialism. In *Vielleicht ist es sogar schön*, for example, Hein describes how his mother, the illegitimate daughter of a 'Halbjude' father, as defined by the Nazis, and an 'ayrian' woman, spent her childhood in hiding to avoid persecution.[37] Throughout the text the narrator recollects his mother's, and subsequently his own attempts to learn about their Jewish heritage, and thereby tackles the problematic fashion in which the Nazi period was addressed in the GDR. He finds, for example, the remnants of a community so decimated that it no longer understands what it means to be Jewish (*V*, 100). At the same time, the narrator highlights the difficulty of attempting to educate a population about its past in an East German state in which history books were routinely given over to political propaganda (*V*, 102).

This problem is explored in some detail by means of an account of the narrator's stay in the United States. In America, he is welcomed with open arms into a Jewish community at ease with its identity and its understanding of its heritage (*V*, 122–30), and on his return to Germany he decides that he will finally embrace his Jewishness and seek out the Jewish community in the now unified Berlin. Yet, he quickly realises that neither he, nor his mother, are Jewish *enough* to be accepted, a fact which, after her death, prevents the family from carrying out her death-bed wishes: 'Before her birth my mother was too Jewish . . . But after her death she wasn't Jewish enough for the Jewish cemetery in Berlin (*V*, 152–3). The narrator can barely conceal his anger as he summarises the treatment of his mother. The specific target of his anger is the present-day Jewish community. However, it is clear that at the root of this community's attitude is what it views as Germany's unresolved past, a legacy that precludes the more relaxed, inclusive notion of Jewishness he finds amongst the American Jewish community.

As many critics have pointed out, GDR literature came late to the question of dealing with Germany's Nazi past, largely because there was no social and historical rupture in East Germany equivalent to the West German student movement of the 1960s. It was not until texts such as Wolf's *Kindheitsmuster* (Patterns of Childhood, 1976), and Christoph (father of Jakob) Hein's *Horns Ende* (Horn's End, 1985) that this process began in

East German fiction. In *Vielleicht ist es sogar schön* we see a continuation and development of this process whereby east Germans confront the Nazi past. Indeed, this is something of a growing trend, as evidenced in recent texts by older writers, such as Christoph Hein's *Landnahme* (Land Seizure, 2004) or Reinhard Jirgl's *Die Unvollendeten* (The Incomplete Ones, 2003), which examine the experience of post-war expellees from the former German regions east of the Oder–Neisse line, a topic that had been taboo in the GDR.

CONCLUSION

As we have seen in this chapter, the GDR remains an important topic for east German writers. At times, we see authors drawing on GDR literary traditions, at times reacting against them, in an attempt to negotiate both present-day problems and the legacy of the East German past. It is, perhaps, still too early to answer the question of whether, into the next decade, it will be possible to identify a strand of German writing that can be defined as 'GDR literature'. However, as the work of Jakob Hein and others intimates, the GDR may already be losing its relevance, as some authors, at least, become ever less concerned with specifically 'east German' issues or with the 'distinctiveness' of an east German experience. Indeed, there is, on occasion at least, little to distinguish Hein or Hennig from young west German 'pop' writers. If this trend continues, a time may well arrive in the near future when GDR literature does indeed, as Brussig insisted in the quotation with which this chapter began, become a redundant category.

NOTES

1. Holger Briel, 'Humor im Angesicht der Absurdität: Gesellschaftskritik in Thomas Brussigs *Helden wie wir* und Ingo Schulzes *Simple Storys*' in Gerhard Fischer and David Roberts, eds., *Schreiben nach der Wende: Ein Jahrzehnt deutscher Literatur 1989–1999* (Tübingen: Stauffenberg Verlag, 2001), 263–73.
2. Heinz Ludwig Arnold, ed., *DDR-Literatur der neunziger Jahre* (Munich: Text+Kritik, 2000); Wolfgang Emmerich, *Kleine Literaturgeschichte der DDR: Erweiterte Neuausgabe* (Leipzig: Gustav Kiepenheuer, 1996).
3. Christa Wolf, *Was bleibt* (Frankfurt: Luchterhand, 1990). Ulrich Greiner, 'Mangel an Feingefühl', *Die Zeit* (1 June 1990), 63. For a survey of views expressed in this debate see Thomas Anz, ed., *'Es geht nicht um Christa Wolf': Der Literaturstreit im vereinten Deutschland* (Frankfurt: Fischer, 1991).
4. See Alison Lewis, *Die Kunst des Verrats: Der Prenzlauer Berg und die Staatssicherheit* (Würzburg: Königshausen & Neumann, 2003).
5. Christa Wolf, *Leibhaftig* (Munich: Luchterhand, 2002), 56, hereafter *L*.

6. Christa Wolf, *Nachdenken über Christa T.* (Mitteldeutscher Verlag: Luchter-hand, 1968), 66.

7. See Stuart Taberner, *German Literature of the 1990s and Beyond* (Rochester: Camden House, 2005), 41.

8. Friedrich Hölderlin, *Selected Poems*, trans. David Constantine (Newcastle upon Tyne: Bloodaxe, 1990), 46.

9. Stephen Brockmann, *Literature and German Reunification* (Cambridge: Cambridge University Press, 1999), 85.

10. Wolfgang Hilbig, *Das Provisorium* (Frankfurt: S. Fischer, 2000), 142, hereafter *P*.

11. Wolfgang Hilbig, 'Kamenzer Rede', *Preis- und Dankreden* (Rheinsberg: Kurt Tucholsky Gedankenstätte, 1996), 13–16, here 16.

12. See Jan Faktor, 'Warum aus uns nichts geworden ist: Betrachtungen zur Prenzlauer-Berg-Szene zehn Jahre nach dem Mauerfall' in Arnold, ed., *DDR-Literatur der neunziger*, 92–106.

13. See David Clarke, 'Störstellen': Architecture in the Work of Reinhard Jirgl' in Frank Finlay and Julian Preece, eds., *Interactions: Contemporary German Literature's Dialogue with the Arts* (Berne: Peter Lang, forthcoming 2007).

14. Ingo Schramm, *Fitchers Blau* (Berlin: Verlag Volk & Welt, 1996), 206.

15. Helmut Schmitz, 'Denouncing Globalisation in Ingo Schramm's *Fitchers Blau*' in Stuart Taberner, ed., *German Literature in the Age of Globalisation* (Birmingham: University of Birmingham Press, 2004), 145–67, here 162.

16. Ingo Schulze, *Simple Storys: Ein Roman aus der ostdeutschen Provinz* (Berlin: Berlin Verlag, 1998), hereafter *S*. For a fuller discussion of this novel, see Paul Cooke, 'Beyond a *Trotzidentität*? Storytelling and the Postcolonial Voice in Ingo Schulze's *Simple Storys*', *Forum for Modern Language Studies*, 39:3 (2003): 290–305.

17. Peter Michalzik, 'Wie komme ich zur Nordsee? Ingo Schulze erzählt einfach Geschichten, die ziemlich vertrackt sind und die alle lieben' in Thomas Kraft, ed., *aufgerissen: Zur Literatur der 90er* (Munich: Piper, 2000), 31.

18. Ingo Schulze, 'Für mich war die DDR einfach nicht literarisierbar', *Freitag*, 6 November 1998.

19. Briel, 'Humor im Angesicht der Absurdität', 268.

20. Quoted in Taberner, *German Literature*, 33.

21. See Jill Twark, 'Mathias Wedel and Matthias Biskupek: Two Satirists "im Wandel der Wende"', *glossen* 10 (2000), http://www.dickinson.edu/ departments/germn/glossen/heft10/twark.html.

22. See Taberner, *German Literature*, 51–4.

23. For a discussion of East German cabaret both before and after the *Wende* see Joanne M. McNally, 'Shifting Boundaries: An Eastern Meeting of East and West German "Kabarett"', *German Life and Letters*, 54:2 (2001): 173–90.

24. Steimel has, for example, worked with Brussig on both the stage version of his novel *Helden wie wir* (see below), and on the film *Heimat 3: Chronik einer Zeitwende* (2004), the screenplay for which Brussig co-authored with the director Edgar Reitz.

25. Thomas Brussig, *Helden wie wir* (Berlin: Verlag Volk und Welt, 1995), hereafter *H*.
26. For further discussion see Kristie Foell and Jill Twark, '"Bekenntnisse des Stasi-Hochstaplers Klaus Uhltzscht": Thomas Brussig's Comical and Controversial *Helden wie wir*', in Paul Cooke and Andrew Plowman, eds., *German Writers and the Politics of Culture: Dealing with the Stasi* (Basingstoke: Palgrave, 2003), 173–94.
27. Thomas Brussig, *Wie es leuchtet* (Frankfurt: S. Fischer, 2004), hereafter *W*.
28. See Paul Cooke, *Representing East Germany Since Unification: From Colonization to Nostalgia* (Oxford: Berg, 2005).
29. Thomas Brussig, 'Mrux, die deutsche Einheit', *Der Tagesspiegel*, 31 August 2003. For further discussion of these television broadcasts see Cooke, *Representing East Germany*, 141–75.
30. See Paul Cooke, 'Performing *Ostalgie*: Leander Haußmann's *Sonnenallee*', *German Life and Letters*, 56:2 (2003): 156–67.
31. Jana Hensel, *Zonenkinder* (Reinbek: Rowohlt, 2002), hereafter *Z*.
32. Owen Evans, '"Denn wir sind anders": "Zonenkinder" in the Federal Republic', *German as a Foreign Language*, 2 (2005), 20–33.
33. For further discussion see Paul Cooke, 'From Dr Seltsam to Lieutenant Surf: The Berlin Vorlesebühnen and Contemporary East German Literature' in Finlay and Preece, eds., *Interactions: Contemporary German Literature's Dialogue with the Arts*.
34. Jakob Hein, *Mein erstes T-Shirt* (Munich: Piper, 2001), 6–13, 107–9.
35. Holger Kreitling and Michael Pilz, 'Die DDR war ein Komplettpaket', *Die Welt* (9 September 2004), 27–29.
36. Wladimir Kaminer, 'Mein erster Jakob Hein', in Hein, *Mein erstes T-Shirt*, 5–7, here 6.
37. Jakob Hein, *Vielleicht ist es sogar schön* (Munich: Piper, 2004), hereafter *V*.

CHAPTER 5

'West German writing' in the Berlin Republic

Stuart Taberner

Writing in September 1990, only a few weeks before the German Democratic Republic (GDR) was set to accede to the *Grundgesetz* (basic law)
of the Federal Republic (FRG), the author Patrick Süskind, best known
for his worldwide best-seller *Das Parfum* (Perfume, 1985), sounded a note
of anticipatory nostalgia not for the soon-to-be defunct communist East
Germany but for the passing of his comfortably familiar, dependably dull,
West German reality: 'It's true, I feel a little sad when I think to myself
that the Federal Republic, that unexciting, unloved, practical little state in
which I grew up, will soon no longer exist.' For West Germans of Süskind's
age, born into the aftermath of the war, 'we forty-year-old children of the
Federal Republic',[1] this was the only system they had ever known. And,
although much criticised – most spectacularly in the late 1960s by Süskind's
generation of student protesters – what would come to be known as the 'old'
Federal Republic had been *theirs*. They had grown up with West Germany,
the unloved offspring of the anti-Soviet alliance, fought it, and reshaped it
in their image.

Süskind's bout of unification-blues notwithstanding, for most of the
1990s it would be the dramatic transformation of the former East Germany
that would prove to be the more compelling focus of media attention
and scholarly scrutiny. The ex-GDR was patently more interesting, the
upheavals far more sensational: east Germans, it was proclaimed time and
again, had been 'colonised', their past obliterated, their culture erased and
their identity denied.[2] The institutions, structures and statutes of the 'old'
FRG had simply been imposed wholesale on the *Neue Länder* (new states)
in the east. In the west, for that reason, very little was assumed to have
changed. 'What, as a west German, could I possibly speak about?', asks
the narrator of Hans Pleschinski's autobiographical *Bildnis eines Unsichtbaren* (Portrait of an Invisible Man, 2002) plaintively.[3] Yet much of the
discussion of Germany's post-1990 'normalisation' – if we take this as convenient shorthand for the interrelated debates on the newly united state's

relationship to the past and its social, political and cultural projections in the present[4] – has focused, from the mid 1990s, on the 'old' FRG to a greater extent than on the ex-GDR. The complaints of some east Germans regarding the loss of social solidarity set aside, a relatively stable consensus exists pertaining to the ex-GDR: although nostalgia for facets of everyday life in the East (*Ostalgie*) may be widespread, this rarely implies a desire for a return of the totalitarian state; at the same time, the efforts of west German conservatives in the early 1990s to demonise the communist regime by equating it with the Nazi dictatorship have failed to prevent the general acceptance of a more balanced view of the GDR's ideals, achievements and undeniable failings. In respect of the 'old' FRG, on the other hand, the past has provoked less unanimity. This is not surprising given that the Berlin Republic is the successor state, in terms of its social, political and cultural complexion, and its political elites, to what is now often termed the Bonn Republic, and tends to define innovations in its self-understanding in relation to *this* history.

In this chapter, two arguments are advanced: first, that there exists a significant corpus of contemporary fiction which takes West Germany as its subject in order, in part at least, to ruminate upon the emerging identity of the Berlin Republic, and second, that this is often related to a debate about 'values', that is to say, about the cultural-political legacy of the 'old' FRG. More specifically, this discussion centres on the close connection between writing and social engagement associated with authors such as Günter Grass, of the *Flakhelfergeneration* (the generation born in the late 1920s who were recruited, aged fifteen or thereabouts, into the German war effort in 1945 as anti-aircraft gun operators and the like, although Grass, as we now know, also served with the *Waffen-SS*), and with 68ers such as Uwe Timm, F. C. Delius and Peter Schneider. In the early 1990s, but continuing throughout the decade, culturally conservative writers such as Martin Walser (formerly part of West Germany's social-democratic intellectual consensus), Arnold Stadler and Botho Strauß thus developed the critique of a left-liberal *Gesinnungsästhetik* (aesthetics of conviction) outlined by columnists Ulrich Greiner and Frank Schirrmacher at the outset of the 1990 *Literaturstreit* (Literature Debate) and, before them, from the mid 1980s, by their mentor, the literary reviewer and scholar Karl Heinz Bohrer.[5] Later in the 1990s, pop authors drawn from the generation that had grown up in the shadow of the 68ers – referred to here as 78ers – and from a younger generation variously known as the 89ers, the Generation Golf or the Generation Berlin similarly took issue with what had commonly come to be termed political correctness. (The popular designations

89ers, Generation Golf and Generation Berlin alluded, respectively, to the younger generation's identification with a less burdened German identity after the fall of the Wall in 1989, their materialism and their association with the resurgence of Berlin in the 1990s.) Only apparently immersed in the ever-changing fads of popular music and dance, fashion and modern-day consumer culture, many of these authors produced texts with a surprisingly socially-critical content whilst also marking their distance from what they saw as the suffocatingly moralising tone of the 68ers. Finally, moving into the new millennium, Grass, Timm, Delius and Schneider – writers well established in the 'old' West Germany and renowned for their politically-engaged narratives – re-emerged to reaffirm the link between the production of literary fiction and the broader democratic *Streitkultur* (culture of public debate) they had helped to shape. The 'aesthetics of conviction' typical of much of the fiction of the 'old' Federal Republic since the late 1950s may have been tempered by a more open, less dogmatic attitude towards topics such as the Nazi past and by a greater focus on aesthetic complexity and ambiguity on the one hand, or on entertainment and readability on the other, but this does not imply the disappearance of 'socially-engaged writing'.

CONFLICTING IMAGES OF THE 'OLD' FRG

Already by the late 1980s, it was becoming relatively routine amongst academics and intellectuals to conceptualise the history of the Federal Republic as an *Erfolgsgeschichte* (success story).[6] After all, this was the first securely functioning democracy on German soil; it was stable, largely free of violent conflict (with the vital exception of the urban terrorism of the 1970s), and affluent. For West Germany's predominantly left-liberal cultural elite, however, this view initially appeared counterintuitive and certainly counter to their own customary characterisation of the FRG as regressive, even crypto-fascist, materialistic and indifferent to the crimes of the Nazi past. For many, including Jürgen Habermas, the forty years of 'successful' West German history between 1949 and 1989 were being 'instrumentalised' by revisionist historians and thinkers as means of relativising the crimes of the twelve years of the Nazi period. For others, praise for the FRG equated to praise for the conservative restoration of the 1950s, the crass materialism of the 'economic miracle', and the refusal to address the past, for Chancellor Konrad Adenauer's cavalier appointment of high-ranking ex-Nazis to his cabinet, Ludwig Erhard's promotion of prosperity over historical reflection, and the state's overreaction to the social upheaval of the late 1960s and early 1970s.

In the early 1990s, however, some older west German writers began to revise their attitude towards the 'old' FRG. It may be that a recognition of their previous naivety vis-à-vis the utopian ideals of the GDR encouraged a reassessment of the system many of them had once rejected. Or, perhaps more likely, the fact that the generation of '68 was set to take power may have prompted a revised narrative in which aspects of West German history once viewed as negative now appeared as necessary elements within a stirring dialectic of a faux-democratic conservative restoration and radical challenge ultimately leading to a successful democratisation. The 1950s and 1960s became the pre-history of the 68ers' principal achievement: the permeation of their values across the social, cultural and political institutions of the 'old' FRG and, all the more so following the election of the Red–Green coalition in 1998, the incipient Berlin Republic.

Two texts may be cited as examples of this shift in attitudes towards the 'old' FRG: Uwe Timm's *Die Entdeckung der Currywurst* (The Invention of Curried Sausage, 1993) and F. C. Delius's *Der Sonntag, an dem ich Weltmeister wurde* (The Sunday I became World Champion, 1994). Timm's novella takes the curried sausage to be found at fast-food stands throughout West Germany and transforms it into a symbol of the reconstruction work of the early post-war years. Thus the role of the 'economic miracle' in creating the conditions for a stable democracy is reassessed. We learn, then, that Timm's protagonist, Frau Brücker, invented the dish in order to allay the melancholy of the navy deserter whom she had taken in towards the end of the war. Seduced by the novel flavours of this West German delicacy and his landlady's charms, Bremer ceases to dream of refighting the lost campaigns of the eastern front and accepts the realities of the post-war present, including the loss of territory and foreign occupation. The comforts of consumerism and the careful channelling of excess libido mean that this German democracy can succeed where the Weimar Republic failed, it seems.

If Timm's novella revises the standard left-liberal view of the 'economic miracle' as an instrument of the conservative restoration of the 1950s, Delius's *Der Sonntag, an dem ich Weltmeister wurde* does much the same for an iconic episode in West German history: the unexpected victory at the 1954 football world cup finals. A sporting triumph usually viewed as a boost for a 1950s' nationalism rooted in post-war regeneration is reconceived as the moment when the youthful narrator begins to connect with West Germany's fledgling democracy. In his rendering of Herbert Zimmermann's famous radio commentary, the narrator describes how two versions of the national anthem were sung by the crowd: 'the forbidden first stanza and the permitted third stanza' – the first verse features the (in)famous line: 'Deutschland, Deutschland über alles', and the third: 'Einigkeit und Recht und Freiheit' (unity and justice and freedom). These latter sentiments are the ones with which he identifies, a statement of commitment that has everything to do with the way the German team played: 'the principle of blind obedience or doing as you're told or conformity or evading responsibility had no place here'.[7]

Timm's *Die Entdeckung der Currywurst* and Delius's *Der Sonntag, an dem ich Weltmeister wurde* consciously rewrite the history of the 1950s in order to create a narrative in which the imperfect democracy of the Adenauer period appears as an unavoidable compromise with historical circumstances; a truly liberal state, it is implied, will be realised by the generation of '68. This more positive view of the *potential* of the early FRG, Timm's narrator concedes, requires him to do some 'work' on Frau Brücker's story: 'I had to be selective, do some straightening out, make connections, abbreviate.'[8] First and foremost, the protests of '68 gain legitimacy as part of a tradition of dissent which extends back to before the foundation of the West German state to include opposition to both the Nazis and Adenauer. The narrator's grandmother, accordingly, is credited with preventing some SS men from beating up a Russian prisoner-of-war; later, in the mid 1950s, she campaigned against West German rearmament.

In the 1990s, the 68ers' claim to have fashioned the 'old' FRG in their image was broadly accepted – this does not imply, however, a similarly universal endorsement of the *nature* of the state which they did so much to create.[9] In effect, the 'old' West German left had appropriated the rhetoric of 'normalisation', which had been seen as the property of conservatives in the 1980s and, immediately following unification, of New Right intellectuals.[10] The key difference now, and particularly following the accession to power in 1998 of one-time student protesters Gerhard Schröder and Joschka Fischer, was that a post-1990 German 'normality' was seen as a continuation of the 'old' FRG: a belief in the constitutional state over the delusions of national chauvinism, a self-critical approach to the Nazi past, and a principled humility and self-restraint. For critics of both West Germany and its successor state, however, this was a kind of 'normality' which implied not an end to Germany's peculiar condition as a nation tainted by Nazi crimes, the way it 'stuck out', as Helmut Kohl put it in 1990,[11] but its banality, philistinism, provinciality and inability to inspire passion – a dismal normality, indeed.

Conservative intellectuals such as Karl Heinz Bohrer had, from the mid 1980s, been deriding the provinciality of the FRG, its preference for a pitiful deference over the exercise of power and influence, and its lack of a 'metropolitan culture'.[12] Bohrer's 1987 treatise 'Die permanente Theodizee' (The Permanent Theodicy), in fact, may be said to have anticipated the arguments advanced by Greiner and Schirrmacher during the 'literary controversy' of 1990 with regard to German culture's reduction of aesthetics to morality: the fascination with evil, the 'proper' subject of literary fiction, Bohrer argued, had been replaced by an obsession with ethical instruction.[13] In 1993, writer Botho Strauß continued in much the same vein in an (in)famous article in *Der Spiegel*, 'Anschwellender Bocksgesang' (A Swelling Goat's Song), in which he indicted the 'bigoted piety of the political, of the critical, of the calling-into-question of everything'.[14] Similarly, the protagonist of *Die Fehler des Kopisten* (The Faults of the Copyist, 1997) dismisses the modern FRG as 'lacking in fantasy, enlightened, entirely unsentimental' and calls for a re-aestheticisation of the cosmos;[15] in *Das Partikular* (The Particular, 2000), which tells of a failed love affair but also reflects on sex, commerce and God, it is only away from the metropolis, on the island of Zehl, that beauty can be experienced. Throughout, Strauß is indebted to what Stephen Brockmann has termed Germany's 'romantic anti-capitalist tradition'.[16] In his penchant for the tormented and the metaphysical, therefore, the author alludes to Schopenhauer, Wagner, Nietzsche, Spengler, Heidegger, and others discredited by their association with Nazism.

Perhaps the most sustained literary critique of the 'old' FRG is to be found in the work of Martin Walser. In *Die Verteidigung der Kindheit* (In Defence of Childhood, 1991), Alfred's obsession with the objects that provide the precarious link to a childhood spent in Dresden before the devastation of the city's baroque glories during the firebombing of February 1945 is framed as an act of resistance against the taboo on open discussion of the destruction of Germany's cultural heritage and division. In *Finks Krieg* (1995), the censure is extended as the eponymous hero battles in vain against the smugly officious FRG in an attempt to reverse his dismissal from the civil service. Finally, in *Der Lebenslauf der Liebe* (The Biography of Love, 2001), we are party to Susi Gern's pathetic efforts, from the mid 1980s into the present, to find spiritual satisfaction in a society lacking all transcendental values.[17] Here, the 68ers' embrace of individual choice has created nothing but a tawdry consumerism and an oppressive libertarianism.

Susi's mortal fear of appearing 'spießig' (bourgeois)[18] when confronted with her husband's enthusiasm for group sex points to the perverse value system of a West German state in which, following the shifts in political sensibilities after '68, an expellee's longing for the homeland he was driven from by the Red Army in 1945 is considered 'more embarrassing than kissing in public', as the protagonist of Arnold Stadler's *Sehnsucht* (Longing, 2000) puts it.[19] Indeed, Walser's protégé Stadler, in his Büchner-prize-winning *Ein hinreissender Schrotthändler* (The Scrap Dealer, 1999),[20] a brilliant satire on the state of the nation after the elections of 1998, had already offered a vision of the Berlin Republic as artificial and rootless; it is only the narrator's recollection of a certain Irmelda Swichtenberg, 'an expellee', that offers some proof 'that there can exist a sense of being at home'.[21] Paradoxically, of course, it was precisely the influx of newcomers that so transformed the province in the aftermath of defeat in 1945 and in the course of West Germany's accelerated modernisation. In *Ich war einmal* (Once I was, 1989), expellees from East Prussia and Italian guest workers inhabit the ugly new settlements now ubiquitous in the Swabian hinter-land. In *Feuerland* (Fireland, 1992), *Mein Hund, Meine Sau, Mein Leben* (My Dog, My Sow, My Life, 1994), and *Der Tod und ich, wir zwei* (Death and I, we two, 1996), Stadler's protagonists travel far and wide in order to resensitise themselves to their own *Heimat* (home) only to discover that mass migration and the spread of western modernity has destroyed all local authenticity.

Frequently implicit in the work of Strauß, Walser and Stadler is the sug-gestion that the devastation of German cities by Allied bombers, the brutal mass expulsions from the east, and the loss of *Heimat* following, as Stadler's narrator puts it in *Ich war einmal* (1989), a 'war that ended badly',[22] con-stitute the true foundational trauma of the Federal Republic but that the 68ers' success in institutionalising commemoration of the Holocaust ren-dered discussion of this *German* suffering taboo. In the post-1990 work of all three authors, accordingly, political correctness with regard to the Nazi past becomes an increasing focus of their critique of the FRG.[23] Where the New Right intellectuals of the early 1990s failed to persuade with highly emo-tive, even aggressive attacks on the status quo,[24] in fact, Walser and Stadler in particular might take some satisfaction that their more ironic, often oblique, but no less provocative, literary engagement with a semi-official commemorative culture has achieved a far greater impact. In *Ein sprin-gender Brunnen* (The Springing Fountain, 1998), a series of quasi-authorial interjections indict a 'one-sided' focus on Nazi crimes but remain just para-doxical enough to allow the writer of the lines to imply that his purpose is to challenge the limits of political correctness rather than deny German guilt: Walser's fictional alter ego concedes that his fantasies of an aesthetic recre-ation of his youth 'minus' the Nazis are just that – 'the destination of wishful thinking'.[25] The author's response in his 1998 *Friedenspreisrede* (Peace-Prize speech) to critic Marcel Reich-Ranicki's complaint that the novel 'omitted' to mention Auschwitz displayed a similar laconic indetermincy: 'Never heard of the basic principle of narration: perspective. Whatever the case: the needs of the present come before aesthetics'.[26] The same elusiveness is evident in *Tod eines Kritikers* (Death of a Critic, 2002), in which Hans Lach ('Lach' = Laugh!) 'borrows' the name Michael Landolf to tell the story of his prosecution for the murder of Jewish literary critic André Ehrl-König (aka Marcel Reich-Ranicki, also in Walser's *ohne einander* (without one another, 1993) as Willi André König), a story, which it turns out, he has invented in order to revive his career – along the way a debate is initiated on sensitivities regarding anti-Semitism, a debate which then spilled over into 'real life'.[27] In Stadler's *Ein hinreissender Schrotthändler*, an asylum seeker, Adrian, most likely from the Balkan conflicts of the early 1990s, knocks at the narrator's door and moves in. Again, a critique of 'politically correct' values rooted in eternal contrition for the Holocaust is channelled via irony: so eager to please are the narrator and his wife that Gabi has sex with Adrian, 'on October 3, the Day of German Unity'.[28]

THE 78ERS AND THE GENERATION GOLF – POP AND POLITICS?

If Strauß, Walser and Stadler appear to reject the centrality of politics to writing in a fashion which itself can only be described as overtly political, younger authors often appear to dispense entirely with 'difficult' subjects such as the Nazi past or the struggle to embed democratic values and to describe more personal, everyday experiences. Indeed, notwithstanding a spate of novels in the first years of the new millennium concerned with the war, such as Tanja Dückers's *Himmelskörper* (Heavenly Bodies, 2003) and Olaf Müller's *Schlesisches Wetter* (Silisian Weather, 2003), and in spite of Dückers's rejection of the label 'fun-generation' in her foreword to a collection of reflections by her peers on the Nazi era, *stadt land krieg. Autoren der Gegenwart erzählen von der deutschen Vergangenheit* (city country war: Young Authors narrate the German Past, 2004), much fiction by younger authors remains narrowly focused on the self.[29] This more subjective perspective is authenticated by references to the fashions, brand names and music of the author's youth, that is, the 1970s or 1980s. Throughout, a determinedly pop sensibility dominates, which draws on Anglo-American influences and a German theoretical engagement with consumer society reaching back to the 1960s.[30] Of the generation of '78, for example, writers such as Rainald Goetz, Andreas Neumeister and Thomas Meinecke reproduce the *sensory* experience of pop culture in what appears to be an entirely immanent language of celebration and imitation: Goetz's *Rave* (1998), for example, invokes MTV, VIVA, the 'DJ mix' and the 'euphoria' of dance music.[31]

The reassuring, often comic, everyday banality of the pre-1990 FRG is the predominant theme in Norbert Niemann's 1998 *Wie man's nimmt* (How you take it): 'Everything is normal. *We are all totally normal.*'[32] Matthias Polityckiʼs *Weiberroman* (A Novel about Women, 1993), which traces the narrator's disastrous affairs and shifts in fashion in the 1980s, likewise alludes to a West German 'normality', as does fellow 78er Andreas Neumeister in *Gut laut* (Good Loud, 1998), a survey of pop music from the Munich Olympics of 1972 onwards, which establishes a West German identity independent of Nazism, post-war reconstruction, and '68, with reference to influential German bands such as Kraftwerk and the global phenomenon of *Krautrock*. Yet an (only) apparently unconditional affirmation of the 'old' FRG's consumer society and a rejection of programmatic social engagement may also be a political statement of sorts. First, the only form of rebellion available to those following in the wake of the generation of '68 is precisely a rejection of politics. In his foreword to a collection of reprints from the youth magazine *Mode und Verzweiflung* (Fashion and Despair, 1998), in fact, 78er Thomas Meinecke notes: 'Saying "yes" to the modern world appeared to us at that time to be the most effective form of political dissidence imaginable.'[33] Second, Germany's post-unification 'normality' implies the loss of the 'old' FRG's cosy 'ordinariness', once despised but now regretted. As Andrew Plowman argues, this embrace of *Westalgie* (by analogy with *Ostalgie*) may respond to post-1990 fears that the social, political and economic consensus that had typified West Germany was on the verge of being shattered by globalisation.[34] In the best-selling *liegen lernen* (Learning to lie, 1999), accordingly, Generation Golf writer Frank Goosen casts back to the relative harmony of the 1980s with a nostalgically innocent tale of teenage anxiety, trivial arguments with parents, appalling fashions and glossy magazines featuring, alternately, naked women or (in retrospect endearingly melodramatic) atomic mushroom clouds on their covers.[35]

David Wagner's *Meine nachtblaue Hose* (My Night-blue Trousers, 2000) tells of what it was like for him and his Generation Golf peers to grow up in the shadow of the 68ers. Similar to *Rückspiel* (Return Match, 1993) by 78er Ulrich Woelk, a novel which depicts the dogmatism of a veteran of '68 from the perspective of his younger brother, or Michael Wildenhain's *Erste Liebe – Deutscher Herbst* (First Love – German Autumn, 1997), set during the terrorism wave of the mid 1970s, but perhaps more subtle and allusive, Wagner's text explores its protagonist's efforts to elaborate a version of his 'Westvergangenheit' (West-history)[36] independently of the former student radicals who had come to dominate its institutions, politics and culture. What is most striking about *Meine nachtblaue Hose* is the contrast established between the way the narrator's ex-68er father claims ownership of the FRG by means of his effortless internalisation of a by-now conventional focus on post-war reconstruction, the Berlin Wall, student protest and, finally, his generation's successful democratisation of the state, and the son's struggle to sustain his own, authentic memory of his childhood. Thus a highly detailed account of the taste of nutella or the feel of nivea, schoolboy rivalry between Adidas-wearers and Puma-wearers, and of locations, smells and flavours, generates an evocative, sensuous recreation of the narrator's youth and an alternative image of the FRG to that propagated by his father in his monologues on the *political* formation of the West German state. Yet, even as he finally establishes his own 'ownership' of the FRG, he is forced to recognise that his tale seems banal in comparison with the stories coming out of the ex-GDR. Correspondingly, his lover Fe, the fairy-muse ('Fee' = fairy) who inspired his reconstruction of their shared adolescence, never leaves Anatol, his East German rival. Indeed, Anatol appears to have become the West German woman's new exotic 'other', replacing the Turks whom his name (Anatolia = Turkey) nonetheless invokes; as such, he exerts a kind of anthropological fascination for Fe. Realising this towards the close of the novel, the narrator is left 'somewhere between boredom and sadness' (*MNH*, 170).

Wagner's *Meine nachtblaue Hose* rejects the determinedly 'political' focus of the 68ers without, however, completely bracketing out contemporary realities. The same is true of much of pop literature by Generation Golf writers in which introspection does not necessarily mean a disavowal of social engagement. The short stories in Karen Duve's *Keine Ahnung* (1999), for instance, detail rape, prostitution and drug-taking in a hard-hitting exploration of the emptiness of modern-day life. Duve's *Dies ist kein Liebeslied* (This is not a Love Song, 2002), likewise dwells on its protagonist's morbid revulsion at her own body, her bulimia and suicidal fantasies, themes already developed in *Regenroman* (Rain, 1999), in which a young woman hopes to escape her past in the east but is found and viciously raped by Harry, on the orders of Pfitzner, a gangster from Hamburg and the embodiment of a new, violently exploitative neo-liberal capitalism; at the close of the narrative, Martina fights back and, along with her east German women friends Kay and Isadora, incinerates Harry and Pfitzner with a flamethrower. Less brutal but equally depressing are Julia Franck's *Liebediener* (Love on Demand, 1999), which depicts a woman's absolute isolation in the city, or Judith

Hermann's short stories *Sommerhaus, später* (Summerhouse, Later, 1998). In the title piece of Hermann's collection, the young narrator exists, as it were, in a twilight zone of indecision, paradoxically alienated within the all-pervading global consumer culture that has displaced the parochial but benign materialism of the 'old' FRG. Even in the literary efforts of Alexa Hennig von Lange, Elke Naters or Tim Staffel, the obsession with fashion labels only momentarily camouflages the dissolution of the self. These authors, in fact, have little in common with Benjamin von Stuckrad-Barre, whose purposely undemanding works are often, and wrongly, taken as exemplary of late 1990s pop.

The work of Duve, Hermann and Franck, and, indeed, of many other younger pop authors from the west, hint at the substitution of the generally circumspect capitalism of the 'old' FRG for a new, more aggressive neo-liberalism. In Tanja Dückers's *Spielzone* (Play Zone, 1999), accordingly, the young female protagonist moves from Neuköln, an area in West Berlin associated, pre-1990, with alternative lifestyles, to Prenzlauer Berg in the east of the city in order to discover a form of community as yet untainted by the fake intimacy of 'American-style' private enterprise. At the end of the text, however, it is rumoured that a McDonald's restaurant is about to be built.[37] Precisely by means of their immersion in modern-day consumer culture, younger writers thus engage directly with one of the key issues of the 1990s and early twenty-first century: globalisation.

Christian Kracht's *Faserland* (Frayed-Land, 1995), which describes the journey of a modern-day *flâneur* from the island of Sylt to southern Germany and finally to Switzerland, perhaps best illustrates the dilemma of the younger generation of writers: how to engage with contemporary society whilst rejecting the moral self-righteousness of the 68ers. Thus the narrator's over-indulgence in drugs, sex and brand names barely represses the incessant nausea he experiences in a world of imitation and simulation. This is a young man disgusted by the triteness of a globalised consumer culture in which, for example, 'guests' are invited to 'meet on board' in the restaurant car of an intercity train or the heart of the once quintessentially German city of Heidelberg is disfigured by a 'shabby Pizza Hut and random sportswear shops'. Hedonism and dedication to the superficial, however, offer a means of undermining the earnest political engagement the narrator associates with the 68ers, even as he is aware that this is an empty gesture. On the one hand, then, his reckless overuse of the word 'Nazi' to describe pensioners, taxi drivers, managers, or anyone whose fashion sense fails to please him,[38] challenges the political correctness of the student movement generation. On the other hand, he cannot deny the extent to which the

68ers have shaped his environment. Glimpsing his reflection in a window display containing a trailer for the war film *Stalingrad* (1993), he is forced to acknowledge that he is lucky to live 'in a democratic Germany in which nobody is made to go to the front at the age of seventeen'. Such ideas may well be 'claptrap of the sort you always get from the Social Democrats',[39] the kind of sentiment that might be uttered by a smug 68er, but this makes them no less true. Just like the narrator of Wagner's *Meine nachtblaue Hose*, Kracht's protagonist implies that the 68ers' claim to speak for all on matters of social and political concern propels his generation into a paradoxical embrace of consumerism; in Kracht's novel, total affirmation to the point of sickening excess may be the only possible means of even hinting at a critique of the vacuousness of contemporary culture.

The authenticity which Kracht's 'pop-modern *flâneur*'[40] seeks is the authenticity of his West German childhood – his voyage from north to south takes him exclusively through the territory of the 'old' FRG. Yet West Germany has faded: memories of the 'colourful plastic spades' and innocent blushes of family holidays on Sylt, for example, appear ever more inaccessible as he becomes caught up in the Berlin Republic's infatuation with designer labels and the consumer society's promotion of global brands over local substance. Finally disgusted with the post-unification Federal Republic, he leaves for Switzerland, 'a part of Germany in which everything is not as bad'.[41]

In Kracht's subsequent novel, *1979* (2001), the attempt to escape from a hegemonic American consumer culture into authenticity is mocked as long since doomed: Kracht's narrator, 'empty' and 'without history',[42] hopes, in the course of the Iranian revolution of 1979, Tibetan Buddhism and a Chinese labour camp, to purge himself of his western decadence but is incapable of transcending his own self-indulgent pose. For this younger west German writer, as for many of his peers, it seems that the impossible attempt to define a literary aesthetic free of the moralising, socio-critical conceit of the 68ers and yet also suitably distanced from the pop consumerism they describe results in a melancholic resignation in which a trivialising ennui alternates with dark despair.

A SOCIALLY COMMITTED LITERATURE FOR THE NEW MILLENNIUM?

By the mid 1990s, concern about too much political correctness was no longer restricted to such figures as Walser, Stadler and Strauß, or to younger pop writers. Former 68ers, too, were engaging with the allegation that their generation had been overzealous. Peter Schneider, in particular, confronted his peers in 1990 with the naivety of their previous sympathies for the GDR as a 'better' alternative to capitalism and with the hypocrisy of their efforts at 'damage limitation';[43] in his Berlin novels, *Paarungen* (Pairings, 1992) and *Eduards Heimkehr* (Eduard's Return Home, 1995), similarly, the author criticises the alacrity with which Germans in the present pass judgment on individuals caught up in National Socialism without any true understanding of the circumstances or even full knowledge of the facts.[44] Less sophisticated perhaps, but hugely successful, was Bernhard Schlink's 1995 *Der Vorleser* (The Reader), in which Michael, looking back from the 1990s, questions his peers' rush to judge his lover, the former concentration camp guard Hanna, at her trial in the early 1960s and intimates that her illiteracy was ignored because it did not fit their image of the perpetrator. Schlink's novel has been regarded by some as attributing a victim status to Nazi functionaries,[45] but it is unclear whether the author wishes his readers to accept Michael's exculpation uncritically.[46] More clear-cut is Hans-Ulrich Treichel's *Der Verlorene* (Lost, 1998). This short novel draws attention to its young protagonist's refusal to acknowledge the pain his parents feel with regard to the son they lost in 1945 on a trek *and* the parents' refusal to recognise their guilt.[47] In *Menschenflug* (Human Flight, 2005), a farcically self-reflexive sequel, the 'author' of *Der Verlorene* is more readily able to talk about his incestuous longings for his sister than about his lost brother – it is more acceptable to indulge in salacious public confession than to address the taboo on 'German suffering'. Yet an awareness of the dangers of overzealousness need not imply the abandonment of a critical stance. F. C. Delius's *Die Flatterzunge* (The Flutter-Tongue, 1999) concedes some ground to the complaints of its trombonist protagonist that he is being persecuted by the media following a tour to Israel during which he signed a bar tab with the name Adolf Hitler, but simultaneously parodies his attempts to paint himself as a victim and as the man who will single-handedly topple the walls of Jericho or, as he sees it, the strongholds of political correctness.

In the early 1990s, as we have seen, former 68ers such as Delius, Timm and Schneider had advanced a generally positive appraisal of their generation's impact on the 'old' FRG; by the end of the decade, however, they were responding to a more differentiated 'historicisation' of the tensions inherent in their youthful rebellion.[48] On the one hand, this meant examining the relationship between idealism, political violence and the urban terrorism of the 1970s, as Schneider does in *Skylla* (Scylla, 2005), or Timm does in

Rot (Red, 2001), a lengthy novel in which Thomas Linde, onetime 68er revolutionary turned jazz critic and funeral orator, offers up an improvised obituary for the radical politics to which he had dedicated himself thirty years earlier and debates whether he should carry out the plan formulated by his recently deceased comrade, Aschenberger, to blow up the 'Victory Column' in Berlin. Or, more surprising, it meant recognising that the explosion of interest in 'German wartime suffering' at the end of the 1990s was not (only) to be attributed to the malign influence of right-wing revisionists set on claiming victim status for Germans but was also a consequence of their own refusal to deal with this aspect of the past for fear of validating revanchism. Most famously, the 'Über-narrator' in Günter Grass's *Im Krebsgang* (Crabwalk, 2002),[49] explicitly identified as the author's alter ego, regrets that the subject of the novella, the treks from East Prussia and the torpedoing in the Baltic of the liner *Wilhelm Gustloff* with the loss of more than seven thousand refugees, had not been addressed by him or his peers: 'In truth, he says, it should have fallen to his generation to give voice to the misery of the East Prussian refugees.' This neglect, it is claimed, simply abandoned the subject to those 'caught up on the right'.[50] Similarly, in Timm's *Am Beispiel meines Bruders* (In my Brother's Shadow, 2003), in which the author tells the story of his older brother, a *Waffen-SS* volunteer killed in 1943, via a painful engagement with his diaries, the emphasis is as much on the origins of the narrator's enthusiasm for the 'anti-authoritarian movement of the student revolt' and his repudiation of his parents' allusions to the firebombing of German cities as on his older sibling: the reference to 'German suffering' lacked an appropriate recognition of the 'chronology and causality of cruelty'.[51]

These recent novels by Grass and Timm reaffirm the link between writing and social engagement. *Im Krebsgang* thus alludes to Grass's interventions, in literary works such as *örtlich betäubt* (Local Anaesthetic, 1969) and *Aus dem Tagebuch einer Schnecke* (From the Diary of a Snail, 1972), in the political debates of the late 1960s and early 1970s with a narrative in which an individual's failure to deal appropriately with the past offers an exemplary lesson of how *not* to overcome melancholia.[52] Measured, critical engagement with past failures is the basis for the incremental internalisation of democratic values. Story-telling is the key: if the narrator Paul had related to his son his own mother's story of her expulsion from East Prussia, he might have inoculated Konrad against the self-righteous outrage he feels once he discovers the extent of 'German suffering' and prevented him from killing Wolfgang, the internet adversary who, in an act of misplaced philo-Semitism, passes himself off as Jewish. Likewise, in Timm's *Am Beispiel meines Bruders*, the narrator relates how, as an adolescent, he began to write as a means of dealing with his fury, trying, inadequately, to 'depict fictional people in conflict situations' (*BB*, 135). In Timm's *Rot*, the pitiably ineffective former 68er Thomas Linde never gets round to blowing up the 'Victory Column' before his own death: he is too busy recounting his friend's life and composing an often feeble essay on the symbolic meanings of the colour red. Here, too, fiction defuses extremism and fanaticism.

Perhaps the most persuasive recent defence of the value of writing as a form of social engagement, that is, its institutionalisation of a self-critical moderation in place of the tradition of fanatical extremism that had previously scarred German history, is to be found in Delius's *Mein Jahr als Mörder* (My Year as a Murderer, 2004). Here, too, story-telling is to be preferred to symbolic acts of political violence. Thus the narrator's plan to murder the Nazi judge Hans-Joachim Rehse, acquitted in late 1968 of any responsibility for the more than two hundred death sentences in which he was implicated during his time at the notorious 'People's Court', is endlessly postponed as he becomes immersed in his research for a book he intends to write on one of Rehse's victims, the doctor Georg Groscurth, and the anti-Nazi group Groscurth founded with Robert Havemann, the future GDR dissident. An exemplary tale of one man's valiant opposition to Nazism is documented – the novel is one of a number in the 1990s by former 68ers to recognise the pedagogic value of such stories, including Peter Schneider's 'und wenn wir nur eine Stunde gewinnen . . .' ('And if we only gain an Hour . . .', 2001) – as is the history of his wife's struggle in the 1950s to have his sacrifice acknowledged and to protest against remilitarisation. Along the way, the narrator offers an insight into the sources of the moral outrage of his generation of student protesters: a sense that *they* were the victims of Nazism, condemned to grow up in a country devastated by war, disgust with their parents' laments on their own suffering, indignation at the presence of ex-Nazis in positions of influence, and the seductive appeal of the revolutionary pose.

In exploring the motives of the 68ers within the context of the 1950s and the imperfect democracy of the 'old' FRG, Delius contributes to the 1990s' debate on the students' legacy to the Berlin Republic. More specifically, however, his narrator's elucidation of the relationship between writing and politics defines one of the key, lasting values of '68: literary fiction as a critical intervention in contemporary society capable of embracing ambiguity, moral complexity, and the frustratingly incremental nature of change:

'until I could see some deliverance: write'.[53] Georg Groscurth was captured while trying to mass-produce oppositional leaflets; this form of engagement, Delius's novel implies, may be as necessary as it is often futile.

CONCLUSION

This chapter has scrutinised a number of examples of post-1990 fiction which focus on the 'old' FRG in order to explore the pre-history of the Berlin Republic. Above all, this focus was framed as a dialogue, a wrangle, or even a conflict, regarding the continuing legacy of politically engaged literature associated with an author such as Günter Grass, in his mid seventies at the beginning of the new millennium, or, more generally, with writers of the generation of '68, of whom Uwe Timm, F. C. Delius and Peter Schneider were offered as examples. The claim made by the 'old' West German left-liberal elite that its role in shaping the democratic culture of the Bonn Republic should be acknowledged in the Berlin Republic is challenged on the one hand by conservatives in a corpus of literary texts which, it is purported, elevate aesthetics over politics and, on the other hand, by younger pop authors with narratives which provocatively and deliberately trash many of the causes so dear to the heart of their protagonists' 68er parents. Yet neither calculated aesthetic complexity nor an only apparently unreflected embrace of consumerism and 'pure entertainment' can disguise the fact that a concern with society remains very much integral to contemporary German fiction. Ten years and more after Süskind's 'unexciting, unloved, practical little state' had ceased to exist, in fact, it seemed that a number of the socially committed writers of the 'old' West Germany were determined to revive and restate their pre-eminence even as they conceded some ground to contemporary critiques of political correctness and adjusted to a present-day preference for individuals' life-stories over historical or philosophical moralising. 'West German writing', if this is taken to mean the peculiar alignment of literary fiction and political engagement typical of the intellectual culture of the 'old' Federal Republic for much of its existence, has certainly been contested, reinterpreted and refashioned in the Berlin Republic, but – in the second decade after unification at least – it remains very much alive.

POSTSCRIPT

In August 2006, as this volume was being prepared for publication, Günter Grass announced in an interview with the *Frankfurter Allgemeine Zeitung* that he had served with the *Waffen-SS* from November 1944 until his capture by American forces in May 1945. In the furore that followed, Grass's critics declared that this revelation meant that the author's more than fifty years of politically engaged writing was now entirely discredited. Grass's *Beim Häuten der Zwiebel* (Peeling the Onion), which appeared at the beginning of September, however, suggests that it was precisely Grass's youthful susceptibility to Nazism that motivated his post-war career as a writer and public figure dedicated to confronting, and learning the lessons of, the past: the text shows how the author's biographical deficiencies are reworked, and perhaps thereby redeemed, in the 'exemplary' stories contained within half a century of fiction, poetry, graphic art and drama. For Grass, at least, there can be no alternative in post-war – and no doubt post-unification – German writing, to politically engaged literature.

NOTES

1. Patrick Süskind, 'Deutschland, eine Midlife-crisis', *Der Spiegel*, 38 (17 September 1990), 118–25, 125 and 123.
2. See Paul Cooke, *Representing East Germany since Unification: From Colonization to Nostalgia* (Oxford: Berg, 2005).
3. Hans Pleschinski, *Bildnis eines Unsichtbaren* (Munich: Hanser, 2002), 175.
4. See Stuart Taberner and Paul Cooke, eds., *German Culture, Politics and Literature into the Twenty-First Century: Beyond Normalization* (Rochester: Camden House, 2006).
5. See Stephen Brockmann, 'The Politics of German Literature', *Monatshefte*, 84:1 (1992): 46–58.
6. See Frank Brunssen, 'The New Self-Understanding of the Berlin Republic: Readings of Contemporary German History', in Stuart Taberner and Frank Finlay, eds., *Recasting German Identity* (Rochester: Camden House, 2002), 19–35.
7. F. C. Delius, *Der Sonntag, an dem ich Weltmeister wurde* (Reinbek bei Hamburg: Rowohlt, 1996 [1994]), 116 and 110.
8. Uwe Timm, *Die Entdeckung der Currywurst* (Cologne: Kiepenheuer & Witsch, 1998 [1993]), 20.
9. See Ingo Cornils, 'Successful Failure? The Impact of The German Student Movement on the Federal Republic of Germany' in Stuart Taberner and Frank Finlay, eds., *Recasting German Identity*, 109–26.
10. See Stefan Berger, *The Search for Normality* (Oxford: Berghahn, 1997).
11. Serge Schmemann, 'Kohl, the Man for the German Moment', *The New York Times* (1 July 1990), 1 and 4.
12. See Jan-Werner Müller, 'Karl Heinz Bohrer on German National Identity: Recovering Romanticism and Aestheticizing the State', *German Studies Review*, 23:2 (2000): 297–316, 297.

13. Karl Heinz Bohrer, 'Die permanente Theodizee', *Merkur*, 41 (1987): 267–86.
14. Botho Strauß, 'Anschwellender Bocksgesang', *Der Spiegel* (8 February 1993), 202–7, 205.
15. Botho Strauß, *Die Fehler des Kopisten* (Munich: Deutscher Taschenbuch Verlag, 1999 [1997]), 16.
16. Stephen Brockmann, *Literature and German Unification* (Cambridge: Cambridge University Press, 1999), 115.
17. See my 'The Triumph of Subjectivity: Martin Walser's Novels of the 1990s and his *Der Lebenslauf der Liebe* (2001)' in Stuart Parkes and Fritz Wefelmeyer, eds., *Martin Walser* (Amsterdam: Rodopi, 2004), 429–46.
18. Martin Walser, *Der Lebenslauf der Liebe* (Frankfurt: Suhrkamp), 121.
19. Arnold Stadler, *Sehnsucht* (Cologne: Dumont, 2002), 287.
20. See my '"Nichts läßt man uns, nicht einmal den Schmerz, und eines Tages wird alles vergessen sein": The Novels of Arnold Stadler from *Ich war einmal* to *Ein hinreissender Schrotthändler*', *Neophilologus*, 87 (2003): 119–32.
21. Arnold Stadler, *Ein hinreissender Schrotthändler* (Cologne: Dumont, 1999), 136.
22. Arnold Stalder, *Ich war einmal* (Frankfurt: Suhrkamp 1999 [1989]), 27.
23. See Sally Johnson and Stephanie Suhr, 'From "Political Correctness" to "*Politische Korrektheit*": Discourses of "PC" in the German Newspaper *Die Welt*', *Discourse and Society*, 14:1 (2002): 49–68.
24. See, for example, Heimo Schwilk and Ulrich Schacht, eds., *Die selbstbewußte Nation* (Frankfurt: Ullstein, 1994), in which Strauß's 'Anschwellender Bocksgesang' is reprinted.
25. Martin Walser, *Ein springender Brunnen* (Frankfurt: Suhrkamp, 1998), 283.
26. Martin Walser, *Erfahrungen beim Erfassen einer Sonntagsrede* (Frankfurt: Suhrkamp, 1998), 7–17, here 19.
27. See Bill Niven, 'Martin Walser's *Tod eines Kritikers* and the Issue of Anti-Semitism', *German Life and Letters*, 56:3 (2003): 299–311.
28. Arnold Stadler, *Ein hinreissender Schrotthändler*, 228.
29. Tanja Dückers, 'Vorwort' in Tanja Dückers and Verena Carl, eds., *stadt land krieg: Autoren der Gegenwart erzählen von der deutschen Vergangenheit* (Berlin: Aufbau Taschenbuch Verlag, 2004), 7–13, 8.
30. See Thomas Ernst, *Popliteratur* (Hamburg: Rotbuch Verlag, 2001).
31. Rainald Goetz, *Rave* (Frankfurt: Suhrkamp, 2001 [1998]), 69. Hereafter *RA*.
32. Norbert Niemann, *Wie man's nimmt* (Munich: Hanser, 1998), 432.
33. Thomas Meinecke, *Mode und Verzweiflung* (Frankfurt: Suhrkamp, 1998), 8.
34. See Andrew Plowman, '"Was will ich denn als Westdeutscher erzählen?": The "old" West and Globalisation in Recent German Prose' in Stuart Taberner, ed., *German Literature in the Age of Globalisation* (Birmingham: Birmingham University Press, 2004), 47–66.
35. Frank Goosen, *liegen lernen* (Frankfurt: Eichborn, 2000 [1999]), 35.
36. David Wagner, *Meine nachtblaue Hose* (Frankfurt: Fischer, 2002 [2000]), 144. Hereafter *MNH*.
37. Tanja Dückers, *Spielzone* (Berlin: Aufbau Verlag, 1999), 191.

38. See Frank Finlay, '"Dann wäre Deutschland wie das Wort Neckarrauen": Surface, Superficiality and Globalisation in Christian Kracht's *Faserland*' in Stuart Taberner, ed., *German Literature in the Age of Globalisation*, 189–208; Christian Kracht, *Faserland* (Munich: Deutscher Taschenbuch Verlag, 2002 [1995]), 82; 85; 97.

39. Kracht *Faserland*, 97.

40. See Anke S. Biendarra, 'Der Erzähler als "Popmoderner Flaneuer" in Christian Krachts Roman *Faserland*', *German Life and Letters*, 55:2 (2002): 164–79.

41. Kracht, *Faserland*, 22; 151.

42. Christian Kracht, *1979* (Munich: Deutscher Taschenbuch Verlag, 2003 [2001]), 34.

43. Peter Schneider, 'Man kann sogar ein Erdbeben verpassen' in Peter Schneider, *Extreme Mittellage: Eine Reise durch das deutsche Nationalgefühl* (Reinbek: Rowohlt, 1990), 54–78, 64.

44. See Colin Riordan, 'German–Jewish Relations in Peter Schneider's Works' in Pól O'Dochartaigh, ed., *Jews in German Literature since 1945: German-Jewish Literature, German Monitor* (Amsterdam: Rodopi, 2000), 625–36, 634.

45. See, for example, Omer Bartov, 'Germany as Victim', *New German Critique*, 80 (2000): 29–40.

46. See Stuart Taberner's introduction to his edition of the novel (London: Duckworth, 2002).

47. See Stuart Taberner, 'Hans-Ulrich Treichel's *Der Verlorene* and The "Problem" of German Wartime Suffering', *The Modern Language Review*, 97 (2002): 123–34.

48. See Ingo Cornils, 'Long Memories: The German Student Movement in Recent Fiction', *German Life and Letters*, 56:1 (2003): 89–101.

49. See Stuart Taberner, ' "Normalization" and The New Consensus on the Nazi Past: Günter Grass's *Im Krebsgang* and the Problem of German Wartime Suffering', *Oxford German Studies*, 31 (2002): 161–86.

50. Günter Grass, *Im Krebsgang* (Göttingen: Steidl, 2002), 87, 99.

51. Uwe Timm, *Am Beispiel meines Bruders* (Cologne: Kiepenheuer & Witsch, 2003), 68–9; 131–2. Hereafter *BB*.

52. See Stuart Taberner, 'Feigning the Anaesthetisation of Literary Inventiveness: Günter Grass's *örtlich betäubt* and the Public Responsibility of the Politically Engaged Author', *Forum for Modern Language Studies*, 34:1 (1998): 71–81.

53. F. C. Delius, *Mein Jahr als Mörder* (Berlin: Rowohlt, 2004), 44.

CHAPTER 6

Literary reflections on '68

Ingo Cornils

One of the constituent debates of the post-unification period has centred on the impact of the generation of '68 – those in their late fifties and sixties at the end of the 1990s who had been active in the student movement of the 1960s – on the culture, politics and society of both the 'old' West Germany and the 'new', post-1990 Federal Republic.[1] While some observers continue to see '68 as a 'watershed' that embedded West German democracy and as a 'cultural revolution' that negated the nation's authoritarian past,[2] others believe it has led to a loss of traditional values and German identity. Equally significant, the discussion has centred on the 68ers' role in shaping West Germany's open and democratic *Streitkultur* (culture of public debate). Above all, the legacy of 'critical engagement' with the Nazi past, arguably the 68ers' most outstanding contribution to the self-understanding of modern-day Germany, has been challenged, as has the continuing dominance in the media, politics and the cultural sphere of a left-liberal elite drawn largely from the ranks of the former student protesters. This chapter examines the debate on '68 and, specifically, the recent explosion of literary texts reflecting on '68 as myth and cultural memory. These texts not only interrogate the values, aspirations and aesthetics of the generation most closely connected with the dramatic events of that period but also endeavour to define its significance for the Berlin Republic.

THE LEGACY OF '68

By the late 1990s, some thirty years after the events of '68, a process of historicisation had begun which, for the most part, appeared to undermine the political agenda and self-image of the former student radicals who had finally achieved power with the election of the Red–Green coalition in 1998. While the government of Gerhard Schröder and Joschka Fischer was keen to portray the 'new' Germany as a 'normal' country that had inter-nalised liberal, democratic values and come to terms with its past,[3] some historians had started to suggest that the 68ers might have a blind spot when it came to their formative years. Ingrid Gilcher-Holtey's *1968: Vom Ereignis zum Gegenstand der Geschichtswissenschaft* (1968: From Event to History, 1998), Wolfgang Kraushaar's *1968 als Mythos, Chiffre und Zäsur* (1968 as Myth, Cipher and Caesura, 2000), Gerd Langguth's *Mythos 68: Die Gewaltphilosophie von Rudi Dutschke* (The Myth of 68: Rudi Dutschke's Philosophy of Violence, 2001) and Gerd Koenen's *Das rote Jahrzehnt* (The Red Decade, 2001) thus all displayed a new, (self-)critical attitude towards '68. Kraushaar in particular, one of the most prolific writers on German protest movements, argued that the 68ers' occasionally dangerous radicalism and illegal actions should be set against their broadly positive impact on civil society; he cautioned, however, that '68 had long been accorded the status of a 'foundational myth'[4] and had become distorted by half-truths, fanciful interpretations and over-simplifications.[5] Gerd Langguth, on the other hand, was far less forgiving: a member of a conservative student association in the late 1960s, Langguth's *Mythos 68* sought to unmask the student rebellion as a dangerous plot hatched by Rudi Dutschke, the leader of the most radical student group in West Berlin, and to demonstrate how events such as the killing of Benno Ohnesorg by a policeman in June 1967 or the attempt on the life of student organiser Rudi Dutschke had been transformed into a 'nostalgic cult'.[6] In the spring of 2001, indeed, the student movement's attitude towards political violence came under the spotlight when foreign minister Joschka Fischer was outed as a former militant who had fought the police and lived next door to a terrorist. The ensuing scandal led to demands in parliament by the CDU leader, Angela Merkel – then in opposition – that the 68ers once and for all denounce the 'misguided' ideals of their youth.

The myth of '68 has been defined by Robert Frank as follows: 'The spirit of '68 is real . . . Over time, however, this spirit has been mythologised. As a symbol of a new political culture characterised by solidarity, a critical and watchful stance and a new set of political practices, this myth of social change functions as a foundational myth, a form of legitimation for the actions of a generation.'[7] The generation in question, of course, is precisely the generation most closely associated with the shaping of the politics, culture and society of the Berlin Republic. From the late 1990s, both the liberal and conservative media began to challenge the myth of '68, and its legitimatory function, even as they themselves contributed to a reductive image of the period; indeed, 1968 has become an 'iconic' year, similar to 1945 or 1989, a crucial moment in time when it was good to be young, when no one worried about the hole in the ozone layer,[8] and when hopes were high that the revolution was possible. Yet the myth of '68 is immensely flexible and adaptable; it is a 'theme with variations'.[9] While some associate it with the dismantling of authoritarian structures in education, others see it as the coming-of-age of West Germany's fledgling democracy or as the (short-lived) victory of romantic, utopian thought over *realpolitik*. And the 68ers themselves are not loath to make use of such allusions, perhaps, it has been suggested, because they have failed so comprehensively in their objectives that they can only survive by fleeing into the realm of fantasy.[10] As a modern myth with heroes, villains, martyrs and an open end, the narrative of '68 is well-suited as a 'core identity' around which disparate groups can coalesce; former adversaries may even unite in the shared ownership of 'their' '68. Sociological studies, in fact, point to a strong sense of a common self-understanding amongst the age group born between 1938 and 1948 that does not exist to the same extent amongst other cohorts.[11] Finally, a myth is far more difficult to challenge than mere 'facts'. Once broadly accepted, it often proves to be resistant to questioning and comes to form part of collective memory.[12]

There appear to be three distinct views with regard to the myth of '68: there are those who claim that the 68ers have falsified history and fooled the public into believing that they had a positive effect on society, those who believe that the 68ers have been misunderstood and that the public needs to be told what really happened, and those who enhance the myth by according the 68ers an epochal significance that will ensure their place in the history books. This threefold engagement with '68 takes place in newspaper editorials, in public debate and in history seminars. In my next section, I explore the ways in which three *literary* representations published in 2001 – Leander Scholz's *Rosenfest* (Feast of Roses), Erasmus Schöfer's *Ein Frühling irrer Hoffnung* (A Spring of Crazy Hope), and Uwe Timm's *Rot* (Red) – responded and added to the discussion.

THE MYTH OF '68

From the early 1970s, writers – often former activists – began to publish novels about the student movement. They soon found themselves in the role of talespinners, keeping the spirit of '68 alive and reminding their readers of the advances in consciousness and social and political enlightenment that, in their view, had been all too quickly forgotten. In the 1990s, in fact, Peter Schneider's *Lenz* (1973) and Uwe Timm's *Heißer Sommer* (Hot Summer, 1974) were still being widely read as testaments to the 'spirit of the age'. A less charitable interpretation is that 'the revolt turned into literature'[13] served to feed the craving of frustrated 68ers to have their 'days of glory' endlessly replayed for them.[14] Whatever the case, by the turn of the century, there had been in excess of forty narratives dealing with '68 or set against the background of '68.[15]

From the end of the 1990s, that is, from around the time that Kraushaar, Langguth et al. were busy historicising '68 in a series of academic and zeit-geist publications, a new wave of literary representations of the era appeared. Three texts in particular were interesting in so far as they appeared at more or less the same time as the 'Fischer affair' was reaching fever pitch. Sig-nificantly, however, hardly any mention of these fictional depictions of the period was made in the course of the debate; this lends credence to Kraushaar's argument that, in the 1990s, '68 had become a cipher for more general conflicts largely unrelated to the era itself. Yet Scholz's *Rosenfest*, Schöfer's *Ein Frühling irrer Hoffnung* and Timm's *Rot*, if any of the partici-pants in the controversy had taken the time to read them, might well have added a useful dimension to the discussion. These three novels, in fact, set out competing interpretations of the aims, ambitions and motivations of the 68ers for a new generation of readers who have no memory of the period itself. Inevitably, of course, this process of bringing '68 to life invests the era with new mythical meanings.[16]

In *Rosenfest*, Scholz narrates the flight of Andreas Baader and Gudrun Ensslin, the founding members of the Red Army Faction (RAF), from the police as an exhilarating road trip. By focusing exclusively on his terrorist protagonists, the author blanks out the ranks of student protesters; the demonstrations of '68, it is thereby implied, led directly to West German terrorism, but the majority of those involved in the street protests of the day were, we are asked to believe, merely a gullible and largely lethargic mass, incapable of understanding that they were being manipulated by the dangerous radicals who would later turn to violence. Thus, when the leader of the Frankfurt Socialist German Students (SDS) propounds their theory of provocation and Baader suggests that the students should organise themselves into criminal gangs, the audience is horrified.[17] For Erasmus Schöfer, on the other hand, '68 possesses an entirely different significance. *Ein Frühling irrer Hoffnung*, part of a tetralogy entitled *Die Kinder des Sisyfos* (The Children of Sisyphus), suggests that – just like the hero of Greek myth – the 68er generation indeed inched humankind forward, only to find itself frustrated, beaten and forced to start over and over. A life-long communist and founder of a writing circle for workers, the author seeks to connect the contemporary reader with '68 via empathy with its utopian yearnings. Viktor Bliss, a former activist, lives as a recluse after the fall of communism, his dreams of a better world seemingly disproved by events, and recounts his experiences to his estranged granddaughter. In this way, Schöfer bridges the gulf between the hopes of the 68ers and – so the author hopes – the latent idealism of a new generation nauseated by western 'leisure and pleasure' ideals that ignore the plight of the poor.[18]

The iconography of the Left also features prominently in the perhaps most thoughtful literary reflection on '68, Uwe Timm's *Rot*. Here, the move of the government from Bonn to Berlin in 1999 is used as a starting point for a funeral oration for the 68ers. As the protagonist, Thomas Linde (a former 68er now working as a freelance funeral orator), floats in limbo in his dying moments, he realises that the youthful passion for the cause he shared with his former comrade, Aschenberger, was not so very foolish after all: he glimpses the sense in Aschenberger's plan to blow up the victory column in Berlin as a protest against Germany's resurgence as a military power in the 1990s. Linde is at pains to explain to his young and ambitious girlfriend, Iris, the dreams and aspirations of his generation and, in doing this, generates a new respect for moral and political ideals that are decidedly out of fashion in the Berlin Republic. The novel is ambivalent, oscillating between sympathy for Aschenberger (literally a 'heap of ashes') and disdain for his yearning for a 'normal' existence which combines a bourgeois existence with apathy. Linde's most authentic moments occur when he delivers his deeply humane, 'alternative' funeral orations. Here, similar to his friend Aschenberger, who used to offer 'alternative' tours around Berlin, Linde continues to challenge established codes of behaviour.

Overall, literary reflections on '68 at the end of the 1990s both replicate and also make concrete the three fundamental positions taken by participants in the wider debates of that time as described at the beginning of this section. Leander Scholz, then, cheerfully chips away at the myth of '68 and portrays the student movement as a precursor to the terrorism of the 1970s, whereas Erasmus Schöfer claims to tell it 'as it really was', although his ideological basis is clear. Scholz thus seeks to undermine the notion that the social and political engagement of '68 should be a primary point of reference for the Berlin Republic; Schöfer, on the other hand, draws a supposedly authentic picture of the period in order to criticise the political apathy of the present. Uwe Timm, alternatively, adds to the myth of '68 through his virtuoso use of imagery drawn from German Romanticism and the nation's liberal-democratic revolutionary tradition. Indeed, the protagonist's name 'Linde' is highly evocative, conjuring up heroic images from the Germanic *Nibelungenlied* as well as harking back to the revolutionary subtext of Richard Wagner's *Ring*-cycle. Similar allusions are evoked by the painting *Saint George and the Dragon* by Paolo Uccello, which adorns Aschenberger's dark flat. By elevating its 'struggle' to a mythical level, Timm acknowledges the fading of the student movement into history but also revives it as the object of literary and aesthetic fascination with socio-political relevance for the present-day Berlin Republic, which is characterised, the author suggests, by an egotistical materialism.[19]

The ongoing fascination of German writers into the new millennium with the 'unfinished business' of '68 is reflected in a number of texts that appeared in the period 2000–5, and particularly by a series of seven novels published in 2004 and 2005: Friedrich Christian Delius's *Mein Jahr als Mörder* (My Year as a Murderer, 2004); Gerhard Seyfried's *Der schwarze Stern der Tupamaros* (the Black Star of the Tupamaros, 2004); Sophie Dannenberg's *Das bleiche Herz der Revolution* (The Pale Heart of the Revolution, 2004); Erasmus Schöfer's *Zwielicht* (Twilight, 2004), Peter Schneider's *Skylla* (Scylla, 2005); Bernd Cailloux's *Das Geschäftsjahr 1968/69* (The Business Year 1968–69, 2005), and Uwe Timm's semi-autobiographical narrative, *Der Freund und der Fremde* (The Friend and the Stranger, 2005). In what remains of this chapter, I analyse three of these texts, namely those by Dannenberg, Schneider and Cailloux (born 1971, 1942 and 1945, respectively), as examples of a substantial shift in the way literature in the by now established Berlin Republic engages with the ongoing controversies surrounding the significance of '68. The most recent German literary fiction dealing with the period continues to reflect on the myth of '68 but now also points to how, as anticipated by Timm's *Rot*, the focus has transferred from political events to a more directly personal assessment of the meaning of the period for individuals. This shift in focus may be the result of the increasing pressure former 68ers experience in the Berlin Republic to justify the choices they made when they were young. Indeed, in the era after the collapse of communism and more particularly in the wake of the terrorist attacks on New York on 11 September 2001, the heady idealism of their youth increasingly appears to many who were not there to be both incomprehensible and naive.

'68 DECONSTRUCTED

Dannenberg's *roman-à-clef* is a searing indictment of the 'crimes' of the 68ers and the psychological damage she believes them to have inflicted on their children and their parents. One of the most vitriolic attacks on the peace-loving and reformist image of the German student movement is her (factually inaccurate) 'reconstruction' of events at the Frankfurt Institute of

Social Research in 1968. Thus Aaron Wisent (aka social theorist Theodor W. Adorno) is coerced by Bodo Streicher (aka Horst Mahler, at that time a lawyer for Baader and Ensslin, more recently a right-wing nationalist) into writing a defence of the notorious flyer 'Burn warehouse, burn', a propaganda text written by members of the radical 'Commune I', which is reproduced in full in the novel. When Wisent refuses to condone this incitement to violence, militant members of the SDS turn against him: 'We don't want to talk, we want to fight . . . We want weapons. We want to know how we can blow up this stupid university, all universities, America Houses, America, the capital.'[20] In this passage, Dannenberg echoes a scene from Timm's *Heißer Sommer*, but while in Timm's novel space is given to an explanation of the 'great refusal' elaborated by Herbert Marcuse, 'the father of the revolution', we learn here of the SDS's 'darker' motives. Thus Dannenberg 'exposes' the 'nihilistic' critical theory promoted by Adorno and Marcuse and embraced by the students as merely another vehicle for corruption and the abuse of power.

The militant minority, described by Dannenberg as lazy, drugged-up, fanatical bullies, not only interrupts Wisent's lectures. Shouting anti-semitic slogans such as 'Pentagon Jew', they throw a Molotov cocktail and Wisent dies in agony (*DBH*, 106). His brilliant assistant, Hieronymus Arber, who tries to save Wisent's life, is later outmanoeuvred by a corrupt coalition of another assistant, the scheming Heinz Müller-Skripski (aka philosopher Jürgen Habermas), and the thugs who quickly manage to find influential posts in government, media and higher education. In an intrigue reminiscent of Dietrich Schwanitz's *Der Campus* (The Campus, 1995), Arber's academic career is thereby torpedoed and he is lucky to find a post at a polytechnic in the provinces.

In a second narrative strand, Dannenberg introduces the reader to Kitty Caspari, who, it seems, has been 'ruined' by the anti-authoritarianism of her 68er parents. Kitty's father, Borsalino von Baguette (aka Klaus Croissant) has resigned as a defence lawyer for RAF terrorist Susanne Albrecht after having been forced by Streicher to smuggle weapons into prison, and has relocated his family to the 'Free Republic of Wendland' (one of the strongholds of resistance against nuclear power plants). Now he makes a living defending the anti-nuclear protesters. From an early age, Kitty has been subjected to what her grandfather describes as permanent brainwashing on the subject of capitalist corruption and the need for permanent revolution. Her home life is stifling: her mother is entirely self-obsessed; she is subjected to harrowing sexual experiments by her father and brother, and sent to a quack therapist when she refuses to accept their view of the

world. It takes years for Kitty to undo the damage caused by her upbringing. She meets Arber, who encourages her to write down her experiences,
but even in the present he is thwarted by his nemesis Müller-Skripski, who
ensures that Kitty's story does not get published.

The novel's third narrative strand deals with the relation between the
68ers and their parents, the 'Nazi generation'. The 68ers have broken all
lines of communication with them, but not, Dannenberg suggests, out of
moral revulsion, but because they lack the curiosity, the empathy and the
willingness to accept their parents' failure. Significantly, it is not the fact
that their parents started the Second World War or that they are responsible
for millions of deaths, but the fact that they lost the war that causes the 68ers
to turn against them. Once again, the 68ers are presented as hypocritical
and self-centred, unable to learn from history and therefore doomed to
repeat it.

In an interview with *Der Spiegel*, Dannenberg suggested that her generation's hatred of the 68ers was as strong as that of the 68ers towards their
parents. She claimed to be disgusted by their 'false anti-fascism', 'sweaty
stench', and 'destruction of traditional values' such as decency, reliabil-
ity and homeliness, and by the 'Pornographisierung der Kindheit' (the
sexual perversion of childhood). Most damaging of all, she argued that
the generation that had invented 'progressive aesthetics' and presented the
RAF terrorists as victims was, at least in part, responsible for modern-day
terrorism: 'there is a direct line from Che Guevara to Al Quaida'.[21] Pre-
dictably, this polemical attack – which echoed the fury of Bettina Röhl's
attack on Joschka Fischer in 2001 – attracted a great deal of media attention, fuelling a controversy about the 68ers' responsibility for all that was
wrong with the country that had re-erupted following the publication of
Gerd Koenen's *Vesper, Ensslin, Baader: Urszenen des deutschen Terrorismus*
(The Origins of German Terrorism, 2003) and a volume of essays entitled
Andreas Baader, Rudi Dutschke und die RAF by the Hamburg Institute of
Social Research (2005).[22]

Dannenberg's attempt to deconstruct the repressive and hypocritical
character of '68 touched many raw nerves. However, in spite of a blanket
panning of the novel (the book was almost uniformly rejected as clichéd,
even 'blasphemous'),[23] she seems to have hit a nerve and to have caused
a crack to appear in the previously seemingly impervious armour of the
68ers. Yet the question remains as to whether *Das bleiche Herz der Revolution*, a vicious satire that implies that the idealism of the 68ers was
synonymous with the emotional brutality of those who would later turn
to terrorism, reflects the view of the majority of Germans in the Berlin

Republic. In reality, it is far more probable that the majority of the wider population – those who are neither beholden to particular interests nor have a partisan political axe to grind – would insist that it is necessary to differentiate between the utopian dreams of the many thousands of ordinary student protesters and the fanaticism of a minority. Moreover, it is perhaps ironic that Dannenberg, born after the events themselves and a product of an 'anti-authoritarian' upbringing which sought to advance the rights of the individual, and especially of women, would use this selfsame freedom against the 68ers.

'68 RE-IMAGINED

Just after the turn of the millennium, with public opinion turning against the 68ers, the pressure for former activists to 'come clean' was growing. The novel *Skylla*, by the well-known '68er' author Peter Schneider, accordingly, is a complex and sophisticated attempt to engage with contemporary debates on the period and its alleged militant tendencies. In addition, it is an essay on Napoleon Bonaparte's observation: 'What is history but a fable agreed upon?' The protagonist is Leo Brenner, a former activist in the student movement, now a successful Berlin solicitor specialising in divorce cases. Fleeing a rainy Tuscany one summer, he buys a plot of land on a hill in Latium and builds a house for his family. He and his young wife, Lucynna, an archaeologist, become involved in a race to reconstruct a sculpture that was the source for the mosaic they discover underneath their terrace whilst exploring the myth of the monster Scylla. Amongst the daily frustrations of house-building in Italy and a second narrative strand that explores the time of the emperor Tiberius, in whose cave in Sperlonga the sculpture was first set, we come to what appears to be a minor narrative detour, but which proves to be the centre of the novel. Brenner encounters an old comrade from his student days, Paul Stirlitz. This down-on-his-luck drifter, who scrapes a living helping affluent 68ers to build their second homes in arcadia, confronts Brenner with his past as an agitator and student leader.

Brenner initially has no recollection of Stirlitz (an indication of the passage of time and his 'successful' integration into bourgeois society), but is forcefully reminded that not all 68ers have managed to leave their past behind. Skilfully reflecting the political debate about the legacy of '68, Schneider has his characters take opposite sides on how to remember the era: for Brenner, therefore, it was a 'wonderful and necessary revolution', for Stirlitz, alternatively, it was a time of 'brutal slogans and formulas for saving the world'.[24] It soon becomes clear that Brenner and Stirlitz are not only arguing about how to historicise their past but also about its very legitimacy.

Stirlitz reminds his former comrade of the time Rudi Dutschke was shot by an individual who had read too many inflammatory headlines in the tabloids published by the Springer press. He wants Brenner to admit that as a leading figure in the movement he had been instrumental in enticing young people to violence with the slogan 'Blow up Springer!' (S, 208). Faced with this 'self-appointed judge', Brenner adamantly refuses to make such an admission of guilt. The reason for Stirlitz's investment in the issue becomes obvious when he confesses that he had interpreted the slogan as a call to direct action. He had prepared a bomb that was intended to damage the Springer headquarters in West Berlin but which instead killed two innocent people. Brenner feebly protests that his slogan had not been a call for violence, that it had simply been a case of following 'the logic of alliteration' (the original German is: 'sprengt Springer', S, 209), but Stirlitz, eaten up by his feelings of guilt, demands that Brenner accept a degree of responsibility for the consequences of his actions.

Initially, the solicitor defends himself vigorously, claiming that he had never suggested that people should plant bombs. The only thing he is willing to accept responsibility for is 'an all too reckless use of words' (S, 214). However, when Stirlitz steals the mosaic and Lucynna disappears, Brenner begins to have doubts. These, in turn, lead to a process of reflection and self-examination.[25] At this point, Schneider widens the scope of his 'archaeological dig'. Brenner meets with one of the archaeologists attempting to recreate the Scylla sculpture, who explains that people want to know where they come from, and, through this process, who they are and where they are going. Historiography, therefore, is a never-ending contest about memory. Each generation creates a new and unique history from the testaments of its forebears: 'The decisive thing is not what happened, but what elements of events are being formulated and captured. A history that has never been written gets lost – in the end, it hasn't even happened' (S, 248–9). Asked by Brenner whether this means that there is no difference between the original and the reconstruction, the archaeologist responds: 'I wouldn't go that far. But when there is no original, not even a copy of the original, the reconstruction will prevail in collective memory. And eventually, the reconstruction replaces the original' (S, 252).

With *Skylla*, Schneider appears to exorcise a ghost. Both the protagonist and the author were actively involved in the student revolt (the name *Brenner* suggests a willingness to play with fire). Both avoided violent conflict but share a certain responsibility for the actions of others whom they might have inadvertently incited to violence. Referring to Schneider's famous speech *Wir haben Fehler gemacht* ('We have made mistakes') of April 1967, *Spiegel* editor Stefan Aust has described the author as 'the quiet agitator' who articulated a tactic of a 'limited breaking of rules' which ultimately led to an escalation of violence.[26] Indeed, Schneider was more involved in the movement than is commonly remembered today. He was part of the group that prepared the 'Springer tribunal' in 1967 and one of the signatories of a pamphlet against Springer's press monopoly in West Berlin.[27] He was also, as he has himself revealed, one of the originators of the 'Wanted' poster displayed during the visit of the Shah of Persia to West Berlin. This poster incited the demonstrations during which Ohnesorg was killed and the subsequent escalation of the conflict between the students and the state.

Over the years, Schneider has distanced himself considerably from the worst excesses of '68, but continues to maintain that the protests were entirely necessary at the time. The message is clear: similar to the myths of the 'monster' Scylla or that of the 'shy' emperor Tiberius, the myth of '68 has undergone numerous retellings and the truth has become unrecognisable beneath countless conflicting interpretations. Just like Tiberius, who attempted to legitimise his hold on power by creating a mythical bloodline to Odysseus, it seems that the 68ers are busy anchoring their legend in collective memory, an activity that has gained urgency with the passage of time and the increasingly critical attitude towards them in the Berlin Republic. Schneider is aware of how much he himself has contributed to the 'mythical' power of 1968. With *Lenz* (1973), to be sure, the author attempted to distance himself from the 'unpoetic' dogmatism and futile violence that had destroyed what had been intended, and yet this text has become one of the 'iconic' texts on the student movement. *Skylla* can be interpreted as a further aesthetic and creative allegory of the movement, linking the personal and the mythical: once a beautiful maiden, corrupted through no fault of her own, she kills those who come too near. Innocence and violence are the two halves of her being, and yet Odysseus thought she was the lesser of two evils.

'68 ILLUMINATED

With *Das Geschäftsjahr 1968/69*, another former 68er, Bernd Cailloux, made an unexpected contribution to the debate. The novel demonstrates that '68 does not have to be portrayed exclusively in terms of its directly political significance. Instead, Cailloux resurrects the year as the time when the concrete utopia of living an 'alternative' life seemed within reach of quite ordinary young people. Three friends – the first-person narrator and Andreas Büdinger, both disillusioned local reporters, and the inventor Achim Bekurz – set up a small business in a garden shed in Düsseldorf. This is a cottage industry with a difference: inspired by the young Josef Beuys and his circle, they wait for an idea that will enable them to become artists themselves, ideally without too much effort. Before long they form the *Muße-Gesellschaft* (leisure society), hoping to create a kind of subversive counter culture whilst making a living outside the rules of the capitalist market. Bekurz is to be responsible for the technical side, while the others take care of logistics and marketing. They agree to take decisions together and to divide profits equally whilst supporting an increasing number of drug-hazed 'friends'.

Their first product is the 'revolutionary' strobe light, which they plan to manufacture for discos and live events. It is an invention that fits the mood of the time perfectly and the alternative scene of young people eager for new kicks and experiences. The friends get their breakthrough in Hamburg's *Golem* disco, where the proprietor plans to cash in on the unique mix of politics, art and lifestyle of the late '60s. The psychedelic lightshow installed by the *Muße-Gesellschaft* creates a euphoric effect that proves a success once Büdinger demonstrates to them the new possibilities: 'He ran through the ring in all his jerking height, as if hit by electric shocks, and twisted his gangly body, his long arms and legs, into rhythmically exact, endlessly flashing strobe-images.'[28] The dancers love the new effects; it is, the narrator comments, as if 'a mental jerk had gone through everyone, dividing time into a Before and and an After'. The owner of the strip club next door is impressed as well, but the *Muße-Gesellschaft*, riding high on the success of their first sale, refuses to deal with a representative of the 'system' they despise.

Even at this early stage, the three friends realise that by selling their product they are selling a part of themselves. They have tripped over the stumbling block at the heart of the 68er philosophy: the realisation that it is impossible to live an 'authentic' life within the falsehoods of the present-day reality. They begin to understand that their dream of a counter-cultural enterprise in a capitalist reality is full of contradictions, for example, when the owner of the *Golem* tries to haggle over the agreed price. It is Büdinger, the most entrepreneurial minded of the three, who papers over the cracks that are beginning to appear in their philosophy. He refuses to take the dream of a non-profit organisation too seriously and pragmatically sets up the *Muße-Gesellschaft* as a limited company. He tells the others that the flash of the strobe light stands for the start of the counter culture: 'We bring a new light into the world, and with it we will change the habits of a whole generation – what more do you want?' (*G*, 48). Yet the narrator is not persuaded. He is aware that the pathos of Büdinger's argument runs counter to his own ideals, but is unable to convince his partners that he is right.

A few months after their début, they get the opportunity to show off their product to a wider audience when they are hired to provide a massive strobe light and the swirling psychedelic images on the screens behind the performing bands at the *Internationale Essener Songtage* (the German equivalent of the Woodstock festival, headlining Frank Zappa and his Mothers of Invention). For all those present, the night of 28 September 1968 proves to be the pivotal moment of their lives:

An event that would stay forever in the memory of those who were there – a fundamental experience and yet only a stolen second in the history of the world, just like the whole windy year of which it was part. Only afterwards, when we tried to give form to this era, did it became clearer that this night marked a turning point, when an avant-garde of future cultural practice broke with old norms and escaped – into lifestyles and behaviour patterns that would ultimately define them and others. (*G*, 66)

In passages like this, Cailloux romanticises the moment, investing it with significance beyond the individual and the singular. He uses the strobe light as a metaphor for the consciousness-changing import of the liberation of young people who feel for an instant that their lives could be so very different. But the moment cannot last. The *Muße-Gesellschaft* is in demand: theatres, artists, manufacturers and advertising agencies beat a path to their door, bringing about the inevitable descent into commercialism. As the narrator begins his own plunge into drug addiction, he realises that his company is doing exactly the same as his dealer: by supplying them with accessories to reach a desired state of mind, they feed and exploit the need of young people to escape reality (*G*, 75).

Eventually, Büdinger becomes the company director, while the narrator anaesthetises his scruples with ever-increasing amounts of drugs. To meet the costs of expansion, the company sells its strobes to the strip-clubs they once abhorred, moves into 'respectable' premises and employs new people, while the narrator is edged out. Unsurprisingly, given his drug addiction, the narrator is unable to oppose Büdinger. Instead, he attempts to justify his continued participation in the company to himself during long car journeys from customer to customer. He still believes that they achieved something without, he says, the aid of 'irgendwelcher studentischer Heißmacher' (any overzealous student agitators). What the students were discussing in theory, he muses, they had already turned into practice and had thereby changed reality (*G*, 111).

And yet the thrill has disappeared. The narrator is sent to open a branch in Hamburg, where he slowly recovers from his addiction and finds love with a woman who correctly sizes him up as a 'hippy-businessman' (*G*, 177). Encouraged by his new independence, he plans to outwit his former business partners, only to be thwarted when he contracts life-threatening hepatitis, a weakness that Büdinger exploits in order to persuade him to sign over his share in the company. Years later, they meet again and laugh off their *Muße-Gesellschaft* as a 'youthful error', sarcastically commenting that '68 had been 'a grandiose, almost ingenious PR campaign, and one that cost almost nothing' (*G*, 236). Yet the narrator has not given up on his ideals. He still believes that they had a unique opportunity to do 'the right thing' and, even though they failed miserably, has no regrets: 'after all, we came up with something useful' – the little flashing light (*G*, 254).

Bernd Cailloux's novel was very positively reviewed and was nominated for the 'German Book Prize'. He is praised, then, for conveying to the reader 'the essence of '68', whilst refraining from jumping on the bandwagon of '68er bashing'.[29] Certainly, the author stays clear of the endless political debates without, however, entirely ignoring their significance. The student protests are always in the background but they do not dominate the plot. Rather, Cailloux focuses on the way the era must have felt to the many people who, most likely, were less interested in pouring over their editions of the writings of Karl Marx than simply having fun and emancipating themselves from the austere and authoritarian norms of the post-war generation. His depiction of milieu, mood and jargon communicates a sense of authenticity, while his imaginative use of the strobe light as a metaphor for the 'spirit of '68' marks him out as a poetic and thoughtful literary witness to the period.

Cailloux's main achievement, perhaps, consists of his novel's representation of '68 as simply another financial year, with the student protests and countercultural ideals a minor irritation for business. Indeed, the manner in which everybody lines up to do deals with the subversive *Muße-Gesellschaft*, adapting and integrating their 'revolutionary' invention into the mainstream, symbolises what became of the cultural revolution of '68 more broadly: it was domesticated, packaged, and later sold as pop culture. The title *Geschäftsjahr* (Business Year) holds another meaning, however: a balance sheet on which those involved can enter the achievements of '68.

For the narrator, a modern Parcival who has invested his whole identity in his ideals, there may be a small personal plus, even though he lost his health. For Büdinger, there may have been financial success, but for him as a person, the entry is empty.

On balance, Cailloux – just like Schneider and Timm – appears to feel that the dominant materialism of the old Bonn and the new Berlin Republic has asphyxiated the utopian potential of '68. What is significant in this narrative is the fact that this materialism is not simply portrayed as part of an abstract 'system' of capitalist exploitation or as a function of the culture industry but is related to real people who make their own choices.

CONCLUSION

In the most recent literary reflections of '68, the historic events and their underlying motivations are recalled and subjected to biting satire, myth creation, or to an audit where the ideals and the reality of the time are recorded on the two sides of a balance sheet. Through the poetic imagination of the writers, the reader is afforded insights into the psychology, emotions and flavour of an era that is fast receding into cultural memory. Moreover, they use the increasing historical distance to focus on uncomfortable truths that even five years earlier would have been impossible to explore. Human failures, be it the inability of the 68ers to connect with their parents or children, their inability to think about the consequences of their actions, or simply the naivety of mistaking a business venture for a utopian dream, are exposed and analysed. As such, the texts make a unique contribution not only to our understanding of the era, but also to the debate about the values that will determine the future direction of German political culture. They contain, even in Dannenberg's deconstruction, the description of an *alternative* to a one-dimensional society, and the memory of a precious personal and collective experience of challenging their parent generation and changing their own lives that has enabled the 68ers to dominate the moral high ground in the old Bonn and the new Berlin Republic.

With the demise of the Red–Green coalition and the end of their long-term 'project' to change political culture from within the institutions, the 68ers have finally entered history. It is doubtful that the supply of books on them will dry up in the near future, however, given the continuing public fascination with their past. The lost utopian dream, the myth of a golden age that may come again, the revolutionary fight for freedom and justice – these elements will always make for a good story. To judge by Uwe Timm's *Der Freund und der Fremde* (The Friend and the Stranger, 2005), a semi-autobiographical narrative relating the life and death of Timm's one-time friend Benno Ohnesorg, we are likely to see many more accounts, increasingly more distanced from the actual events and yet at the same time much more personal than what we have seen so far. For Timm, '68 was all about a new aesthetic and a new consciousness: 'No lies. No false emotions. Talk about everything. Look at things closely, without turning away.'[30] This is the true legacy of the 68ers for the Berlin Republic.

NOTES

1. See Ingo Cornils, 'Successful Failure? The Impact of the German Student Movement on the Federal Republic of Germany' in Stuart Taberner and Frank Finlay, eds., *Recasting German Identity: Culture, Politics and Literature in the Berlin Republic* (Rochester: Camden House, 2002), 107–26.

2. Andrei Marcovits and Philip Gorski, *The German Left: Red, Green and Beyond* (Oxford: Oxford University Press, 1993), p. 4. See also Ingo Cornils, 'The German Student Movement: Legend and Legacy', *Debatte*, 4:2 (1996), 47–9.

3. See Stuart Taberner and Paul Cooke, eds., *German Culture, Politics and Literature into the Twenty-First Century: Beyond Normalization* (Rochester: Camden House, 2006).

4. See also Ingeborg Villinger, '"Stelle sich jemand vor, wir hätten gesiegt": Das Symbolische der 68er Bewegung und die Folgen' in Ingrid Gilcher-Holtey, ed., *1968: Vom Ereignis zum Gegenstand der Geschichtswissenschaft* (Göttingen: Vandenhoeck & Ruprecht, 1998), 239–55.

5. In his most recent book, Kraushaar appears to change his mind, after uncovering evidence that suggests that Rudi Dutschke had formulated the idea of an urban guerilla as early as 1966.

6. See Ingo Cornils, 'Folgenschwere Schüsse: Die Kugeln auf Benno Ohnesorg und Rudi Dutschke im Spiegel der deutschen Literatur', *Jahrbuch für internationale Germanistik*, 35:2 (2005), 55–73, and also Cornils, '"The Struggle Continues": Rudi Dutschke's Long March' in Gerard DeGroot, ed., *Student Protest: The Sixties and After* (London: Longman, 1998), 100–14.

7. Robert Frank, '1968 – ein Mythos?' in Gilcher-Holthey, ed., *1968*, 301–7, here 307.

8. See Daniel Cohn-Bendit and Reinhard Mohr, *1968: Die letzte Revolution, die noch nichts von dem Ozonloch wußte* (Berlin: Wagenbach, 1988).

9. Hans Blumenberg, *Arbeit am Mythos* (Frankfurt: Suhrkamp, 1979), 40.

10. Peter G. Spengler, 'Mit 1968 Staat machen? Anmerkungen und Zweifel zu einem Fluchtpunkt des Zeitgeistes', http://www.jahrbuch2000.studien-von-zeitfragen.net/Thema_1967/ thema_1967.htm (accessed 28 September 2006).

11. See, for example, Heinz Bude, *Das Altern einer Generation: Die Jahrgänge 1938–1948* (Frankfurt: Suhrkamp, 1995).

12. See Edgar Wolfrum, '"1968" in der gegenwärtigen deutschen Geschichtspolitik', *Aus Politik und Zeitgeschehen* 22–23 (2001): 28–36.

13. Ralf Schnell, *Geschichte der deutschsprachigen Literatur seit 1945* (Stuttgart: Metzler, 1993), 420–30.
14. See Ingo Cornils, 'Looking back: Piwitt, *Rothschilds* and the German Student Movement' in David Basker, ed., *Hermann Peter Piwitt* (Cardiff: University of Wales Press, 2000), 47–64.
15. See Ingo Cornils, 'Writing the Revolution: The Literary Representation of the German Student Movement as Counter-Culture' in Steve Giles and Maike Oergel, eds., *Counter-Cultures in Germany and Central Europe: From Sturm und Drang to Baader–Meinhof* (Bern: Peter Lang, 2003), 295–314.
16. See Ingo Cornils, 'Long Memories: The German Student Movement in Recent Fiction', *German Life and Letters*, 56:1 (2003): 89–101.
17. Leander Scholz, *Rosenfest* (Munich: Carl Hanser Verlag, 2001), 98.
18. Erasmus Schöfer, *Ein Frühling irrer Hoffnung* (Cologne: Dittrich Verlag, 2001), 10.
19. See Ingo Cornils, 'Uwe Timm, der heilige Georg und die Entsorgung der Theorie' in Frank Finlay and Ingo Cornils, eds., *(Un-)erfüllte Wirklichkeit: Neue Studien zu Uwe Timm* (Würzburg: Königshausen & Neumann: 2006), 55–71.
20. Sophie Dannenberg, *Das bleiche Herz der Revolution* (Munich: Deutsche Verlagsanstalt, 2004), 64. Hereafter *DBH*.
21. Interview with Sophie Dannenberg in *Der Spiegel online* (18 November 2004), http://www.spiegel.de/kultur/literatur/0,1518,327028,00.html (accessed 15 March 2006).
22. See Ingo Cornils, 'Joined at The Hip? The Representation of the German Student Movement and Left-Wing Terrorism in Recent Literature', *German Monitor* (forthcoming 2007).
23. Katrin Hillgruber, 'Ein Kommunist braucht kein Deodorant', *Frankfurter Rundschau* (1 September 2004).
24. Peter Schneider, *Skylla* (Reinbek: Rowohlt Verlag, 2005), 125. Hereafter *S*.
25. See Christiane Schott, 'Die Vergangenheit ist nicht tot', *Stuttgarter Zeitung* (17 June 2005).
26. Stefan Aust, 'Betreten verboten', in Paul Michael Lützeler, ed., *Festschrift für Peter Schneider zum 65. Geburtstag* (Berlin: Rowohlt, 2004), http://www.peterschneider-autor.de/freunde.htm (accessed 28 September 2006).
27. Martin Watson and Peter Schneider: 'Über die Mühen des Kampfes in Deutschland', http://www.uni-essen.de/literaturwissenschaft-aktiv/nullpunkt/pdf/schneider_muehen.pdf.
28. Bernd Cailloux, *Das Geschäftsjahr 1968/69* (Frankfurt: Suhrkamp, 2005), 58. Hereafter *G*.
29. See Gerrit Bartels, 'Blitz der Subversion', *taz* (20 June 2005); Florian Felix Weyh, 'Eine ganz normale Epoche', *dradio.de* (7 July 2005); Bernd Wagner, 'Rasante Reise in die 60er Jahre', *dradio.de* (10 July 2005).
30. Uwe Timm, *Der Freund und der Fremde* (Cologne: Kiepenheuer & Witsch, 2005), 63.

CHAPTER 7

Pop literature in the Berlin Republic

Sabine von Dirke

In response to the question, 'When is literature pop?', the author Georg M. Oswald, whose work occasionally is categorised as such, articulates the problem most succinctly: 'Since a definition is lacking, the question can only be answered empirically. It's pop, when people call it pop.'[1] This was the case in the 1960s when Rolf Dieter Brinkmann, Jörg Fauser and Hubert Fichte, but also more established authors such as Peter O. Chotjewitz, Elfriede Jelinek and Peter Handke, were denounced as 'pop' because they had left the ivory tower and mingled with the popular and trivial articulations of life and culture. Some thirty years later, an advertising campaign in late 1998 was credited with the revival of the pop label in the Berlin Republic.[2] It grouped the latest publications of three Suhrkamp authors (so called on account of their connection with the high-brow publishing house of that name), Andreas Neumeister's *Gut laut* (Good Loud, 1998), Rainald Goetz's *Rave* (1998) and Thomas Meinecke's *Tomboy* (1998) under the term 'pop' because popular music was central for these texts.

Thanks to the fast and furious pace of the cultural sections in the newspapers and arts programmes on radio and television, the pop label quickly and quite literally gained currency beyond the marketing departments of the book industry and a media debate on pop literature ensued, lasting from the late 1990s into the first three years of the new millennium.[3] Thematic definitions dominated, such that the designation was applied to any text featuring the quotidian life of the twenty-something set in which sex, drugs and rock 'n' roll ruled supreme. Combined with a fascination with biography that attached the tag 'pop' to practically all writers from this cohort, this approach generated a diffuse list of authors. Indeed, the very term 'pop literature', as Eckhart Schumacher argues, seemed to be 'an equally indeterminate and over-determined expression of despair'.[4]

My discussion of pop literature in the Berlin Republic addresses two issues: its definition and its controversial reception. From an analysis of both, I maintain that several features distinguish a pop-literary aesthetic from the literary-aesthetic paradigms privileged in West Germany after 1945, that is, from the moralist-realist writing dominant in the Bonn Republic, and from the new narrative fiction emerging in the 1980s. With these features as its basis, the label pop literature can indeed be used as a meaningful category and establish a cohesive group of texts for which the term makes sense.

Secondly, an examination of pop literature rebuts the widely propounded criticism that it lacks social and historical awareness and shows how this literature addresses the impact of the changing social structures brought about by the New Economy, or, to put it in broader sociological terms, addresses the impact of the 'risk society' on individual and collective life in the Berlin Republic. I argue that pop literature has successfully recycled the pop aesthetic of the 1960s in order to participate in a provocative manner in two formative discussions in the Berlin Republic: the debate on the state of literature in the wake of unification and the generational discourse on the legacy of '68 and the social, cultural and political influence of the former student protesters – now top politicans, leading intellectuals and media personalities – claiming pre-eminence in the shaping of contemporary German society.

WHAT IS POP LITERATURE?

Critics and authors alike have acknowledged the continuities between pop literature in the 1960s and the 1990s.[5] Taking the pop aesthetic of the 1960s as a backdrop, we can discern six features which many of the later texts share to various degrees and which provide a structure for describing pop literature more precisely: first, the focus on daily life; second, the aesthetic of the surface and immediacy which rejects a hermeneutics of depth and refrains from ascribing a deeper meaning to the phenomena depicted; third, the non-narrative structure of the texts; fourth, the formal emulation of the electronic media; fifth, the challenging of the high/low culture dichotomy; and sixth, a new understanding of the position and function of the author within the media society.

Rainald Goetz's internet project, *Abfall für alle* (Trash For Everyone, 1999), represents the most striking example of the continuities between the two moments of pop literature.[6] The title not only refers back to the aesthetic programme of the 1960s, alluding to Warhol's infamous 'from the garbage into the book', but can also be read as a re-appropriation of the derogatory term which the cultural establishment has applied to the *Null Medien* or 'trash' electronic media.[7] Under the web address

www.rainaldgoetz.de, Goetz published for a year vignettes of his daily routine, his thoughts on various topics and transcriptions of random publicly
accessible texts ranging from summaries of television shows to quotations
from high culture artefacts. This mode of writing captures the moment
through the citation, copying and indexing of culture without assigning
meaning. Consequently, there is no narrative structure in this 'Novel of a
Year', as the subtitle of the book version reads, and no coherent ideological
agenda that might create a unified whole. Indeed, pop literature's universe
encompasses, as Anke Bienderra proposes, 'daily life, pop music, lifestyles
and life crises after a shopping trip gone wrong, in short, everything that
literature had previously marginalized is now represented in a register of
quotidian speech marked by its "literary orality"'.[8]

Secondly, pop literature adopts a mimetic, spontaneous and associative
perspective that purports merely to record what *is* and which refrains from
ascribing a deeper meaning to the world it depicts in all its randomness and
bleakness.[9] Starting from the observation that appearance is everything in
the media-saturated consumer society, pop literature explores this surface
and attains immediacy through a double-strategy of emulation and re-
coding of the proliferating signs typical of today's society.[10] This goes hand
in hand with the third feature, namely pop literature's attempts to emulate
the representational structure of popular culture and the electronic media
characterised by an accelerating pace and the accidental ordering of perception. Consequently, pop literature's representational flow dispenses with a
coherent narrative structure and privileges series of fragments, snapshots
and sound bites.

This non-narrative structure – the third feature of pop fiction – is well
illustrated by the lack of a story line or even of an identifiable protagonist in
Goetz's *Abfall für alle*. Pop texts de-emphasise traditional elements of narrative such as plot and character development. Hence, contemporary pop
writing, for the most part at least, can be distinguished from the emphasis on story-telling, sophisticated literary technique and reading pleasure
that originated in the 1980s with authors such as Patrick Süskind and Sten
Nadolny. Instead of developing suspenseful plots and ingeniously intricate narrative resolutions, pop literature's mimetic neo-Realism provides
detailed descriptions of the materiality of its time. In the case of Benjamin
Stuckrad-Barre's début novel, *Soloalbum* (1998), Moritz Bassler correctly
maintains that the protagonist's separation from his girlfriend is the only
epic element in the novel[11] and merely represents the pretext for the narrator's sour observations about various milieus and issues in the 1990s.[12] The
story line does not amount to more than a chronicle of the protagonist's

descent into excessive alcohol and television consumption after his girlfriend left him, his last-ditch efforts to get her back, and his re-emergence
from his lethargic retreat from the world.

Elke Naters's first novel, *Königinnen* (Queens, 1998), has an even slimmer
narrative arc. Alternating between the perspectives of the two first person
narrators, Marie and Gloria, the novel describes the relationship of these
two 'best' friends. The only plot twist comes about when Marie, who
envies Gloria for having found Mr Right and for already having children
with him, meets a man who she hopes will be her Prince Charming. The
novel thematises the two characters' discontent with the state of their lives –
the single and married life – which they try to remedy by buying into the
sales pitch of a consumer culture that links brand names with lifestyles and
happiness even though they cannot properly afford this world of luxury
goods.

The Suhrkamp authors Goetz, Neumeister and Meinecke, already relatively well established by the late 1990s, but also the younger Austrian
writer Kathrin Röggla, embody the most radical articulation of the fourth
feature: the emulating of popular music and the electronic media, specifically the adaptation of musical rhythms and DJ sampling into literature.
As is typical for all pop literature, Neumeister's 1998 novel *Gut laut* thus
dispenses with all elements of narrative in the traditional sense. Indeed,
Gut laut has no plot to speak of, no fully fledged characters, just voices: the
book consists primarily of diverse reflections on music and of snapshots
of the life of a young man in West Germany during the 1970s and 1980s
for whom popular music is the ultimate point of reference. In this way,
Neumeister's text seeks to establish a sense of the immediacy of memory
and of the present. The author does not want to tell a story or explain the
past but uses language to compose *Sprachmusik* (language music) in order
to express memories steeped in popular music culture with the utmost
directness. In a similar vein, Goetz turns literary fiction into Techno prose,
in *Rave* and elsewhere. Yet the work of Neumeister and Goetz also demonstrates that pop literature does not necessarily result in the easy reading we
might expect from pop literature. The same holds true for Röggla's novels *Abrauschen* (Taking Off, 1997) and *Irres Wetter* (Crazy Weather, 2000),
which are more reminiscent of Hip Hop than of Techno, and for Meinecke's
use of the sampling technique of the modern-day DJ, in *Tomboy* but also
particularly in *Musik* (2004). These texts are hermetic in their own right
and develop a complex multi-layered prose that requires the same erudite
familiarity with music, politics and theoretical discourse as high art does.
This may explain why this 'advanced pop' was spared some of the ire of the

cultural establishment in comparison to the publications of some of their peers.

The fifth feature is pop literature's challenge to high culture's insistence on hermetic art as the only possible means of articulating a critique of the existing order and to its concurrent dismissal of all products of the culture industry as pure deception. And finally, as a sixth characteristic, pop authors acknowledge that there is no position outside the market place and that they and their writing are as subject to market forces as any other product. Consequently, pop authors, most of whom have extensive experience as journalists, in the media or in the advertising industry, employ marketing strategies calculatedly and openly in order to maximise their publishing success. These qualities are explored further in the following sections.

POP LITERATURE AND THE NEW ECONOMY

Published around the time of the Frankfurt Book Fair in 1999, Iris Radisch's negative review of pop literature in the weekly *Die Zeit* is a good point of departure from which to explore further the meaning and style of pop literature while examining the ideological bias of criticism hurled against it. Radisch bases her assessment primarily on four books: the 1999 anthology, *Mesopotamia* (1999), whose authors constitute a 'Who-is-Who' of pop literature, Stuckrad-Barre's two novels, *Soloalbum* (1998) and *Livealbum* (1999), the conversation compilation *Tristesse Royale* (1999), and Goetz's internet project *Abfall für alle*. Here, Radisch echoes the thrust of the critics' dismissal of pop texts as superficial and denies them any value in so far as they engage with an aesthetic of surface, an aesthetic on which, it is claimed, the mundane world of consumer culture and the media have always thrived:

> That the world, while fictional, is what it is, articulates the contemptible Realism of a generation of richly endowed heirs. Others have explained the world, now it is a matter of talking about it. And not as one imagines it from the secure citadel of high literature, but it comes into the house as news of the day, as a real-existing game show, as a recording of one's daily routine . . . news from the headquarters of music, the media and fashion, messages from TV, the cultural section, or the fax machine.[13]

Radisch's review betrays the privileging of a high modernist aesthetics. Accordingly, Kafka, a prime representative of the modernist canon, is presented as the yardstick for her devaluation of pop literature. Nor does she forget to list the other oft-noted supposed deficits of pop literature: a lack of historical consciousness as well as a failure to address social problems and provide viable alternatives, if not a social utopia, or, in more general terms, pop literature's refusal to articulate a position. Yet does a closer look at pop-literary texts indeed support this blanket criticism?

The pop revival in the 1990s certainly deviates from the conventional definition of mainstream post-war German literature, at least since the 1960s, as a socially responsible cultural form that exposes society's ills, condemns the reluctance to learn from the Nazi past and speaks up for the disenfranchised. Measured against this paradigm, pop literature can be described as narcissistic, as it focuses on the everyday and the concerns of a middle class that is still relatively affluent and privileged in comparison with other social classes and minority groups. The predominantly first-person narrators and protagonists have typically been raised in a solidly bourgeois milieu with access to higher education. For example, the narrator of Christian Kracht's *Faserland* (Frayed-Land, 1995) attended an elite boarding school in West Germany and is now able to travel without having to worry about money. The protagonist of Meinecke's *Tomboy*, Vivian Atkinson, and her friends are almost all graduate students at the University of Heidelberg. And Stuckrad-Barre's narrators in *Soloalbum* and *Livealbum* attended *Gymnasium*, the preparatory school for higher education, and have experienced university life. Although it is more difficult to determine the sociological position of Naters's characters, the linguistic register they use and their range of cultural references indicate that they too hail from the educated middle class.

In spite of their middle-class upbringing, however, some of the protagonists of contemporary pop novels *do* experience financial difficulties on account of the fact that they are either unemployed or only semi-employed. Not surprisingly, then, a discussion of money is a recurring theme in pop-literary texts. For instance, one of the protagonists in Elke Naters's *Königinnen* is on welfare support, but she still falls prey to consumer culture and buys a pair of expensive designer shoes, which she cannot rationally justify. Stuckrad-Barre's contribution to *Mesopotamia*, 'Saisonarbeiter' ('Seasonal Worker'), moreover, articulates a changed attitude towards professional careers and money: 'For me and most of my friends, there is no causal relationship between what we call our work, our careers, and earning a living. You can always get some money somewhere, not much but enough to get by. Money is no more than a means of transportation, and if necessary, one can steal a ride.'[14] Kathrin Röggla's first novel, *Abrauschen*, presents another example of how pop literature thematises the increased material uncertainty brought about by the global New Economy. Thus *Abrauschen* examines contemporary public debates on what the author calls, in a lower-case prose clearly influenced by the terseness characteristic of the electronic media, the 'erbengeneration' (the 'generation of heirs' who stand to inherit the wealth accumulated by their parents and thus, it was claimed, feel little need to work) and points out the increasing socio-economic differentiation and re-stratification that shapes life in the present. The narrator does not deny the significance of material values for her generation but she insists that only the parental generation is truly rich, 'while the younger set has nothing left but to scream with rage'.[15]

It is her inheritance, the sale of the parental condominium in Salzburg, that takes her back to the town where she grew up. The nasty vignettes about the sale of the condominium in the novel point to an important social issue: the lack of affordable housing in urban areas owing to the speculative value now attached to property. Both unemployment and the absence of reasonably priced accommodation affect young Germans from the very bottom of the socio-economic ladder to the middle class. Yet even those who do not have to grapple with financial problems fail to experience true happiness – the consumerist '*Spaßgesellschaft*' (fun society)[16] generates nothing but boredom and deceitful interpersonal relationships. Naters's 2002 novel *Mau Mau* thus tells of a group vacationing in a tropical setting: two couples and a single woman who go through the entire gamut of group and couple dynamics. While the text does not present an overt critique of the five friends, it does exhibit two aspects of life in the 'fun society' in a most unflattering manner: the omnipresence of the performance principle, that is, the need to be successful,[17] and the emptiness, isolation and violence this engenders.

In the pop literature of the 1990s, the New Economy brings forth a mentality marked by narcissistic detachment from the world and overindulgence in luxury goods. The detachment from which protagonists suffer and their hedonist materialism point to the psychological toll exacted by the consumer society. Sibylle Berg's pop novel *Ein paar Leute suchen das Glück und lachen sich tot* (A Few People in Search of Happiness Laugh Themselves to Death, 1997), for instance, illustrates well the way in which detachment may be deployed as a strategy for survival. Only the one character who manages to separate herself entirely from her husband and her daughter and to find comfort in the role of the observer, in letting the world pass by while drinking a *café au lait*, survives the turmoil. All the other characters experience violent deaths, even when they finally come to recognise happiness in making a true commitment to another person. The pop literature of the 1990s does not, therefore, provide a rosy picture of this middle-class world and life in the New Economy or in the contemporary 'fun society'.

The bleak descriptions of contemporary life that characterise the prose of Naters and Berg, as well as of many other pop authors, do not allow for a pleasurable reading experience but rather evince disgust. Yet pop texts neither take an overt position on the world they depict nor project any alternative future; only occasionally do they betray their protagonists' yearning for an escape from this empty, phoney life. The narrator of Stuckrad-Barre's *Soloalbum*, for instance, claims that his life as a single man is not satisfactory in comparison with a stable, long-lasting relationship.[18] The unease which such pitiless depictions of daily life at the turn of the millennium provokes begs the question as to why pop literature is so often derided as an affirmative embrace of consumer culture. The answer lies in another key feature of the form – the challenge it presents to the high/low culture paradigm.

POP-MODERN JAMMING

The pop revival in the Berlin Republic emulates the aesthetic challenge to the high/low culture dichotomy initiated by pop artists in the 1960s. It is not, therefore, surprising that pop literature in the 1990s, as in the 1960s, draws on the archive of both popular and high culture. However, present-day pop fiction is different from its predecessor in so far as an appreciation of pop culture is no longer confined to a subculture or the underground but has been internalised by the broad mass of middle-class youth. Most protagonists in pop texts of the present day are as avid connoisseurs of high culture as they are of modern music and shopping. In spite of his extensive and intensive consumption of television and music, the narrator of *Soloalbum*, for instance, reads widely, including Peter Handke, Charles Bukowski and Jörg Fauser, and thereby connects the pop project of the 1990s back to the high-point of pop literature in the 1960s (*S*, 128).

Several of the contributions to the pop anthology *Mesopotamia* follow a similar pattern. Alexander von Schönburg's narrator attends Bruckner's *Seventh Symphony* and refers to Thomas Hobbes's *Leviathan* and Ortega y Gasset's *Revolt of the Masses*.[19] In his contribution, Kracht's obscure first-person narrative alludes to classical music, referring to Grieg's *Holberg Suite*, denigrating Mahler's *Song of the Earth*, and quoting at length from Purcell's *Dido and Aeneas*, compositions to which the narrator listens on the plane.[20] Carl von Siemens's ruminations on colonialism in the same volume cite not only Salman Rushdie's *Midnight's Children* but also drop the name of the early twentieth-century British author Edith Sitwell, who famously explored the links between poetry and the popular music of her time, namely jazz.[21] These texts, representative of many others, replay the Leslie Fiedler tune from the 1960s, 'cross the border, close the gap'.[22] In other words, they intentionally blur the distinction between high and low culture so dear to the literary establishment. Pop literature in the 1990s suggests that high and low culture serve the same functions, or have become interchangeable in terms of their use-value at least. Here, two examples illustrate this point: Moritz von Uslar's contribution to *Mesopotamia* and Naters's second novel, *Lügen* (Lies, 1999).

In the short story 'Davos', Uslar has his two characters listen to pop music ranging from Elton John via Johnny Cash to Bon Jovi while driving to the famous skiing resort. All of a sudden, they insert Wagner's opera *Tristan and Isolde* into the car's tape deck. This, however, is a very specific version, a recording from 1952 which demonstrates the first-person narrator's knowledge of high culture:

Why is it that suddenly we need to listen to the entire third act of *Tristan and Isolde* in a specific recording – Suthaus / Flagstad / Wilhelm Furtwängler – from 1952? Now! Immediately now! Quickly now! It is not just listening, but, please, we need to give it our most intense listening, we need to feel it, be deeply touched. True love! Now! Immediately! That is asking a lot, it is exhausting. However, it has to be, it has to be.[23]

The ironic commentary on the appropriate mode of reception of Wagner's opera in comparison to the mode of reception for popular music postulates that there is no difference in terms of the themes and function of high and low art. Both deal with the same and everlasting theme of love, articulate it equally well and soothe the pain love causes. The difference is only presumptive and discursively constructed, the story implies, via the high/low culture dichotomy. In Naters's *Lügen*, likewise, the narrator insists emphatically on the significance of reading for her understanding of life and lists canonical titles such as Flaubert's *Madame Bovary*, Stendhal's *Red and Black*, as well as Dostoyesky's *Crime and Punishment*, all novels from the nineteenth-century Realist tradition. Yet when the mother of the narrator's best friend dies, the films of Hollywood director Douglas Sirk, and particularly his melodrama *Imitation of Life*, provide a more appropriate means via which the daughter of the woman who died and indeed the narrator herself can articulate feelings of grief.[24]

One of the representational strategies of pop literature – the so-called 'label crashing' modelled on modern-day American pop literature such as Bret Easton Ellis's oeuvre – has generated much critical ire and exemplifies the continuing potency of transgressions of the high/low culture paradigm.[25] The derogatory term 'label crashing', then, refers to the frequent and deliberate use of brand names in pop literature. In the opening paragraphs of Kracht's *Faserland*, for example, the narrator is described as standing at 'Fisch-Gosch', a famous fish deli on the island of Sylt, in his 'Barbourjacke' drinking a 'Jever'-beer. In the same section, he refers to 'Salem', an expensive boarding school as well as to two famous night spots in Hamburg and Munich respectively, 'Traxx' and 'P1', without further explanation – the reader, it seems, is expected to be familiar with these cultural icons. Critics have interpreted the extensive use of brand names in this vein throughout pop literature as an affirmative celebration of consumer culture. Yet, as Moritz Bassler has argued, such allusions are not gratuitous but part and parcel of a mimetic, neo-Realist representational strategy that attempts to convey contemporary life in an immediate, unsublimated way. 'The key to the new principle is the archived brand name: it is not about primordial words, but about the import and processing of already existing terms that have long been charged with encyclopaedic meaning, with phrases, discursive connections and conceptual complexes in literature.'[26] Label crashing hence reflects the extent to which designer labels have permeated present-day culture. Pop texts use brand names in order to characterise a specific milieu, protagonist or historical moment quickly and economically and in order to signal that, in today's world, there is no space outside the market and marketing.

The brand names pop literature so vigorously cultivates tend towards the higher end of the market and demand that we interpret their presence in the text. Above all, the brand name represents an attempt to differentiate oneself through style from the masses and to hold on to the status symbols of the middle class precisely at a moment in time when social decline appears likely. Furthermore, the embrace of the world of luxury is intended as a provocation of the social-democratic, moralising culture of consensus that developed in the wake of '68 and which condemns conspicuous consumption. This notion is explored further in the next section.

TRISTESSE ROYALE, OR THE TRIUMPH OF MARKETING

Pop authors in the late 1990s skilfully utilised marketing strategies and, more specifically, the strategy of self-presentation typical of the 'event culture' emerging at the time. Thus they styled themselves as brand names in an increasingly overcrowded book market, or rather in a market increasingly dominated by the electronic media and in which books appeared to be losing their appeal.[27] Yet the true scandal, for their critics, was that pop authors admitted their allegiance to market principles (The preface to Berg's *Ein paar Leute suchen das Glück* is a typical, if heavily satirical, acknowledgment of the economic reality of contemporary authorship: 'Thanks. With every one of my books you buy, you help me finance my future home in the Tessin. Please do recommend this book to your vast circle of friends and your parents').[28] Nowhere were critical sensibilities more ruffled than in the furore that followed the publication in 1999 of *Tristesse Royale: Das popkulturelle Quintett* (Tristesse Royale: The Pop-Cultural Quintet), the protocol of a weekend of indolent conversation and navel-gazing at Berlin's Hotel Adlon produced by self-proclaimed 'pop dandies' Joachim Bessing, Christian Kracht, Eckhart Nickel, Alexander von Schönburg and Benjamin Stuckrad-Barre.

The title *Tristesse Royale: Das popkulturelle Quintett* is, of course, a parody of the name of the television talk show *Das literarische Quartett* (The Literary Quartet) hosted by the renowned literary critic Marcel Reich-Ranicki. Hence the book appeared to promise a serious, high-brow analysis of contemporary cultural trends. Certainly, the proclaimed purpose of the event, namely to give a snapshot of the attitudes and lifestyle of the younger generation of twenty-somethings, was taken at face value by commentators in spite of the playful relativisation of all possible positions enacted by the five participants, and in spite of the deliberately exaggerated rhetoric employed by the speakers in large parts of *Tristesse Royale*. Yet the photograph of the pop quintet on the jacket of the first edition should have provided critics with an obvious visual clue that the five were in fact staging a performance. Exquisitely dressed but in a clearly affected pose, the picture shows the pop quintet impersonating the *fin-de-siècle* dandy. The frequent use of the term *ennui* in the volume itself, deployed to describe the crisis faced by their generation, also alludes back to the existential emptiness experienced by a cultural elite at the end of the nineteenth century, as do the swigs of absinth, the hallucinatory drug of choice for the bohemian, which Bessing takes from his brand-named hip flask.[29]

The setting for this 'Snobismus Revival' (snobbery revival),[30] the new Hotel Adlon, has great symbolic value. Erected on the site of the original Adlon at the Pariser Platz, a stone's throw from the restored parliament building, the Reichstag, the hotel is a brand new building with state-of-the-art engineering and technology hidden beneath a monumental, late nineteenth-century façade. This choice of architectural style for a hotel which serves both high-status foreign visitors to the German parliament and international celebrities may metaphorically reconnect the Berlin Republic of the 1990s with the unencumbered national pride and bombasticism of the Wilhelminian Empire.[31] Some of the statements in *Tristesse Royale* can indeed be understood as a resuscitation of late nineteenth-century elitist class structures and reactionary virilism: the exclusion of women from the all male circle of the pop quintet and the numerous homophobic statements combined, paradoxically, with a demonstrative homo-sociability. Alexander von Schönburg's fascination with the First World War generation, his resentment of liberalism's validation of individualism, and his elitist justification for marrying within aristocratic circles account for much of the reactionary venom in the volume.

At the same time, however, the participants' denigration of the Adlon – the set for their demonstratively over-the-top performance of the zeitgeist of the present day – as 'hollow' (*TR*, 60) may reveal a keen sense of the problem of authenticity inherent in a postmodern media society. It is difficult to gauge just how seriously this critique of the consumer culture is to be taken. After all, ambivalence is a characteristic of pop and raging against inauthenticity may itself be an inauthentic pose. Yet the book nonetheless raises a series of important issues: the extent to which the proliferation of media images has affected society; whether any values remain following the postmodern proclamation that 'anything goes'; the stagnation which a culture of consensus produces, and, finally, a contemporary discourse that pits the younger generation against that of '68. Indeed, *Tristesse Royale* contains a number of precise and insightful analyses of present-day Germany and beyond. For example, who would quibble with Bessing's denunciation of a global consumer society in which customers perform more and more services themselves and thus become unpaid labour for the corporate world, 'under the pretext of gaining more freedom' (*TR*, 36). The quintet's negative description of the 'new professions', that is, the explosion of jobs in the media industry, similarly exploits the insider's perspective in order to strip away the supposed glamour and excitement of these careers.

POP AGAINST THE GENERATION OF '68

Whether the *Tristesse Royale* event was intended as a serious cultural critique or simply as an exercise in postmodern games-playing, it is difficult to understand the aggressive response it provoked. In fact, it is only in the context of the generational dynamic which permeated both the intellectual musings of the pop quintet and the larger debate on pop literature in the 1990s that the controversy surrounding the text makes sense. In the words of Georg Oswald, accordingly, 'this book claims to interpret the world for its own generation and thus enraged those who have made the same claim once upon a time'.[32] More specifically, it is the generation of '68 that is the target of the impertinent ridicule elaborated by the pop quintet and, indeed, by pop literature more broadly.

This aspect is thematised in the chapter 'Der Kulturchef' (The Head of the Cultural Section), which opens the second part of *Tristesse Royale*, 'In the Mirror of the Media'. Here, a freelance writer attempts to sell a story about the younger generation's obsession with consumer culture and luxury goods to the head of the cultural section at a major newspaper; this individual is fifty-six and thus (in 1999) part of the sociological cohort of '68. He dismisses the freelancer's insights and refers dismissively to the generation of twenty-somethings of his son (and the freelancer) as the 'flea-market generation' on account of the fact that they actually appear to prefer a rather scruffy, lower-class look from the 1970s to designer labels. More important, he claims that it is *his* generation that is being described: 'I am 56 and it is my generation that you are describing. Look at me: my vest is from Hermès . . . and so is my shirt . . . My jeans are Versace . . . and the shoes are handmade from horse leather. – Well, it is actually me about whom you are talking' (*TR*, 72). In this section, *Tristesse Royale* responds to the criticism hurled at pop authors and, more generally, at the mindless consumerism and self-indulgence of the so-called 'Generation Golf' to which they belong (the term comes from Florian Illies's bestselling zeitgeist publication of that name of 2000). Thus we are presented with the double standard of those 68ers who strike a countercultural pose while embracing consumer culture just as completely and as eagerly as any other group.

At the same time, *Tristesse Royale* signals that a significant difference exists between the Generation Golf and the generation of '68. While the head of the cultural section is sitting pretty on his Eams chair, that is, he has a professional position which affords him his designer-label comforts, the younger generation has to confront a fast-paced global economy in which there is precious little job security. Unlike the 68ers, they will not benefit from the cosy socially responsible market economy of the Bonn Republic with its promise of unlimited material comforts. Perhaps even more damning, the pop quintet holds the generation of '68 responsible for the shape of contemporary Germany and the mentality of its younger generations. The lack of binding values they bemoan is seen as a result of the sweeping countercultural protest of the 1960s. Since this protest eroded all social taboos, there is now no longer any opportunity for transgression at all. This 'results', according to Stuckrad-Barre, 'in the kind of freedom that totally enslaves people' (*TR*, 121). This position of the pop quintet re-articulates the conservative perspective that '68 represented a fall from grace and not the democratic redemption that this generation believes itself to have effected.

Perhaps the most shrewd dismantling of the self-image of the generation of '68 is the pop quintet's provocatively apolitical reception of the history of countercultural protest in the Federal Republic since the late 1960s. As the pop quintet takes a brief walk outside the Adlon, the five accidentally become embroiled in a protest rally against Germany's participation in NATO's military campaign against Serbia which the epitome of the now mainstreamed counterculture, the then Secretary of State, Joschka Fischer, was championing at the time. The subsequent discussion of the event does not make any reference to the political content of the protest but rather evaluates it only in terms of its appearance, that is, in terms of fashion. 'However, the old aesthetic of the protest marches, when you could see men with good haircuts in suits or cool jeans, photographed by William Klein, throwing stones in May '68 in Paris, this is gone for good' (*TR*, 95). Even the Arafat shawls worn by the militant protesters of the 1970s and 1980s, it is claimed, demonstrated a greater appreciation of style than the 'shapeless mélange of colours that has found its home in the alternative milieu' of the present (*TR*, 96). With this purely aesthetic perspective on political protest, the pop quintet, like many of their contemporaries, refuses to enter public discourse on terms set by the 68ers.

Pop literature's approach to history, and particularly to the Nazi past, similarly rejects the overt, even ostentatious, political engagement of the 68ers. Critics, in fact, condemned younger authors' superficial ahistoricism, and it is certainly true that pop texts' often apparently rather offhand references to Germany's troubled past, as, for example, in Kracht's *Faserland* with its inflationary use of the term 'Nazi', may be problematic.[33] Yet Lorenz Schröter's contribution to Kracht's *Mesopotamia* anthology, 'Bellersen', perhaps gives a hint of what such a seemingly casual disregard for historical awareness might say about the younger generation's response to the paradigm of critical engagement inaugurated by the generation of '68. This short prose text tells, then, of how the small town of Bellersen – most likely a play on the name Bergen Belsen, the site of the infamous concentration camp – became caught up in the contemporary discourse on the Nazi past. The problem begins when a medieval inscription, 'To the Dead Jew', is uncovered during the renovation of the local inn. The simple question posed by Anna's small son: 'What are Jews?',[34] to his 68er mother causes her to panic and stutter instead of giving an answer. In fact, Anna's inability to utter the word 'Jew' – because she experiences it as 'anti-Semitic' – illustrates the extent to which discussion of the Nazi past may be subject to a stultifying political correctness imposed by the 68ers. The normative discourse of the generation of '68 is not only outdated, it seems, but is also ill-suited to the needs of the younger generation.

CONCLUSION

To dismiss pop literature as representing nothing but an ahistorical superficiality devoid of any awareness of social and political issues and, therefore, as uncritical, is misguided. As this chapter has demonstrated, pop fiction in the 1990s and beyond exhibits a keen sense of the historical, socio-political and technological forces that shape today's world, and, more specifically, the Berlin Republic. For the pop generation, for whom the optimism of '68 concerning socio-political change has been invalidated by the reality of the New Economy, direct political commitment appears futile. Instead, pop authors turn to the consumer paradise of brand names and designer labels in order to stage their dissent by means of an only apparently affirmative thematisation of fashion and lifestyle. This strategy may have had at least temporary success, as the response to pop in general, and to the pop quintet's performance of the *Tristesse Royale* event in particular, shows. The irony is that those who grew up in the shadow of '68 should choose to mobilise aspects of the historical inauguration of West Germany's counterculture – a pop aesthetic of provocation – against those who once practised it themselves, and to stage their challenge, at the very moment when the 68ers' long march through the institutions finally brought them, thirty years later with the election of the Red–Green coalition in 1998, to social, political and cultural pre-eminence in the newly established Berlin Republic.

NOTES

1. Georg M. Oswald, 'Wann ist Literatur Pop? Eine empirische Antwort' in Wieland and Winfried Freund, eds., *Der deutsche Roman der Gegenwart* (Munich: Fink, 2001), 30.
2. Eckhard Schumacher, *Gerade Eben Jetzt: Schreibweisen der Gegenwart* (Frankfurt: Suhrkamp, 2003), 11.
3. See www.single-generation.de (last accessed 28 September 2006).
4. Schumacher, *Gerade Eben Jetzt*, 15.
5. See Thomas Ernst, *Popliteratur* (Hamburg: Rotbuch, 2001) and *Text & Kritik* 10 (2003), special issue on *Pop-Literatur*.
6. Andreas Neumeister's *Angela Davis löscht ihre WebSite* (2002) represents another interesting example of pop literature confronting the electronic media.

7. Eckhard Schumacher, 'From the garbage, into the Book: Medien, Abfall, Literatur' in Jochen Bonz, ed., *Sound Signatures: Pop-Splitter* (Frankfurt: Suhrkamp, 2001), 193.

8. Anke Bienderra, 'Der Erzähler als "popmoderner Flaneur" in Christian Krachts Roman *Faserland*', *German Life and Letters*, 55:2 (2002): 164–5.

9. See Moritz Bassler's *Der deutsche Pop-Roman: Die neuen Archivisten* (Munich: C. H. Beck, 2002).

10. Jörgen Schäfer, 'Neue Mitteilungen aus der Wirklichkeit: Zum Verhaltnis von Pop und Literatur in Deutschland seit 1968', *Text & Kritik* 10 (2003): 14–17.

11. Bassler, *Der deutsche Pop-Roman*, 103.

12. See Hubert Winkels, 'Grenzgänger: Neue deutsche Pop-Literatur', *Sinn und Form*, 4 (1999): 581–610.

13. Iris Radisch, 'Mach den Kasten an und schau. Junge Männer unterwegs: Die neue deutsche Popliteratur', *Die Zeit* (14 October 1999).

14. Benjamin von Stuckrad-Barre, 'Saisonarbeiter', in Christian Kracht, ed., *Mesopotamia: Ein Avant-Pop-Reader* (Stuttgart: dtv, 2001 [1999]), 203.

15. Kathrin Röggla, *Abrauschen* (Salzburg and Vienna: Residenz Verlag, 1997), 12–13.

16. See Harald Martenstein, 'Die Spaßgesellschaft: Warum sie so verhasst ist und wie man sie kritisieren könnte', *Merkur* 641/642, 9/10 (2002): 906–11.

17. Martenstein, 'Die Spaßgesellschaft', 911.

18. Benjamin von Stuckrad-Barre, *Soloalbum* (Cologne: Kiepenheuer & Witsch, 1998), 24–5. Hereafter *S*.

19. Alexander von Schönburg, 'In Bruckners Reich' in Christian Kracht, ed., *Mesopotamia*, 39 and 41.

20. Kracht, 'Der Gesang des Zauberers' in Kracht, ed., *Mesopotamia*, 301–5.

21. Carl von Siemens, 'Im Schatten des Tigers' in Kracht, ed., *Mesopotamia*, 131. This reference establishes a particularly interesting continuity between the avant-garde of the early twentieth century and pop literature of the 1990s. Sitwell was known for her unique, performance-like poetry recitals as well as for recording these and her poetry.

22. Leslie Fiedler, 'Cross the Border – Close the Gap' in *Collected Essays of Leslie Fiedler* (New York: Stein and Day, 1971 [1968]), vol. II, 461–85.

23. Moritz von Uslar, 'Davos' in Kracht, ed., *Mesopotamia*, 18.

24. Elke Naters, *Lügen* (Cologne: Kiepenheuer & Witsch, 1999), 37; 186.

25. Mathias Mertens, 'Robbery, Assault, Battery: Christian Kracht, Benjamin V. Stuckrad-Barre und ihre mutmasslichen Vorbilder Bret Easten Ellis and Nick Hornby', *Text & Kritik*, 10 (2003): 201–7.

26. Bassler, *Der deutsche Pop-Roman*, 186.

27. Heinrich Kaulen, 'Der Autor als Medienstar und Entertainer: Überlegungen zur neuen deutschen Popliteratur', in Hans-Heino Ewer, ed., *Lesen zwischen Neuen Medien und Pop-Kultur: Kinder- und Jugendliteratur im Zeitalter multi-medialen Entertainments* (Munich: Juventa, 2002), 214.

28. Sibylle Berg, *Ein paar Leute suchen das Glück und lachen sich tot* (Leipzig: Reclam, 1997), preface.

29. Joachim Bessing, ed., *Tristesse Royale: Das popkulturelle Quintett* (Berlin: Ullstein, 2005 [1999]), 33. Hereafter *TR*.
30. Bassler, *Der deutsche Pop-Roman*, 121.
31. Stuart Taberner, *German Literature of the 1990s and Beyond: Normalization and the Berlin Republic* (Rochester: Camden House, 2005), xiv–xvi.
32. Oswald, 'Wann ist literatur Pop?', 36.
33. See Frank Finlay, ' "Dann wäre Deutschland wie das Wort Neckarrauen": Surface, Superficiality and Globalisation in Christian Kracht's *Faserland*' in Stuart Taberner, ed., *German Literature in the Age of Globalisation* (Birmingham: Birmingham University Press, 2004), 189–208.
34. Lorenz Schröter, 'Bellersen,' in Kracht, ed., *Mesopotamia*, 173–90, 177.

CHAPTER 8

Representations of the Nazi past I: perpetrators

Bill Niven

Considering post-unification German fiction from the perspective of its portrayal of Nazi perpetrators would seem, at first, an uncomplicated task. There are characters who could be designated as such: Hanna in Bernhard Schlink's novel *Der Vorleser* (The Reader, 1995), for instance, is a former concentration camp guard implicated in the killing of Jews, while the figure of the grandfather in Marcel Beyer's perplexing novel *Spione* (Spies, 2000) is linked with the activities of the Legion Condor during the Spanish Civil War. In another novel by Beyer, *Flughunde* (The Karnau Tapes, 1995), we are even treated to a portrayal of the Goebbels family and, briefly, of Hitler. In addition, we could point to characters who allow themselves to 'slip' into the Nazi system, become involved in supporting its ideological superstructure and lend their ideas to its racist praxis: in *Flughunde*, Karnau's interest in the relationship between sound and the physiology of its articulation soon meshes with Nazi Germanisation ideology, while in Jens Sparschuh's novel *Der Schneemensch* (The Yeti, 1993), another aspiring academic with a research interest in a supposed *Ursprache* – a kind of original esperanto – soon becomes embroiled in an absurd plan of the *SS-Ahnenerbe* (SS Ancestral Heritage Organisation) to locate and communicate with the legendary yeti in Tibet. Even the ordinary soldier has come under literary scrutiny: Uwe Timm's autobiographical, yet at the same time literary *Am Beispiel meines Bruders* (In My Brother's Shadow, 2003), seeks to understand the role and mentality of Timm's brother, a *Waffen-SS* member, during the Second World War; and Ulla Hahn's novel *Unscharfe Bilder* (Blurred Images, 2003) investigates the role of a father in the *Wehrmacht*. The role of the not-so-ordinary soldier, such as the *Wehrmacht* general in Thomas Medicus's literary (auto)biography *In den Augen meines Großvaters* (In the Eyes of my Grandfather, 2004), has not escaped attention either. A further example of such literary explorations of the role of fathers during the war is Dagmar Leupold's *Nach den Kriegen* (After the Wars, 2004).

In fact, anything other than a degree of post-unification literary interest in the activities of the so-called *Tätergeneration* (perpetrator generation) in the Third Reich would be a surprise. The theme of German perpetration was brought forcefully into the public realm in 1996 with the publication in Germany of Daniel Jonah Goldhagen's *Hitler's Willing Executioners* (1995),[1] a book which sets out to demonstrate that Germans had murdered Jews largely on grounds of a shared ideology of aggressive anti-Semitism, not just because they were 'following orders'. And the long-running exhibition 'War of Annihilation: Crimes of the *Wehrmacht* 1941–1944', which travelled from city to city between 1995 and 1999, also focused the attention of millions of today's Germans on the involvement of the 'ordinary soldier' in the murder of Jews, partisans and Soviet POWs.[2] In German historiography, many books have appeared that explore the role of bureaucracies in the Holocaust, and their anti-Semitic motivation.[3] Thor Kunkel's controversial novel *Endstufe* (Last Phase, 2004) about the *SS*'s link to the pornography industry is, for all its originality, unthinkable without this broader awareness of the involvement of *SS* and *SS*-connected bureaucracies. No stone of the Nazi system has remained unturned in the search to identify the extent of anti-Semitic concurrence and collaboration.

Yet the works I have listed above can hardly be classified, primarily, as novels about Nazi perpetration – despite the fact that they certainly feature Nazi perpetrators and collaborators. Essentially, Uwe Timm's *Am Beispiel meines Bruders* sets out to explore the biographies of Timm's father and mother, and the impact on their lives, and indeed on Uwe's own post-war life, of the death of the brother (among other factors). Marcel Beyer's *Spione* is arguably more interested in the figure of the grandmother and her disappearance from family memory than it is in the grandfather. Moreover, it might even be claimed that some of these works – at first sight, at least – cast doubt on the perpetrator status of their perpetrator characters. Hanna in Schlink's *Der Vorleser* is depicted, some have argued, more as a victim of her illiteracy and the machinations of her co-defendants in her post-war Nazi trial than she is as a perpetrator. Ulla Hahn's novel *Unscharfe Bilder*, in which a daughter so self-righteously questions her father about his role in the army, seems more concerned to exculpate that father; however, towards the end the father would seem to admit his guilt. And Marcel Beyer's *Spione* depicts the grandfather as possibly the victim of a plot by his second wife to sever all contact between him and his offspring. Even Karnau in Beyer's *Flughunde* and certainly the protagonist in Sparschuh's *Der Schneemensch* could be viewed less as full-blooded persecutors and more as the tools of the Nazi organisations which use them.

My contention in this chapter is that there is no post-unification fiction which is about Nazi perpetration as a theme in its own right. Instead, fictional explorations of National Socialism – undertaken by writers who could be classified as members of the second or third or even fourth generations – are often more focused on the problems and processes of addressing that period than they are on this past itself. Given the specific conditions of the needs, interests and perspectives of later generations, given the epistemological scepticism of post-modernity, given too the sheer physical distance in terms of temporality between *now* and *then*, this focus is perhaps to be expected. To take but one example: the difference between the precise reconstruction of the past typical of historiography and the elaborate play with versions of the past which characterises Beyer's *Spione* could hardly be greater. Whether the grandmother in the novel really was an opera-singer, whether the grandfather's second wife is still alive, or indeed whether the grandmother herself is still alive – all of this remains uncertain in a subjective interplay of imagined recreations which results in confusion. The final scene of the novel, in which the Legion Condor grandfather – if it is indeed the grandfather – and the narrator stand with their cameras directed at one another sums it all up: characters appear to spy on each other, driven by their own agendas of self-interested investigation and only able to see what they seek to grasp through a limited and framing lens.

The dissolution of the past into subjective, fragmentary and contradictory images in Beyer's case is extreme. But its imperviousness to accurate reconstruction is a common theme, as Uwe Timm's *Am Beispiel meines Bruders* shows. The brother's irregularly maintained and often staccato-style diary provides, ultimately, no clear answer as to his role in the *Waffen-SS*. Indeed, fiction dealing with National Socialism reveals a deep-seated concern as to the past's *material* accessibility. Often this concern focuses on photographic records, on their unreliability, or on their absence. In Ulrich Treichel's novel about the post-war lives of German expellees, *Der Verlorene* (Lost, 1998), the photographs of the second son in the family album are small and show only parts of him, making him hard to identify; it is as if his parents took only minimal and partial notice of him – as if, indeed, he hardly existed. The family album in Beyer's *Spione* contains no portraits of the grandmother, giving rise to the suspicion that a deliberate attempt was undertaken to eradicate her from family memory by destroying the photographs of her. Hollbach, the *Wehrmacht* lieutenant in Klaus Modick's novel *Der kretische Gast* (The Cretan Guest, 2003), may have burnt photographs pointing to his involvement in criminal reprisal measures against

Cretan civilians; in *Spione*, photographs of the grandfather's involvement in the Legion Condor are also conspicuous by their absence. It is what extant photographs *fail* to reveal, rather than what they show, that forms the fictional focus. Fiction seeks to discover those parts of the past hidden 'between' the photographs, although Beyer, for one, would doubt that it can succeed.

To be sure, there are also examples of post-unification fiction in which the finding of photographs acts as a stimulus to narrative developments: here one might point to Ulrich Woelk's novel *Rückspiel* (Return Match, 1993), or Ulla Hahn's *Unscharfe Bilder*, where the chance sighting of a photograph in the *Wehrmacht* Exhibition triggers the daughter's determination to confront her father about his past. But even in the case of Woelk and Hahn, the ultimate value of the photographic discovery is limited. In *Unscharfe Bilder*, images of *Wehrmacht* criminality elided from private memory emerge in the public realm only for the novel, ultimately, to prevaricate on the issue of whether or not such images really tell the whole story about the killers. Neither what photographs show, nor what they do not show, is truly representative.[4]

HISTORICAL CONTEXT AND RELATIVISATION

For all its frequent scepticism, post-unification German fiction dealing with the Nazi past nevertheless seeks to provide a framework in which National Socialism can be understood. In the remainder of this chapter, I wish to focus on the question of historical contextualisation, a process at work in many post-unification novels. Different forms of contextualisation can be identified. In the case of Kunkel's *Endstufe* and Modick's *Der kretische Gast*, the policies and conduct of National Socialist Germany are compared with the policies and conduct of the Allies, a form of synchronic contextualisation which seeks out questionable parallels and comes close to relativising, perhaps even trivialising Nazism. By contrast, Woelk's *Rückspiel* and Schlink's *Der Vorleser* are literary examples of a *diachronic* contextualisation: the Nazi past is viewed through the lens of later generations, a process which highlights the aforementioned problems adhering to any attempt to reconstruct this past, but also one which reveals continuities and differences between the 1933–45 period and the Federal Republic. In the course of analysing these forms of contextualisation, I shall also consider a third variant – namely the exploration in novels such as Beyer's *Flughunde* of the context in, and conditions under which individuals exposed to Nazism became criminals.

Thor Kunkel's *Endstufe* is in many ways a remarkable novel because it is the first to risk an almost comical portrayal of the *SS*.[5] The narrative follows the pornographic activities of members of the *SS*'s Racial Hygiene Institute. The focus on sexual corruptibility and corruption, dubious financial machinations and petty internal conflicts between members of the *SS* and the Gestapo captures well the atmosphere of general ethical corrosion that certainly characterised these bodies. The novel's main character, Fussmann, with his interest in biomagnetism and the 'New Man', is preoccupied with higher bioethical visions, the hypocrisy and pseudo-grandeur of which are utterly exposed by his rampant and near self-destructive sexual excess. Yet Kunkel's novel says nothing about Nazi barbarity; the official activities of the Hygiene Institute's members do not seem to extend beyond looking for something to do to justify their existence, such as inventing a malaria crisis among the troops in Africa. This should not be taken in itself as a criticism of *Endstufe*, yet such an omission appears significant in view of the fact that the final 100 pages contain damning indictments of the Soviets, British and Americans, indictments emanating in part from the minds of Kunkel's corrupted German characters, but in part also from the figure of the narrator; the Soviets and the Americans themselves appear as profoundly unsympathetic.

One or two examples will suffice here. Describing the impact of the advancing Red Army on Germany in 1945, the narrator is not lost for drastic words: Soviet soldiers 'rain down on the treks of fugitives and on East Prussian villages like the arrows of a demented Eros'. Into Berlin, the Soviets import 'palaeolithic morals'; and they organise 'the hunting down of women, gangbangs, orgies among the rubble lying in the streets' (*E*, 496). Nor does the narrator spare the Americans: 'your average GI Joe didn't really care two hoots about the liberation of the world . . . What he really cared about was sleeping with as many women as possible. Even black soldiers finally got their hands on what they'd always secretly called *white meat*' (*E*, 518). If one adds to this mix the critical commentary provided by the novel on the Allied bombing of Hamburg, Dresden and Hiroshima, and on the killing of German civilians in the East Prussian village of Nemmersdorf by the Soviets, it becomes hard to avoid the impression that Kunkel would agree with the words of one of his characters, Lotte: 'it's not the *just* who have won the war, but the brutal' (*E*, 562). At the very worst, Kunkel's novel implies that the greater criminals were the Allies. Certainly, *Endstufe* implies a continuity between Nazism, and the Soviet and American liberators, who appear as obsessed with sex and pornography and as intent on the abuse of women as the Nazis. That Fussmann finds a job in the United States experimenting on human prisoners in an attempt to examine the link between smoking and cancer merely serves to underpin this construed continuity.

There is a historical revisionism at work here: the Second World War is no longer viewed primarily as a conflict between Germans and the Allies, but largely as one episode in a twentieth-century history of international machismo, global pornography, ruthless capitalism and experimentation in the name of progress. Lines of long-term continuity overshadow short-term differences. Indeed, given the primitivism of the Americans and Soviets as portrayed in *Endstufe*, the collapse of Nazism appears to usher in an even more degenerate form of degeneracy. A similar, if less strident example of relativisation is provided by Klaus Modick in *Der kretische Gast*.[6] On one level, Modick's novel is a conventional tale about a son seeking to establish the truth about his father – an investigative model, sometimes involving grandchildren and grandfathers, underlying many post-unification novels on the Nazi past. In discovering that his father, Friedrich Hollbach, was personally responsible for crimes against Cretan civilians, Lukas completes his quest. Yet the novel has another level. Its main character is Johann Martens, a member of a German archaeological institute who goes over to the Cretan resistance during the war. While *Der kretische Gast* does not shirk from horrifying portrayals of German atrocities, it also suggests on more than one occasion that the British collaborated with the Germans on Crete in an attempt to crush the communist partisan movement while at the same time supporting the non-communist partisans; it thus implies British responsibility for fomenting civil war on Crete, and it also claims there was a lack of British interest in saving Crete's Jews from the Holocaust. Significantly, after the German surrender the British recruit the services of Hollbach, who accuses Martens of cooperating with the communist partisans and kills him as he tries to flee.

Here again, similarities bridge the fault-lines dividing the Germans from their opponents: in this case, it is shared anti-communism, the mutual respect of one traditional army for another, and even indifference to the fate of the indigenous population – including Jews – which link the Germans and British. Modick's novel is aesthetically committed to encouraging in the reader the perception that things are never quite what they seem. In a sense, then, *Der kretische Gast* also flirts with postmodern scepticism: Modick, it could be argued, seeks to undermine the modernist view of history that divides the Germans and the Allies into the aggressors and the righteous, the regressive and the progressive. To be fair to the author, he also depicts British support for the partisans as courageous and important. In the final analysis, however, Modick's pursuit of an aesthetic agenda of undermining stereotypical classifications results in a new historiography – one which seeks to understand history in terms of what bound the Germans and the Allies, whether this be a common anti-fascist commitment linking Martens with the partisans, or, more importantly, a common programme of anti-bolshevism connecting the British and the German commanders. Reconciliation also appears to be a goal of the novel. Martens marries a Greek woman; their daughter – brought up by the Englishman Bates – falls in love with Hollbach's son, Lukas. The daughter of a renegade German and the son of a German Nazi are united.

In contrast to Kunkel's and Modick's novels, *Flughunde* by Marcel Beyer pursues a form of literary-historical contextualisation which highlights German guilt rather than relativising it. At the centre of *Flughunde* is the scientist Karnau, whose commitment in life is to producing a comprehensive cartography of human sound; in the course of the Third Reich, he becomes caught up in SS racial experiments on concentration camp prisoners. Yet Karnau is not the cynical and mechanical scientist we might imagine Nazi scientists to have been. His interest in the production and range of human sound is marked by a passionate hypersensitivity to which he gives high-flown literary expression, and which would appear to stand in sharp contrast to the utter insensitivity of his ruthless experiments on human beings. His increasing emotional attachment to the Goebbels children, for whose threatened innocence and fragility he certainly does have compassion, also stands in contrast to this insensitivity. Beyer shows that criminality among scientists was possible in the Third Reich because the Nazis removed ethical barriers on experimentation. He also shows that a total lack of ethical scruple and human concern on the part of a scientist when conducting experiments need not imply a state of general emotional anaesthesia; professional indifference to human suffering could coexist with sensitivity and humanity in the private sphere. Beyer's portrayal of Karnau is certainly a critique of a tradition of scientific materialism which just seems to have been waiting for the chance provided by Nazism. Yet it is also a critique of a world of ethical double-standards and partial moral vision; responsibility remains firmly with the individual for his or her wilful self-delusion, all the more striking in Karnau's case because he seems to be largely free of racism. Yet his commitment to science is as absolutist as that of Hitler to anti-Semitism. The absurdity of his commitment is demonstrated both by the sacrifices it costs – at points in the novel Karnau expresses the hope that his sound map might contribute to human progress – and by its fruitlessness when he learns that no recording machine or indeed human being can register the ultrasonic.

One of the most typical forms of literary contextualisation of the Nazi period since 1990 is the exploration of the interaction of individual and society. Writers examine the impact on the individual of the Nazi accession to power, of Nazi totalitarianism, ideology, Nazi idealism, Nazi murderousness and criminality. Martin Walser's *Ein springender Brunnen* (The Springing Fountain, 1998) suggests that it was possible for a community, and for the children within that community, to remain immune from the grip of the regime, a belated affirmation, it seems, of the principle of inner emigration. Other authors show rather the inescapability of that grip. Ulla Berkéwicz's novel *Engel sind schwarz und weiß* (Angels are Black and White, 1992) shows how it was possible for young children in the early years of the Third Reich to fall prey, in their naive enthusiasm, to the illusion that Nazism simply embodied a romantic and patriotic revivalism, and to fail to understand its true meaning. But Berkéwicz also shows how this failure, in the case of the main character, Reinhold Fischer, gives way over time to a very acute understanding of Nazism's true brutality, an understanding which in Reinhold's case inspires him to desert the army and befriend a family of Russian Jews who help him hide.[7] Similarly, Johann Martens in *Der kretische Gast* undergoes a process of painful enlightenment as to Nazism's true nature before he joins the partisans. Jens Sparschuh's interest in *Der Schneemensch* (The Yeti, 1993), and Beyer's in *Flughunde*, is rather in showing how individuals are seduced by Nazism, drawn into it. Whatever the differences between the above works, they have an investigative interest in points of intersection between the individual and Nazism in common, and, taken together, portray a range of possible responses. A more positive view of Kunkel's *Endstufe* might contend that his aim, too, is to explore this intersection and to reveal another mode of response: namely a spiral of constant sensual self-titillation which simultaneously constitutes a blindness and indifference to Nazi crimes.

CONTEXTUALISATION AS CRITICAL TOOL

There are forms of historical contextualisation in post-unification German prose writing which eschew questionable relativisation. In these cases, the Nazi past is examined more from the diachronic perspective of what came *after*: namely the early history of the Federal Republic, the reactions of the generation of '68, and the subsequent responses of later generations.

The most notable example here is Ulrich Woelk's 1993 novel *Rückspiel*,[8] in which the narrator, Stirner, a member of the post-1968 generation, goes in search of the National Socialist past of a former teacher who, in his love for a woman, may have been responsible for removing a rival suitor, Masol, by denouncing him as a Jew (*RS*, 86). Kampe, the teacher, clearly continues to have Nazi sympathies but the novel, ultimately, equivocates on the issue of Kampe's guilt, with regard to both Masol and Klausen, one of Kampe's erstwhile pupils. Following his expulsion from school in 1969 – Klausen had called Kampe 'a useful idiot of imperialism' – Klausen committed suicide. The narrator's brother effectively accuses Kampe of having direct responsibility for Klausen's death. But when Stirner confronts Kampe with his probable guilt, Kampe argues for a much more complex chain of cause and effect in the case of Klausen's death and Masol's emigration from Germany (*RS*, 239ff.). The reader, and Stirner, are left uncertain as to what really happened, and as to Kampe's degree of responsibility.

Woelk's interest is in the arguably undifferentiated nature of the accusations raised against the Third Reich generation by the 68ers – of whom Stirner's brother and his brother's contemporary, Johnny, are the representatives. Yet the novel also explores the disorientation of the post-'68 generation as represented by Stirner himself, who is eight years younger than his brother. Stirner's obsession with delving into Kampe's Nazi past is conveyed by Woelk as a somewhat laboured attempt on the part of the narrator to overcome his own sense of detachment both from the ideals of his brother and from the history and identity of the society in which he lives. Significantly, the narrator works as an interior designer, while being 'homeless' himself. He appears to represent a generation that is more sceptical, rational, pragmatic and emotionally distanced than that of his brother. Yet his attempt to understand his brother by understanding Kampe not only fails, it also severs him from the present; the fall of the Wall in 1989 finds him still in pursuit of Kampe, and his failure to grasp the historical moment represented by 1989 leads to a rift between him and his girlfriend. In seeking to understand history, he fails to understand the present.

Woelk's novel, as already indicated, illustrates the difficulties attached to any attempt to reconstruct the past, and the dangers of an over-indulgence in such an attempt. Its main focus is on the intergenerational judgmentalism that hinders this attempt; neither Stirner's generation (whose cynicism blunts its sensitivity), nor that of his brother, nor that of Kampe is capable of a truly judicious assessment of other generations. As a result, the past and present are viewed through the distorting lens of self-interest, mutual resentment and prejudice as the generations battle for moral supremacy – a battle whose bitterness is only enhanced by self-defensive blindness to the fact of failure. Kampe, and especially his contemporary, Kulisch, cling to nationalist and Nazi values as if they had never been discredited. Stirner's brother also continues to spout the wisdoms of the generation of '68 despite the fact that his lofty ideals have given way to a tame collaboration with the state and with the values he once rejected. Thus Stirner's brother's idealism ends in the once despised haven of marriage, which he had described as the 'grave of love' (*RS*, 115), and in employment in the civil service. Such blindness to change, and to the need for a critical self-examination which it implies, also characterises Stirner in his failure to respond commensurably to the events of 1989.

Rückspiel's evocation of an apparent parallelism between generations so keen to stake out their differences is strengthened by symmetries between relationships, processes and events in the distant and more recent past. Kampe appears to denounce Masol, while the narrator's brother denounces Kampe, and Johnny appears ready to 'sell' his girlfriend for fifty marks – the dehumanising instrumentalisation of others is not a characteristic of Nazism alone. Masol's competition with Kampe for Elsa Kirch's love represents only one of three unfortunate love triangles in the novel. Klausen, so the narrator ultimately seems to believe, was in love with Johnny's girlfriend, while she only had eyes for Johnny; and the narrator himself loses his girlfriend, Lucca, to Johnny. The general impression of symmetricality is enhanced by the novel's repeated association of festive events with negative developments. The blonde at the centre of Klausen's amorous interest falls from a window during a school-leaving party, Stirner's brother's wedding turns into a family éclat, while the estrangement between Lucca and Stirner occurs during fall-of-the-Wall celebrations on 9 November and 31 December 1989.

For all its interest in the moral and emotional congruence between generations, and for all its elaborately plotted networks of associations, *Rückspiel* is too self-consciously constructed a novel to invite the reader's uncritical identification with such symmetry. We are never allowed to forget that the novel is a first-person narrative and that Stirner's perspective is that of an obsessive organiser whose preoccupation with symmetry is almost pathologically extreme – as when he suggests that the only difference between Kampe and Klausen is that Kampe had the opportunity 'to denounce Masol as a Jew and get rid of a competitor' whereas 'Klausen never had such a chance' to get rid of Johnny (*RS*, 280). Yet the novel reveals little of Elsa Kirch's feelings towards Kampe, and whether Klausen would have acted like Kampe under different circumstances is a moot point. The novel gives considerable weight to Lucca's growing impatience with Stirner's obsession with the past. She suggests that he uses the few fragments of that past he has managed to unearth to 'land people in trouble because you envy them because they are alive, and when someone betrays someone, then at least they're living'. She reproaches Stirner with being 'invulnerable', adding: 'if someone killed you, you wouldn't even notice' (*RS*, 270). In the final pages, Stirner appears to turn away radically from his previous preoccupation with reconstruction, arguing that 'everything which, in my head, is history never happened' (*RS*, 294). He comes to replace this preoccupation with an equally questionable conviction that everything he has been recording in his story is but the expression of the moment which ceases to have meaning as soon as he lifts his fingers from the keyboard. Now, he describes his recording process as 'without system' (*RS*, 295), turns away from the notion of the past and gives himself over to an eternal present – a far cry from the beginning of the novel, where he told the reader 'the present is nothing' (*RS*, 7).

Rückspiel interprets an act of supposed denunciation in the Nazi period through a set of generational prisms, uncovering generational parallels without subscribing to the view that parallels necessarily imply equivalence.

Bernhard Schlink's worldwide best-seller *Der Vorleser* also sets out to portray a member of the Third Reich generation through the eyes of a member of a later generation.[9] While one could argue as to whether Kampe should be classified as a 'perpetrator' or rather as a 'fellow-traveller' with an instinct for exploiting the system, there is no doubt about Hanna Schmitz in *Der Vorleser*. As a concentration camp guard both at Auschwitz and in a small satellite camp near Cracow, she clearly belongs to the category of 'perpetrator'. In contrast to Kampe, however, who is condemned out of hand by Stirner's brother and Johnny, and even, at first, by Stirner himself, Hanna is portrayed with some sympathy by the first-person narrator of *Der Vorleser*, Michael Berg. The reason seems clear: as a fifteen-year old boy, Michael, without knowing that Hanna had once served as a camp guard, had a sexual relationship with her. Years later in the early 1960s – in the course of the West German trial against Hanna and other women who stand accused of allowing hundreds of female prisoners to burn to death in a church – Michael makes the discovery that Hanna is illiterate. This appears to explain the fact that Hanna used to insist that Michael read aloud to her as part of a sexual ritual. Hanna's readiness to burden herself with more guilt than might actually accrue to her in order to conceal her illiteracy from the court seems to heighten his sympathy for her and moves him to consider whether he should inform the judge of her predicament – something, however, he ultimately decides not to do.

That Schlink should have opted to portray Hanna through the emotionally prejudiced eyes of Michael has been held against him by several commentators on the novel. Critical opinion is divided on *Der Vorleser*, with a number of critics arguing that it effectively constitutes a kitsch-laden defence of Hanna, who may be condemned by the court, but whom we are invited to forgive by the novel. That she spends her prison years learning to read and write and then commits suicide shortly before her release would perhaps suggest that literacy is a prerequisite of moral awareness and responsibility, a corollary of which would be that the inability to read or write prevents the development of a sense of right and wrong.[10] Hanna, then, is not really to blame for her conduct as a camp guard. For some critics such as William Collins Donahue, '*Der Vorleser* is more concerned to establish Hanna as victim than as perpetrator',[11] while historian Omer Bartov even perceives in the novel a view of 'Germany as victim' (in the figures of both Michael and Hanna).[12] Schlink's novel thus apparently fits into what some see as a worrying new trend in German culture whereby Germans are presented as victims, either of circumstance, or of Nazism, even of the Allies.[13]

While there undoubtedly is such a trend, Schlink's *Der Vorleser* is not really an example of it. Critical reviews overlook the fact that the novel is written in the first person, and that Michael's position of emotional involvement is one of which the reader is constantly aware. This could hardly be otherwise, given that he is aware of it himself, while never achieving proper distance. Throughout the novel, he vacillates between feelings of love towards Hanna, feelings of guilt towards her, feelings of anger and indignation, and feelings of shame for having loved her; he feels both that he has betrayed her (for instance by turning away from her towards his peers as a teenager (*V*, 72)), and at the same time that she has exploited and betrayed him (e.g. *V*, 153). He never extracts himself from this emotional entanglement, indeed it is exacerbated by his half-hearted attempts to help her both during her trial and when she is in prison. Thus while he sends her cassettes with recordings of himself reading novels aloud, he never visits her in person until shortly before her release; his readings assist her in learning to read and write, but this was not his intention, and he fails to support her emotionally. Her suicide appears related to her sense of disappointment in him. While Michael was certainly the teenage victim of Hanna's predatory sexuality and her ritualistic exploitation of his reading skills, he never assumes responsibility for endeavouring to overcome the damage done to him – any more than Hanna assumes responsibility for her illiteracy during the Third Reich.

Michael seems untypical of the late 1960s' student generation of which he is part. His father, a philosophy professor, was discriminated against under the Nazis (see *V*, 88); he does not, therefore, effectively symbolise the parental generation against which the student movement rebelled. Moreover, while Michael seeks to integrate into his peer group as it grapples with the Nazi past, he simultaneously remains aloof. In addition, his erotic relationship as a teenager with a Nazi perpetrator certainly makes an exception of him. At one point in his narrative, Michael claims that, for those children who could not or did not want to reproach their parents, the confrontation with the National Socialist past was not merely a form of generational conflict, 'but the actual problem' (*V*, 161). Michael is unable to use the Nazi past as a weapon against his father in any potential generation conflict. Robbed of such an opportunity to instrumentalise it, he feels more constrained to confront it directly. This confrontation is made all the more painful by his emotional and sexual involvement with Hanna, an involvement which brings him so close to the Third Reich generation that he is more inclined to see himself as tinged with its guilt than as in a position to condemn it (*V*, 162). Michael is thus far from able to avail himself of the easy rejectionism of his peers.

On the other hand, his struggle to defend Hanna, and his attempts to understand her, mark him out as different. It is this differentness that enables Schlink to use Michael as a foil to highlight problematic tendencies inherent in the process of *Vergangenheitsbewältigung* (coming-to-terms with the past). Michael's desire to comprehend Hanna brings him into conflict with the prevalent impulse amongst his generation to condemn, a conflict he internalises: 'I wanted both to understand Hanna's crimes and to condemn them' (*V*, 151). At the same time he feels that attempting to understand violates another accepted wisdom: namely that 'we should not think we can understand what is incomprehensible, and should not compare what is incomparable' (*V*, 99). Schlink is not arguing for a relativisation of the horrors of the Holocaust. The perspective here is *Michael's*. If he could only convince himself it were socially acceptable to seek to understand, then he could allow himself even more empathy with Hanna, which in turn would reduce his sense of guilt for loving her. His disappointment that it is not 'permitted' to compare his initial emotional numbness during the court scenes with that of Holocaust victims (*V*, 97–8) is similarly motivated: he wishes to pity himself by universalising the problem. Moreover, while his dissatisfaction at the court's affixing of the lion's share of blame to Hanna leads him to identify genuine weaknesses in judicial *Vergangenheitsbewältigung*, it stems largely from his wish to defend Hanna. Schlink makes us aware of Michael's moral and emotional self-interestedness, while using that self-interestedness to throw into relief the question of possible taboos in coming to terms with Nazism (on understanding, empathy and comparison). The novel does not sanction Michael's views on this process, nor does it seek to discredit the latter. Rather it appears committed to exploring the existence of a disjuncture between public memory of the Holocaust and Michael's private position.

That critics have frequently failed to recognise Michael's status as a 'questionable narrator' is surprising – especially as Michael is given to questioning the meaning of the events he is describing. In the course of the novel he asks himself well over a hundred questions, for most of which he is unable to provide an answer. Moreover, the novel contains passages in which Michael's assessments are undermined by the text. This is particularly the case with regard to the court scenes. When the judge asks Hanna about prisoner transports for Auschwitz, which she and the other defendants put together, she appears unable to understand that she was drawing up death lists. Rather, for her, it was a technical issue: 'new prisoners arrived, and we had to make room for the new ones' (*V*, 106). In frustration, she asks the judge what he would have done. His answer is precise and measured: 'there are things one should simply not get involved in and from which, provided there is no personal risk to life or limb, one should distance oneself' (*V*, 107). This places the moral responsibility squarely, and fairly, upon Hanna. Michael's subsequent dismissal of the judge's comments as simplistic and helpless is patently misguided and biased (*V*, 107–8).

Hanna may or may not be anti-Semitic; the novel tells us little about the degree of her racist motivation. If anything, she seems to have opted for her role as guard to hide her illiteracy. Yet this does not exonerate her. The court-room exchanges between Hanna and the judge reveal not only Hanna's struggle to continue to conceal her illiteracy, something Michael picks up on, but also her attitude to her role as camp guard – an attitude Michael either fails to or will not grasp. The dialogue cited in the paragraph above is one good example of Hanna's mechanistic and functional thinking. Later, when asked by the judge why she did not release the prisoners from the burning church, she answers – honestly – that she did not see how she and the few remaining *SS* women could have prevented the prisoners from fleeing: 'that was our job after all, to guard them and stop them from fleeing' (*V*, 122). Hanna is a perfect embodiment of the Nazi perpetrator as imagined by the structuralist school of historians. For many Nazis, the

'Jewish question' was often a technical one; faced with problems posed by population transfers or overfilled ghettos, murder became an act of convenience. For Hanna, guarding prisoners is also a purely functional question: this has to be done, and where it cannot, prisoners have to die. Hanna's mindset is that of the subaltern functionary for whom operability is the issue, not ethics. Her indifference to ethical perspectives is arguably more shocking than the self-defensive machinations of her fellow-defendants, who at least seem able to recognise that society now adjudges their actions to have been wrong.

At no point does the novel imply that Hanna's inability to read or write signifies moral ignorance and therefore innocence. Awareness of morality, after all, is hardly dependent on reading and writing alone. Central to *Der Vorleser* is Hanna's selfishness: she self-obsessively places her concern with avoiding supposed stigmatisation above the welfare of others (her flight into functionality both as concentration camp guard and tram conductor can be read as a desperate attempt to find security in efficiency of performance). Nor should her development from illiterate to avid reader of Holocaust literature in prison be seen as an argument for an equivalence of literacy and moral sensibility. It is Hanna's overcoming of the source of her sense of shame which unblocks her capacity for empathy, which may be enhanced by reading, but is not engendered by it. Certainly, *Der Vorleser* would appear to confirm the need for the individual to take responsibility for getting to grips with his or her own weaknesses. But it steers clear of portraying Hanna's autodidacticism as particularly successful. When Michael visits her shortly before she is to be released, he sees her sitting on a bench. She holds a book in her hands, but peers over it, watching a woman throwing breadcrumbs to some birds (*V*, 184). There could hardly be a stronger metaphor of her wish to be spoon-fed once more. Meeting Michael again, it becomes clear to her, however, that the days of being read to are over (*V*, 186). Her suicide is as much an expression of her reluctance to face life outside the prison cell as it is of a presumptuous wish for absolution. Unsupported by society – which imprisons Hanna but leaves her to herself – her development remains flawed and half-hearted.

CONCLUSION

That post-unification German works of fiction should not focus on Nazi perpetrators as their main theme is, as stated at the outset, not so surprising. For later generations, it is how these perpetrators are remembered and *were* remembered that is an issue. Many years have passed since the end of the Third Reich, and several generations have come and gone. As a result, *Vergangenheitsbewältigung* has taken on new dimensions, coming to mean – for literature and for society at large – not just the confrontation with Nazism but also the metadiscursive exploration of the parameters in which this discourse of confrontation has operated since 1945. In a sense, what we have here is a coming-to-terms with the problems adhering to the process of coming-to-terms. This is particularly the case with Beyer's *Spione*, Schlink's *Der Vorleser* and Woelk's *Rückspiel*. In all cases, generational bias, emotional self-interest and intergenerational conflicts impact on views of the Nazi past, acting as distorting mirrors. The post-modern habitus of such novels and their historiographical scepticism can be seen as problematic. If views of the Nazi past are so much indebted to the tendentiousness of later generations, what remains of the objective truth of that past, of its didactic force as a warning? It is to the credit of Schlink, Beyer – particularly in *Spione* – and Woelk that their scepticism stops short of proposing the abandonment of the past to a kind of memory anarchy.

On the contrary, these three writers combine their examination of generational (mis)representations of the Nazi past with an attempt to understand Nazi perpetrators in terms of their own personal motivations and circumstances, and in terms of the moral, social and intellectual universe in which they became perpetrators. A possible corollary of critically examining the post-'68 discourse of *Vergangenheitsbewältigung* is an attempt to free the perspective on National Socialism from the blinkers of past generations. Yet it must also be pointed out that, in the case of some writers, the interest is not so much in seriously reviewing this discourse as in establishing a dubious counter-discourse. Kunkel's *Endstufe* in particular disseminates a form of relativisation which in fact replicates the post-war mythology according to which Germans saw themselves as victims of the Allies rather than as perpetrators. Reviewing the way the past was remembered after '68 need not mean jettisoning the fundamental distinction between the Germans and the western Allies during the war; that it has come to mean this for some writers is apparent, however, from Helmut Schmitz's contribution to this volume.

1. Translated as Daniel Jonah Goldhagen, *Hitlers Willige Vollstrecker: Ganz gewöhnliche Deutsche und der Holocaust* (Munich: Siedler, 1996).
2. See Hamburger Institut für Sozialforschung HIS, ed., *Vernichtungskrieg: Verbrechen der Wehrmacht 1941 bis 1944* (Hamburg: Hamburger Edition, 1996).

3. For example, Michael Wildt, *Generation des Unbedingten: Das Führungskorps des Reichssicherheitshauptamtes* (Hamburg: Hamburger Edition, 2002); Christian Gerlach, *Kalkulierte Morde: Die deutsche Wirtschafts- und Vernichtungspolitik in Weissrussland 1941–1944* (Hamburg: Hamburger Edition, 1999).

4. Harald Welzer, Sabine Moller and Karoline Tschnuggnall distinguish between the mental 'albums' of family memory, which focus on heroism and victimhood, and the 'encyclopedia', a socially agreed compendium of knowledge about the Nazi past, which focuses more on crime. See Harald Welzer, Sabine Moller and Karoline Tschuggnall, *'Opa war kein Nazi': Nationalsozialismus und Holocaust im Familiengedächtnis* (Frankfurt: Fischer Taschenbuch Verlag, 2002).

5. Thor Kunkel, *Endstufe* (Berlin: Eichborn, 2004). Hereafter *E*.

6. Klaus Modick, *Der kretische Gast* (Munich: Piper, 2005 [2003]), 150–1.

7. For a discussion of these novels by Walser and Berkéwicz, see Helmut Schmitz, *On Their Own Terms: The Legacy of National Socialism in Post-1990 German Fiction* (Birmingham: University of Birmingham Press, 2004).

8. Ulrich Woelk, *Rückspiel* (Frankfurt: Fischer, 1995 [1993]), 102. Hereafter *RS*.

9. Bernhard Schlink, *Der Vorleser* (Zurich: Diogenes, 1997 [1995]). Hereafter *V*.

10. See Sally Johnson and Frank Finlay, '(Il)literacy and (Im)morality in Bernhard Schlink's *The Reader*', *Written Language and Literacy*, 4:2 (2001), 195–214, here 196–7.

11. William Collins Donahue, 'Illusions of Subtlety: Bernhard Schlink's *Der Vorleser* and the Moral Limits of Holocaust Fiction', *German Life and Letters*, 54:1 (2001), 60–81, here 72.

12. See Omer Bartov, 'Germany as Victim', *New German Criticism*, 80 (2000), 29–40.

13. For particularly dismissive opinions of *Der Vorleser*, see Jeremy Adler, 'Bernhard Schlink and "The Reader"' [Reader's Letter], *Times Literary Supplement* (22 March 2002), 17; Frederic Raphael, 'Bernhard Schlink' [Reader's Letter], *Times Literary Supplement* (8 March 2002), 17; Lawrence Norfolk, 'Die Sehnsucht nach einer ungeschehenen Geschichte', *Süddeutsche Zeitung* (27–28 April 2002), 16.

CHAPTER 9

Representations of the Nazi past II:
German wartime suffering

Helmut Schmitz

The decade after German unification witnessed the institutionalisation of a culture of public commemoration of the Holocaust. In the 1990s, moreover, a series of debates on Germany's Nazi legacy took place which, at the time, were taken by many observers to signal the final phase in the process of coming-to-terms with the past (*Vergangenheitsbewältigung*).[1] It was no longer a matter, for the most part at least, of confronting an unwilling population with an uncomfortable historical reality but of integrating the Nazi period into the cultural memory of post-1990 Germany. Thus, by the end of the 1990s, a kind of national 'ownership' of the Nazi period, with an emphasis on German responsibility, seemed well established.[2] At the same time, the accelerating growth of a memorialisation culture in post-1990 Germany, as evidenced by the almost obsessive presence of the Nazi past in the mass media, and especially television, has arguably transformed the Third Reich into a 'heritage' site.

Since the turn of the millennium, however, there appears to have been a shift in German memory discourse away from a resolute focus on German responsibility for the Holocaust and towards a focus on the Allies' devastating aerial bombardment of German cities, the mass rapes of German women during the Soviet advance, and the expulsions of ethnic Germans from East Prussia, Silesia, Pomerania and the Sudetenland at the end of the war. 'German suffering', a topic which had long been regarded as the preserve of right-wing historical revisionists, was suddenly a mainstream media issue. For example, Guido Knopp's five-part TV documentary on the expulsions, *Die große Flucht* (The Great Flight), attracted an audience of five million in 2001. Both Knopp's series and Günter Grass's novella *Im Krebsgang* (Crabwalk, 2002) were accompanied by a series in *Der Spiegel* on 'Germans as victims'.[3] Jörg Friedrich's book on the Allied bombing campaign, *Der Brand* (The Inferno, 2002), moreover, sold more than 200,000 hardback copies; a year later, his book of photographs *Brandstätten* (Sites of Destruction, 2003) sold over 30,000.

The debate on German 'victims' traversed the left–right dichotomies of the 'old', pre-1990 Federal Republic. It was accompanied by a number of highly controversial attempts to reshape the established discourse on Nazism. During a series of debates on the Allied bombing campaign, for instance, some asked whether the obliteration of German cities might not constitute a war crime. This hinted at a change of emphasis in the broad consensus that German crimes had been unique – was the British fire-bombing of Dresden, for example, to be equated with the Holocaust? Just as contentious was the *Zentrum gegen Vertreibungen* (Centre against Expulsions) proposed by the *Bund der Vertriebenen* (League of Expellees), to be built in Berlin as a permanent exhibition on the expulsions of 'ethnic' Germans and twentieth-century expulsions in general. In recent years, the *Bund der Vertriebenen* has also been demanding compensation for expropriated property; this demand, for many observers, implied an analogy with the compensation given (reluctantly) to eastern Europeans enslaved as forced labourers by the Nazis. Indeed, there is no memory of 'German suffering' that is not also immediately part of a highly politicised discourse.

This shift from a more-or-less institutionalised emphasis on responsibility for the Holocaust to a concern with 'Germans as victims' reveals the discrepancy between public memory and private or family memory, as well as between victim-centred and perpetrator-centred memory. While public representation has been largely focused upon the crimes of National Socialism, private and family memory tends to insist on the hardship, suffering and loss endured by individual Germans without regard for the larger context of German responsibility.[4] The victim-centred approach in public commemorations of the Nazi period, with its emphasis on the Holocaust, appears, by definition, to exclude the experiences of the overwhelming majority of (non-Jewish) Germans. Indeed, the story of discrimination, deportation and extermination suffered by Nazi Germany's victims cannot be easily integrated into a single coherent narrative with the travails endured by 'ordinary' Germans who, even if they were not fanatical Nazis, were safe from racial persecution; a focus on the one seems always to be at the expense of the other.

These issues had already been touched upon in 1998 in the wake of author Martin Walser's *Friedenspreisrede* (Peace-Prize speech) and particularly during what later came to be known as the Walser–Bubis affair when Walser suggested to Ignatz Bubis, the then President of the Central Council of Jews in Germany, that the language of commemoration which had become established in relation to the Holocaust was all too frequently instrumentalised by (Jewish) survivors, amongst others, in pursuit of their political interests in the present.[5] Walser's subsequent insistence upon his right to deal with the memory of the Nazi era in his own way, that is, on his right to prefer the less judgmental perspective elaborated by private conscience to a public discourse focused on German guilt, signalled an attempt to break with a victim-centred approach. The massive support Walser received following his admission that he often desired to 'look away' when confronted with images of the Holocaust seemed to indicate that two distinct forms of memory existed alongside one another, the first related to public memory, the second to private memory.

Recent representations of 'German wartime suffering' appear to substitute a semi-official public memory of the Nazi period for a set of images passed down in the family from generation to generation. The emergence of such images from the late 1990s, it is frequently claimed, implies the overcoming of a long-standing taboo imposed by the generation of '68, that is, by the one-time student protesters who, in the late 1960s, had railed against their parents' inability to confront their complicity in National Socialism. The 68ers, then, are accused of having declared it inadmissible to express empathy with 'German suffering'; this they did, it is argued, on account of their feelings of shame for their parents' real or imagined participation in Nazi crimes. If the older generation had repressed their engagement with National Socialism, the student movement is alleged to have similarly repressed any empathy with their parents' wartime experiences and to have cast them exclusively in the role of perpetrators. This suggestion is present in a range of non-fictional and fictional texts, including Bernhard Schlink's *Der Vorleser* (The Reader, 1995), the *Spiegel* series 'Germans as victims', and fellow author and former 68er Peter Schneider's contribution to the volume *Ein Volk von Opfern?* (A People of Victims?, 2003).[6] The implicit argument is that the taboo on empathy with 'German suffering' should be dissolved and the image of Germans as perpetrators be replaced by a more differentiated account of the complexities of the wartime period.

These developments need to be considered within the context of the recent re-emergence of 'intergenerational' fiction.[7] Certainly, the most consistent feature of recent literary works dealing with 'German wartime suffering' is their focus on the relationship between the generations. Grass's *Im Krebsgang*, Marcel Beyer's *Spione* (Spies, 2000), Tanja Dückers's *Himmelskörper* (Heavenly Bodies, 2003), Stephan Wackwitz's *Ein unsichtbares Land* (An Invisible Country, 2003), and Thomas Medicus's *In den Augen meines Großvaters* (In the Eyes of my Grandfather, 2004) thus all focus on the transmission of wartime experiences across three generations. Ulla Hahn's

Unscharfe Bilder (Blurred Images, 2003) and Uwe Timm's *Am Beispiel meines Bruders* (In My Brother's Shadow, 2003), on the other hand, focus more narrowly on the relationship between the wartime generation and their children, that is, those who, in the late 1960s, would take part in the student movement. In the collection *stadt land krieg* (city country war, 2004), edited by Tanja Dückers and Verena Carl, alternatively, the grandchildren begin to appropriate the wartime period. In contrast to the 'father-literature' of the mid to late 1970s, such novels are often written from a perspective of empathy with the parents or grandparents in conjunction with a reassessment of the highly judgmental perspective of the 68ers.

In what follows, I analyse a number of key literary works, each of which deals with a different aspect of the German wartime experience, and relate them to the various contexts outlined above. In particular, I am interested in exploring the extent to which the kind of empathy promoted in some of the texts I examine might differ from the 'didactic empathy' promoted by historians such as Christopher R. Browning or Harald Welzer, whose efforts to 'understand' the perpetrators strives to illuminate the decision-making processes which accompany genocidal acts.[8] Whereas 'didactic empathy' is driven by a desire for greater insight but remains conscious of the broader context of German responsibility for the crimes of the Nazi period, some of the literary texts I examine, representative perhaps of broader trends, may be motivated by the desire to establish empathy with 'German wartime suffering' as an emotional and highly sentimentalised foundation for a national collective and a renewed sense of an 'unburdened' German national identity.

THE AIR WAR: DIETER FORTE'S *DER JUNGE MIT DEN BLUTIGEN SCHUHEN*

In his 1997 lectures *Luftkrieg und Literatur* (Aerial Warfare and Literature, published in 1999), W. G. Sebald argued that post-war German writing had failed to inscribe the experience of the Allied bombing campaign into collective memory.[9] Furthermore, the 'destruction, on a scale without historical precedent' (*LL*, 11), he claimed, had never been the object of a public debate. Sebald suspected that the reason for the collective acceptance of the destruction and humiliation lay in the complex intertwining of traumatisation and feelings of guilt which compelled the Germans to silence, both about their implication in Nazi atrocities and their own painful experiences. The catalyst of German post-war silence, the scholar, literary critic and author went on to argue, was 'the stream of psychic energy that has not dried up to this day, and which has its source in the well-kept secret of the corpses built into the foundations of our state' (*LL*, 13).

Sebald's lectures about a *historical* failure as a result of the complex post-war emotional landscape of guilt, denial, traumatisation and continuities of Nazi mentality were received by the German press as breaking with a supposed taboo on public discourse about 'German wartime suffering' and as legitimising a *present-day* debate. Sebald's was a provocative thesis, and one which was challenged, for example, by Volker Hage, chief literary critic at *Der Spiegel*, in his *Zeugen der Zerstörung: Die Literaten und der Luftkrieg* (Witnesses to Destruction: Writers and the Air War, 2003) and *Hamburg 1943: Literarische Zeugnisse zum Feuersturm* (Hamburg 1943: Literary Depictions of the Fire-storm, also 2003).[10] In the course of the debate, however, Sebald's suggestion that the purported taboo had been self-inflicted, a consequence of Germans' feelings of guilt, disappeared from view in favour of a more emotive emphasis on traumatisation itself. Jörg Friedrich's *Der Brand* and *Brandstätten* thus operate with a narrative that describes the inhabitants of German cities as the objects of an Allied desire to exterminate Germany; both, moreover, mobilise imagery more usually associated with the Holocaust. Furthermore, in the focus on the undoubted horrors of the firestorms, the distinctions between Germans, workslaves and concentration camp inmates often disappear – all appear as the victims of both Hitler and the Allies simultaneously. While it is true that Sebald's lectures also describe the destruction of the German cities as 'without historical precedent', a formulation conventionally associated with Nazi atrocities, they are free from the subtext of a national tragedy that characterises Friedrich's narrative.

Dieter Forte's novel about the Allied air assault on Düsseldorf, *Der Junge mit den blutigen Schuhen* (The Boy with the Bloody Shoes, 1995),[11] shares several features with both Sebald's *Luftkrieg und Literatur* and Friedrich's *Der Brand*. The novel is the second instalment of Forte's autobiographical trilogy, *Das Haus auf meinen Schultern* (The House on my Shoulders), the first part of which, *Das Muster* (The Sample), had appeared in 1992; the third, *In der Erinnerung* (Within Memory), would appear in 1998. The most striking feature of the trilogy, apart from the detailed description of the bombings in *Der Junge mit den blutigen Schuhen*, is the inclusion of the Second World War within a transhistorical narrative of suffering throughout the ages. Forte's trilogy, which, in a similar way to Grass's *Die Blechtrommel* (The Tin Drum, 1959), operates with a worm's-eye perspective, thus presents almost the entirety of modern European history as 'dark fate full of terror and disaster' (*JBS*, 15), that is, as a natural catastrophe outside human control.

In *Der Junge mit den blutigen Schuhen*, Forte sets out to inscribe the experience of the air raids on Düsseldorf, which he experienced as a child, into collective memory. Throughout, the author uses a poeticising style to render the essence of both National Socialism and the bombing campaign. In addition, the novel chronicles the effect of all aspects of the air war on the *living* body: 'The sirens howled, screamed their monotonous melodies . . . quickly ascending to a painful treble that pervaded the ears, entered the brain and stuck there, never to leave the body, so that you heard them when the sirens were quiet' (*JBS*, 134). The most striking difference from Friedrich's *Der Brand*, however, lies in Forte's avoidance of Holocaust imagery. Friedrich explicitly parallels the firestorms with the gas chambers; in *Der Junge mit den blutigen Schuhen*, the bombs simply bring about 'the demise of the world' (*JBS*, 131 and 138). The novel is characterised, in fact, by a mythologising narratorial voice striving to condense 'lived' history, as Forte claimed in an interview with Volker Hage, into 'iconic' and 'lasting' images.[12]

Forte's desire to preserve and hand down the past indicates a self-conscious commitment to communicative memory: 'In the story the past was present and the present was past, because the present was being entrusted to the future in the act of story-telling' (*JBS*, 109–10). It is significant in this respect that the novel lays particular emphasis on the importance of oral narrative. *Der Junge mit den blutigen Schuhen* is thus first and foremost concerned with the transmission of 'lived' experience, as the author notes in an essay in his volume *Schweigen oder sprechen* (To Remain Silent or To Speak, 2003): 'If it is not passed on from generation to generation by poeticising narration, so that it enters deep memory and becomes an unforgotten image of horror in the act of story-telling, it will be lost for the descendants.'[13] Indeed, the work is an example of what Jan Assmann has termed 'mythical memory': 'It is only remembered history that is important for cultural memory, not factual history. One could say that in cultural memory factual history is transformed into remembered history and thus into myth.'[14] Yet Forte's mythical tone raises concerns with respect to agency and historical responsibility: National Socialism appears to come upon Germans as a misfortune not of their making. Indeed, within the working-class district of Düsseldorf-Oberbilk – depicted in the novel as an idyllic multicultural space – National Socialism appears as an 'alien' body, as an intruder. The Third Reich, moreover, appears as a gigantic prison in which there is no substantive difference between the German collective and the victims of Nazi persecution: 'Forced labourer or drafted labourer, there was no difference, the guarding was the same, the food rations were the same, death was the same' (*JBS*, 208). Such a conflation of autobiographical memory and grand mythical narrative may result in an exculpation. In the presentation of Germans as 'victims' of both Hitler and the Allies and in the erasure of the distinctions between 'ordinary' Germans, POWs and camp inmates, the novel perhaps rewrites history.

Forte's *Der Junge mit den blutigen Schuhen* attempts to frame the bombing raids as the 'original' German trauma. Moreover, the novel's stylisation of the bombing campaign as a 'total break in the history of civilisation' appears to equate it with the Holocaust as a foundational moment, as a radical break in history which determined everything that follows.[15] This foundational narrative is rooted in the author's profound and lasting childhood traumatisation. Echoing Wolf Biermann's statement that the experience of the Hamburg fire-storm had stopped his inner life-clock at the age of six and a half years, in fact, Forte noted in his interview with Hage: 'My clock of life, too, came to a standstill then and everything that happened afterwards was not very important.'[16] This is a narrative, then, that is more than a straightfoward attempt to document the horrors of the bombing campaign: *Der Junge mit den blutigen Schuhen* locates 'German suffering', and specifically the Allied bombing of German cities, as the repressed origin of the present. As such, the centrality of the Holocaust to contemporary cultural memory is challenged by a highly charged and vivid representation of Germans as victims.

THE EXPULSIONS FROM THE EAST: GÜNTER GRASS'S *IM KREBSGANG*

Similar to Sebald's *Luftkrieg und Literatur*, Grass's novella *Im Krebsgang* (2002) was initially regarded as a bold and – given the resolutely left-wing credentials of its author – unexpected attempt to overcome the supposed taboo on another aspect of 'German suffering', that is, the expulsion from the eastern territories.[17] The novella, which for a brief period pushed two Harry Potter novels from the top of the *Spiegel* bestseller list, is a complex reflection on three generations of discourse on 'German suffering' and its relationship to the broader enterprise of 'coming-to-terms with the past'. Taking the sinking of the refugee ship *Wilhelm Gustloff* with the loss of thousands of lives off the coast of Gdansk by a Soviet submarine in January 1945 as a central metaphor, *Im Krebsgang* reviews the ship's complex history during National Socialism, the reception of its tragedy in post-war Germany and the current rise of neo-Nazism, particularly on the internet.[18]

It is not difficult to see what attracted Grass to the story of the *Wilhelm Gustloff*. Gustloff, after whom the ship is named, was the Nazi Party's Swiss representative and was transformed into a 'German' martyr after his assassination at the hands of a Jewish student. The ship was first used as a holiday ship by the *Kraft-durch-Freude* (Strength-through-Joy) organisation and then as a transport ship for the *Luftwaffen-Flak-Regiment 88* of the *Legion Condor*, the regiment infamous on account of its actions during the Spanish civil war. At the time of its sinking, the *Wilhelm Gustloff* was, as we are reminded in the novella, an 'armed passenger liner under the command of the navy' and thus not strictly speaking a civilian refugee ship.[19] The date of the ship's sinking, 30 January, is also the date of Hitler's rise to power and the birthday of Wilhelm Gustloff, a fact that the author exploits as a complex metaphor for the interdependence of 'German suffering' and guilt.

An extremely intricate and overdetermined narrative, *Im Krebsgang* presents three generations of German memory discourse as personified by Tulla Pokriefke, survivor of the *Gustloff* tragedy and resident of the former East Germany, her son, Paul, a failed West German journalist, and her grandson, Konrad. Tulla, a character also featured in Grass's *Katz und Maus* (Cat and Mouse, 1961) and *Hundejahre* (Dog Years, 1963), returns manically to the origin of her trauma, her near-death on the sinking *Gustloff*. Her devotion to her son has a single purpose: 'That's all I live for – so's my son can bear witness one of these days' (*K*, 15). Tulla's obsession with her past contrasts with the official silence on these matters in the ex-GDR where the fate of millions of German refugees from East Prussia and elsewhere were anathema. Referring to his mother throughout the novella as a 'has-been' (*K*, 50), in contrast, Paul distances himself from her obsession with the *Gustloff*, a rejection of German wartime trauma that aligns him with the student movement. *Im Krebsgang*, in fact, suggests that the second generation failed properly to empathise with their parents' traumatisation, preferring instead to condemn them for their supposed complicity in Nazism; it is further suggested that what is repressed by the second generation will return in the third. Accordingly, the grandson Konrad, tired of the perpetrator-centred image of National Socialism in public discourse and frustrated when his interest in the 'German experience' of the war is blocked at school, creates a website and chatroom on Wilhelm Gustloff, both the man and the ship. The increasing intimacy between Tulla and Konrad, and the exclusion of Paul, mirrors the replacement in public debate of a conventional emphasis on Nazi atrocities by family stories relating to individual *German* suffering. Konrad, who comes to believe that the discourse on the Nazi past is part of a Jewish conspiracy, ends up shooting his internet chatroom adversary, 'David', a boy of his own age who, in a misconceived philo-Semitic gesture, had taken on the name of Gustloff's Jewish killer. This act of 'vengeance' takes place, appropriately enough, at the dilapidated Nazi memorial to Gustloff.

By means of this highly symbolic construction, *Im Krebsgang* exposes all established discursive positions on the memory of National Socialism as inadequate and one-sided. In the course of the narrative, all the various agents and their fixed narrative stances are revealed as unreliable and compromised. Tulla's exclusive focus on her status as victim, while legitimised by her trauma, is relativised by the anti-Semitism which she passes on to Konrad. Paul, on the other hand, displays an excess of political correctness and withdraws empathy not only from Tulla but from his own history in so far as he rejects his own origin in the *Gustloff* catastrophe: 'All those years . . . I managed to leave the circumstances of my birth out of it' (*K*, 29). And Konrad's interest in the wartime experience of 'ordinary' Germans increasingly turns into a defence mechanism which renders him blind to the complexities of history; he ends up as a voice for far-right propaganda on the internet with his attacks on the 'world Jewish conspiracy, and the 'Jewish-controlled plutocracy' (*K*, 85).

Grass's *Im Krebsgang* tells of three generations of defective German memory discourse in a sober, reflective manner. In its relating of *this* history, however, an alternative, more appropriate mode of remembering both the Nazi past and the undoubted trauma of 'German suffering' is elaborated. This is achieved via the account of the history of the *Gustloff* and its reception which Paul finally manages to establish: a narrative which acknowledges 'German suffering' without investing it with sentimentalised metaphysical meaning. The elaboration of this alternative mode of remembrance is prompted by a character referred to as 'the old man' (*K*, 28), a thin disguise for the author Günter Grass, who employs Paul to write down the ship's story. The 'old man' in fact suggests that the successive failures of memory discourse in post-war Germany is, in part at least, the result of the failure of a generation of writers, including Grass, adequately to address the German wartime experience, and in particular 'German suffering': 'Never, he said, should his generation have kept silent about such misery, merely because its own sense of guilt was so overwhelming . . . with the result that they abandoned the topic to the right wing' (*K*, 103).

In suggesting that it was feelings of guilt that kept Grass's generation from addressing the topic of Germans as victims, such that the topic was relinquished to the (far) right, *Im Krebsgang* subscribes to the notion of a left-wing taboo on 'German suffering': 'No one wanted to hear the story, not here in the West and certainly not in the East. For decades the *Gustloff* and its awful fate were taboo on a pan-German basis, so to speak' (*K*, 29). However, as a metaphor for the post-war discourse on 'German suffering' in general and the flight from the east in particular, the *Wilhelm Gustloff* is somewhat unsuitable. While Paul's assessment of the lack of public attention concerning the *Gustloff's* story might be accurate, this is clearly not so with respect to both flight and expulsions. In truth, the fate of the Germans in the eastern provinces has been part of German literary, media and public discourse throughout the history of the Federal Republic. Indeed, the integration of the millions of expellees into West German society was often hailed as one of the FRG's success stories.

In a similar vein to Forte, Grass, in *Im Krebsgang*, relocates the origins of the German present in the trauma of 'German wartime suffering' rather than in the Holocaust. Konrad's shooting of 'David' has a cathartic effect on Paul which leads him, for the first time, to empathise with his own history; empathy with *German* suffering is seen as necessary in order to pre-empt German revanchism. Having always avoided any engagement with the story of his birth, Paul is thus now able to accept the entanglement of his existence with the death of the drowning passengers of the Gustloff, 'whereupon the cry of the countless thousands blended with my first cry' (*K*, 191). The significance here is that Paul, a member of the first post-war generation, is able to acknowledge, by means of a tentative empathy with his own history, the birth of post-war Germany out of trauma.[20] Like Forte's *Der Junge mit den blutigen Schuhen*, Grass's *Im Krebsgang* is a foundational narrative which situates the origin of the present not in the Holocaust but in the German experience of the horrors of the war. However, the 'thrice cursed' date of Paul's (and of present-day Germany's) birth also recalls the date of Hitler's rise to the position of Chancellor of the Reich. In contrast to Forte's text, *Im Krebsgang* relates the two complexes of German memory – Germany's historical failure and 'German wartime suffering' – to one another and remains mindful of the problematic nature of public discourse on the Nazi past.

THE FRONTLINE SOLDIER: *UNSCHARFE BILDER* AND *AM BEISPIEL MEINES BRUDERS*

The exhibition 'War of Annihilation: Crimes of the *Wehrmacht* 1941–1944', which travelled from city to city between 1995 and 1999, had a cathartic impact on the relationship between generations unlike any other event of the last decade. Initially designed to document the involvement of the regular German army in Hitler's extermination policies in eastern Europe, the exhibition had the 'profoundly positive' effect of opening up a dialogue between those who participated in the war and their children.[21] It was here that the re-evaluation of the student movement's supposed indifference to the suffering of 'ordinary' Germans was most evident.

The *Wehrmacht* exhibition serves as a starting point for Ulla Hahn's novel *Unscharfe Bilder* (2003).[22] Thus the novel stages a confrontation between Hans Musbach, a young participant in Hitler's war in the east, and his daughter, triggered by the exhibition. The daughter, who thinks she may have recognised her father in one of the photographs, presents her father with the exhibition catalogue in an attempt to get him to admit to his involvement. For his part, the father dismisses the images in the catalogue as 'useless' (*UB*, 44) and 'incomplete' (*UB*, 73) and insists on his status as 'part of the German war machinery and simultaneously its victim' (*UB*, 27). While Hahn's novel is an attempt to supplement the images of perpetrators which fill the exhibition with a more balanced representation of both perpetration and victimhood, the father's memories of his own trauma come, in the course of the novel, to dominate the narrative. By the close of the text, the daughter's instinctive condemnation of the mass of Germans as Nazi perpetrators has been substituted for a rather more forgiving empathy with the suffering endured by 'ordinary' German soldiers. In effect, Hahn re-establishes the narrative authority of those who participated in the war by challenging the moral superiority of those who came later. Germans of the author's own 68er generation, then, are accused of being wedded to a form of *a-posteriori* judgment that is necessarily ignorant of the complexities of the actual historical situation; the novel further challenges their right to insist on answers and to pass judgment: 'You have a right to ask but not always the right to an answer' (*UB*, 66).

In order to secure its credibility, *Unscharfe Bilder* draws on historiographical research on the frontline soldier on the east front and other documents such as letters and diaries. Hahn's particular use of these sources, however, exposes her agenda. Hence a substantial amount of Musbach's story is based on extracts from the 1952 edition *Kriegsbriefe gefallener Studenten 1939–1945* (War Letters of Fallen Students 1939–1945),[23] yet the ideological entanglement of the soldiers whose letters appear there, manifest in their bombastically nationalist and racist verbosity, is entirely absent from Musbach's voice. The sixty-year gap between the Nazi period and the time of Musbach's narration appears to have stripped all such ideological baggage from the narrative; Musbach appears simply as 'the traumatised soldier'.[24]

As such, the novel indulges in a form of historicisation which aims to present the Third Reich more 'objectively', more comprehensively, and 'free' of the moral judgments of the present; much the same, of course, was attempted by conservative historians in the mid-1980s in the series of texts which provoked the *Historikerstreit* (Historians' Controversy). Yet, implicitly or explicitly, the ultimate aim of this historicisation is a sentimentalised empathy with the 'German experience'.[25] In this perspective, 'ordinary' Germans appear predominantly as victims – whether as victims of Hitler, of the Allies, or of forces beyond their control. Accordingly, Musbach describes himself as 'prisoner of his own country' (*UB*, 107). A historicist agenda, moreover, all too often promotes a kind of 'heritage' perspective on the past and thereby a rather easy appeasement with a troubled and difficult history. The daughter in Hahn's novel, for example, becomes convinced that Germans born after the war should come to see the suffering of those who participated in the war as their 'inheritance' (*UB*, 145). Here, it is perhaps worth noting that a similar perspective is implied by Oliver Hirschbiegel's film *Der Untergang* (Downfall, 2004), praised by historians as well as the viewing public for its 'realistic' picture of the demise of Berlin.[26] At the time of the film's release, in fact, Bernd Eichinger, the producer, stressed its supposed 'authenticity' as well as its objective 'to illuminate our history ourselves'.[27] It is never mentioned, however, that one of the film's central figures, the SS doctor, Ernst-Günther Schenck, was involved in human experiments at Mauthausen concentration camp.

Hahn's *Unscharfe Bilder* furnishes the empathy that the student movement is said to have withheld from the wartime generation. Indeed, it is probably true that the traumatic experiences of the eastern front soldier have typically been shrouded in a silence, within public commemorative culture at least, which is comparable to the lack of official memorialisation of the Allied devastation of German cities since the 1970s. Similar to the air war, the reason is most likely the fact that the horrific experience of the German army in the east cannot be detached from Hitler's 'second genocide' of the indigenous population.[28] In addition, the extent of the traumatisation, the post-war phase of manic reconstruction, and the heavily politicised discourse about the Nazi past from the mid-1960s onwards left little room for a narrative, empathetic rendition of the soldiers' experience. In attempting to redress the balance, however, Hahn's novel goes to the other extreme and excludes all perspectives which might imply a judgment on, or condemnation of, 'ordinary' German soldiers' motives or actions; the didactic value of historical empathy is increasingly substituted for an unreflected pity. As a consequence, the likely involvement of the father in war crimes is overwhelmed by the extent of his self-evident traumatisation. *Unscharfe Bilder*, moreover, demonstrates the way in which a focus on 'German suffering' may lead to a decoupling of National Socialism from the Holocaust. In the face of the daughter's insistence on the historical context of her father's experience, Musbach demands to know: 'Was it not possible that a German from his generation could tell his totally private story without the question "And the Jews?" being raised at some point?' (*UB*, 100). Once the fate of 'the Jews' is set aside, all that remains of the experience of the wartime generation, is a 'private' family story. This narrative 'cleansing' of the Holocaust from the German experience may be observed, in fact, in a great many of the texts that attempt to represent Germans as victims of war and expulsion.

This presentation of Germans as victims via the 'privatisation' of political experience also features in Uwe Timm's *Am Beispiel meines Bruders* (2003). Timm's short memoir attempts to shed light on the private and political selves of his older brother, who died on the Eastern front in 1943 at the age of nineteen as a soldier in an *SS* death's head division. Timm's account is a fragmented narrative, consisting of extracts from his brother's sparse diary, historical documents and reflections, all embedded within a differentiated account of the experience of the war and the impact of defeat on his own family in the post-1945 period. What emerges is not so much a clearer, less ambiguous image of the brother as an impression of the historical and family context in which Timm himself grew up. *Am Beispiel meines Bruders* thus combines a compassionate approach to the brother's individual fate with a critical reflection on his own experience of life in the 1950s and early 1960s. The post-war West German family, with its internalised authoritarianism and obsession with defeat, is remembered as the origin of the rebellion of Timm's '68er generation.

Throughout his account, Timm remains focused on the broader historical and political context. A personal memory of the Hamburg firestorm is followed first by an extract from his brother's letter voicing his disbelief at the 'wicked' destruction of Hamburg and then by the sober, factual statement: 'Jews were prohibited from entering the air raid shelters'.[29] The effect of this montage technique is to identify 'ordinary' Germans as members of the Nazi 'people's community' even as the reader is confronted with the traumatic nature of their wartime experience. As such, Timm draws attention to the simultaneity and interconnectedness of 'German suffering' and German complicity. This insistence on historical integrity is comparatively rare in representations of the 'German experience'.

In his account of the post-war period, Timm chronicles the transformation of the experience of horror into formulaic language and anecdotes within the extended family, the latent violence in the family, at school and in society, and the continuing presence of Nazi jargon. War stories, it is suggested, made it possible for Germans to cope with the damage to their self-worth caused by the loss of the war. Timm's memoir is thus a reminder of the continuities, psychological and discursive, between wartime and post-war mentalities. The penetration of language by Nazi jargon, the 'mutilated language', is correlated with the visible physical mutilations, the narrator saw all around him, 'the limping, those who walked on crutches, the empty jacket sleeves, the upturned trouser legs, the squeaking artificial limbs' (*BB*, 101).

Timm reveals the manner in which the self-exculpatory narratives of those complicit in National Socialism serve not only to defer any engagement with guilt but also to give meaning to the suffering endured by this generation: 'Language was not only abused publicly by the perpetrators but also by those who said of themselves *we escaped by the skin of our teeth*. Thus they allocated themselves the role of victims' (*BB*, 107). The focus on the various deceptions employed by the parental generation, however, does not preclude the narrator's empathy with his father's suffering as a soldier. The narrator thus recalls one of the few occasions on which his father communicated a genuine sense of horror without resorting to the self-pity and grandiloquence that define his post-war self: 'As he was standing there crying, something of the horror of memory was present, not self-pity, an unspeakable suffering, and to my questions he just shook his head again and again' (*BB*, 103). Both Timm and Hahn are concerned with the rift between the generations. In *Am Beispiel meines Bruders*, however, a belated empathy with what an older generation of Germans suffered during the war is not allowed to degenerate into exculpation.

CONCLUSION

The Holocaust has been central to the public commemoration of National Socialism in Germany since the Auschwitz trials in Frankfurt in 1963, and all the more so from the late 1960s. In the 1980s, conservative historians such as Ernst Nolte, Andreas Hillgruber and Michael Stürmer attempted to detach 'ordinary' Germans' experience of the National Socialist period from the history of the Holocaust; this was only truly achieved, however, in the course of the debate about 'German wartime suffering' in the late 1990s and into the new millennium. Recent representations of 'German suffering' thus frequently tend either to deny the causal relationship between the trauma inflicted upon the victims of Nazism and the suffering endured by 'ordinary' Germans, or, as in the case of Forte, to blur the distinctions between them. The focus on 'German suffering', as such, frequently elides a critical confrontation with the Nazi past and serves instead to promote a sense of a collective national experience. This is certainly the case in Hahn's *Unscharfe Bilder*, which sentimentalises the trauma of German soldiers on the eastern front as part of a national heritage. In contrast, Grass's *Im Krebsgang* and Timm's *Am Beispiel meines Bruders* eschew an overly emotional identification in favour of a more complex historical picture.

In general, the debate about German wartime victims is a challenge to the cultural hegemony of the 68ers and to the conventional emphasis on German guilt. Indeed, a younger generation, which has grown up with images of Nazi atrocities, is now beginning to show an increasing interest in the German 'experience'. As the historical and political realities of the period recede, moreover, and become incomprehensible to a postmodern audience within the global consumer culture, the 'emotional immediacy' of wartime suffering is increasingly being marketed for contemporary Germans' consumption and entertainment. Germany, it seems, may be shedding its status as the 'perpetrator nation' in order to join an emerging global 'victim culture'.

NOTES

1. See Bill Niven, *Facing the Nazi Past* (London: Routledge, 2001).
2. Niven, *Facing the Nazi Past*, 2.
3. 'Die Deutschen als Opfer', *Der Spiegel*, 13 (25 March 2002), 36–64; 14 (30 March 2002), 58–73; 15 (8 April 2002), 56–66; 16 (15 April 2002), 62–68 and Clemens Höges, Cordula Meyer, Erich Wiedemann and Klaus Wiegrefe, 'Die verdrängte Tragödie', *Der Spiegel*, 6 (4 February 2002), 192–202.
4. See Harald Welzer, Sabine Moller and Caroline Tschuggnall, *Opa war kein Nazi: Nationalsozialismus und Holocaust im Familiengedächtnis* (Frankfurt: Fischer, 2002).
5. See Niven, *Facing the Nazi Past*, 175–93.
6. See Peter Schneider 'Deutsche als Opfer: Über ein Tabu der Nachkriegsgeneration' in Lothar Kettenacker, ed., *Ein Volk von Opfern? Die neue Debatte um den Bombenkrieg 1940–45* (Berlin: Rowohlt, 2003), 158–65, esp. 162–3.
7. See Friederike Eigler, *Gedächtnis und Geschichte in Generationenromanen seit der Wende* (Berlin: Erich Schmidt Verlag, 2005).

8. See Christopher R. Browning, *Ordinary Men: Reserve Police Batallion 101 and the Final Solution in Poland* (New York: HarperPerennial, 1992) and Harald Welzer, *Täter: Wie aus ganz normalen Menschen Massenmörder werden* (Frankfurt: Fischer, 2005).

9. W. G. Sebald, *Luftkrieg und Literatur* (Frankfurt: Fischer, 2001 [1999]), 1–2. Page numbers refer to the translation by Anthea Bell, 'Air War and Literature' in Sebald, *On the Natural History of Destruction* (London: Hamish Hamilton, 2003). Hereafter *LL*.

10. Volker Hage, ed., *Zeugen der Zerstörung: Die Literaten und der Luftkrieg* (Frankfurt: Fischer, 2003) and Hage, ed. *Hamburg 1943: Literarische Zeugnisse zum Feuersturm* (Frankfurt: Fisher 2003).

11. Dieter Forte, *Der Junge mit den blutigen Schuhen* (Frankfurt: Fischer, 1998 [1995]). Hereafter *JBS*.

12. See Forte, "Alles Vorherige war nur ein Umweg", interview with Volker Hage in Forte, *Schweigen oder sprechen* (Frankfurt: Fischer, 2002), 45–68, here 46.

13. Forte, 'Luftkrieg im Literaturseminar', in Forte, *Schweigen oder sprechen*, 31–36, here 33.

14. See Jan Assmann, *Das kulturelle Gedächtnis: Schrift, Erinnerung und politische Identität in frühen Hochkulturen* (Munich: Beck, 1997), 78.

15. Forte, "'Alles Vorherige war nur ein Umweg'", 62.

16. Forte, "'Alles Vorherige war nur ein Umweg'", 63.

17. See Helmut Schmitz, *On Their Own Terms: The Legacy of National Socialism in Post-1990 German Fiction* (Birmingham: University of Birmingham Press, 2004).

18. For a discussion of the presence of the internet in Grass's novella, see Kristin Veel, 'Virtual Memory in Günter Grass's *Im Krebsgang*', *German Life and Letters*, 57:2 (2004): 206–18.

19. Günter Grass, *Im Krebsgang* (Göttingen: Steidl, 2002), 108–9. Hereafter *K*. All page numbers refer to the translation by Krishna Winston (London: Faber & Faber, 2003).

20. See Stuart Taberner, "'Normalisation", the New Consensus on the Nazi Past and the Problem of German Wartime Suffering', *Oxford German Studies*, 31 (2002): 161–86, here 179.

21. See Bill Niven, *Facing the Nazi Past*, 143–74, here 144.

22. Ulla Hahn, *Unscharfe Bilder* (Munich, DVA, 2003). Hereafter *UB*.

23. *Kriegsbriefe gefallener Studenten 1939–1945*, ed. Walter Bähr and Hans W. Bähr (Tübingen: Wunderlich, 1952).

24. For a detailed discussion of Hahn's problematic use of historical sources see Helmut Schmitz, 'Reconciliation between the Generations: The Normalisation of the Image of the Ordinary German Soldier in Recent Literature' in Stuart Taberner and Paul Cooke, eds., *German Culture, Politics and Literature into the Twentieth Century: Beyond Normalization* (Rochester: Camden House, 2006), 151–66.

25. See Helmut Schmitz, 'The Birth of The Collective by The Spirit of Empathy' in Bill Niven, ed., *Germans as Victims: Remembering the Past in Contemporary Germany* (Basingstoke: Palgrave, 2006), 93–107.

26. See *Der Spiegel*'s report on the reception of *Der Untergang* at the German Historians' Conference, http://www.historikertag.uni-kiel.de/pressemit/SPIEGEL160904.htm (accessed 28 September 2006) and the internet forum *filmszene.de* for a popular reception of the film: http://www.filmszene.de/kino/u/untergang.html.

27. See Joachim Fest, Bernd Eichinger, *Der Untergang: Das Filmbuch* (Reinbek, Rowohlt, 1004), 458.

28. See Hans-Joachim Schröder, 'Erfahrungen deutscher Mannschaftssoldaten während der ersten Phase des Rußlandkrieges', in Bernd Wegner (ed.) *Zwei Wege nach Moskau: Vom Hitler-Stalin-Pakt zum Unternehmen 'Barbarossa'* (Munich: Piper, 1991), 309–325, here 321.

29. Uwe Timm, *Am Beispiel meines Bruders* (Cologne: Kiepenheuer & Witsch, 2003), 40. Hereafter *BB*.

CHAPTER 10

German literature in the Berlin Republic – writing by women

Lyn Marven

'Writing by women' potentially encompasses women writing, women writers and women's writing, that is, the social and cultural conditions regulating women's production of texts (and the further we go back in history the more significant this is);[1] the reception – and, more recently, marketing – of women as writers; and the thematic and aesthetic specificities (whatever may exist of these) of texts that are designated, or designate themselves, as women's writing. While it is difficult to separate completely the biographical and sociological from the thematic, particularly where women writers are concerned, this chapter focuses largely on textual matters, as well as interrogating critical discourse and approaches to writing by women.

Women are amply represented in post-*Wende* (after the fall of the Berlin Wall) German-language literature, especially in a younger generation of writers; the spurious designation *literarisches Fräuleinwunder* (literary girl-miracle) – intended to reflect the prominence of these younger writers – and the marketing of Judith Hermann in particular demonstrate, however, that the promotion and popular reception of women authors has not necessarily afforded them equal treatment.[2] Recent academic volumes also do not start from an assumption of equality achieved: Chris Weedon and Jo Catling's survey volumes have taken a non-essentialist, but still separatist approach in order to correct an imbalance which may now lie more in criticism of literature than in its production.[3] Other volumes by Leslie Adelson, Stephanie Bird, and Brigid Haines and Margaret Littler draw on a shift both in women's writing and in theoretical approaches to it: although they focus exclusively on women writers' texts, they look beyond 'woman' as a homogenised, privileged category of identity, instead working with an understanding of subjectivity derived from theory (often feminist theory) which emphasises positionality – the multiple discourses in and through which the subject is constructed and constructs itself.[4] This chapter recognises the importance and validity of both of these tendencies: the need to ensure that women writers (continue to) get commensurate coverage, and the need to go beyond categorisation and analysis on the basis of biography and biology.

It is clear that analyses of women's writing have not only raised significant questions for the study of literature, and played a role in feminist debates outside literature, but they continue to highlight relevant concerns, among which is the relevance of the author's sex (nationality, religion, etc.) for our reading.[5] This chapter does not want to have its cake and eat it – that is, by refusing to accept that women writers should be defined by their sex while drawing attention to women writers just because they are women – instead it exists because women writers continue to receive less attention than they may deserve, partly through a simple lack of recognition, and partly through the choice of parameters of study which – wrongly or rightly – exclude or minimise treatment of women writers. Moreover, it uses texts by younger women writers to interrogate the way in which these are read, and in order to allow for the serious themes highlighted through analysis of texts by women to be given attention in wider contexts.

Recent texts by older women writers focus on (usually first-person) woman narrators or on communication and relationships between women, and continue to thematise the coming to language of a female, or feminine, voice and form. Christa Wolf's first-person narrator in *Leibhaftig* (In Person, 2002) struggles to find language and her self in the wake of serious illness, and has a mentor and guide in the nurse, Cora Bachmann, whose name alludes to the intertextual influence of Ingeborg Bachmann on Wolf's work. Irina Liebmann's *Die freien Frauen* (The Free Women, 2004) is about relationships between women, both fictional and real; her protagonist has an imaginary correspondence with Sonja Trotzkij-Sammler and attempts to trace her alter ego Olga in Katowice. In *Endmoränen* (Terminal Moraines, 2002), Monika Maron's narrator is writing a biography of Wilhelmine Enke, lover of Friedrich Wilhelm II, and trying to come to terms with the loss of significance her writing has in unified Germany. Ulrike Kolb's *Diese eine Nacht* (This One Night, 2003) presents the opposite of Wolf's semi-conscious narrator: her text is the liberating stream of consciousness of a woman talking to her former lover, who is in a coma. While these texts do centre on, and take their form from, communication between women, they by no means exclude men – Wolf's protagonist depends on her husband as interlocutor; Liebmann's text ends with a renewed relationship between mother and son. What is most striking about these texts is, in fact, their representation of generational (including maternal) concerns: perhaps unsurprisingly, gender is far less significant than age for these protagonists and authors.

While these writers uphold a feminine aesthetic, a more distanced and ironic relation to feminist ideas can be seen in younger writers, particularly in recent texts by Karen Duve and Kathrin Schmidt. Their use of fantasy, as well as their representations of female characters, can be read as either tongue-in-cheek parody or uncritical pastiche. Karen Duve is undoubtedly one of the most commercially successful authors of recent times, though her work has been controversial, not least for its presentation of contentious subjects such as bulimia and its graphic depictions of violence. Moreover, it is disconcertingly difficult to decide whether the texts are parodic or simply formulaic, in their depictions of characters as well as their relationship to specific genres.[6] In Duve's take on the romance, *Die entführte Prinzessin* (The Princess who was Kidnapped, 2005) the princess of the title, Lisvana, is a feisty young woman who refuses to marry the prince who abducts her.[7] Duve's version has some funny and modern touches – one prince is a vegetarian, and there is opium and pre-marital sex – but it does not tackle the gendered conventions of the genre itself;[8] she sees no need to take a feminist stance, playing instead with what are clearly stereotyped characters and a knowing narrative voice. I return later in the chapter to Kathrin Schmidt's début novel, *Die Gunnar-Lennefsen-Expedition* (The Gunnar Lennefsen Expedition, 1998), a magical realist epic which associates woman and body to an extent, and in ways, that might be considered either essentialist or postfeminist. As in Duve's work, the question is whether the irony in the text masks a return to problematic values, or is critical of these even while citing them.

This adoption of 'genre' writing is a form of distancing, which is also evident in the many contemporary texts that use multiple narrators. Earlier women writers used the confessional first-person narrative form to delineate or construct a feminine subjectivity, and women's writing has often been associated with authenticity. These texts not only show the construction of the text through woven stories – a textuality which Wolf among others claims as a feminine form (particularly in the fourth lecture in *Kassandra*, 1983); they also represent a move into writing in role, something apparent in the choice of male narrators, and other devices which distance narrator and author. The distrust of over-arching, individual narratives which these forms may show is not limited to women – Ingo Schulze's *Simple Storys* (1998; see Paul Cooke's chapter in this volume for a discussion of the deliberate 'misspelling' of the title) is a novel in patchwork form – but perhaps represents a new development for women's writing. Wolf's *Medea* (1996) is a relatively early example of this form. Its subtitle, *Stimmen* (Voices), highlights the polyvocalism of the text's structure, though this is challenged by some critics, who note the privileging of Medea's story above the other characters' versions, as well as the constancy of Wolf's own distinctive voice.[9] Tanja Dückers's Berlin novel *Spielzone* (Play Zone, 1999) interweaves characters and places, giving multiple perspectives, in first and third person narratives with a wide range of narrators and focalisers, male, female, young and old. Julia Franck similarly presents a range of voices, including an old Polish woman and an American man, in *Lagerfeuer* (Campfire, 2003). Katja Lange-Müller's *Die Letzten: Aufzeichnungen aus Udo Posbichs Druckerei* (The Last Ones: Notes From Udo Posbich's Printworks, 2000) has a framework narrative within which are male voices, doubly ventriloquised by narrator Püppi and the author; and the perspective of Schmidt's *Koenigs Kinder* (Koenig's Children, 2002), almost entirely in *style indirect libre*, relates the thoughts of several characters revolving around the gay lawyer, Marl, at the same time as constructing a very different narrative through their connections to Koenig.

As the furthest step away from authenticity and the representation of women's experience in literature, staging a clear difference between author and narrator, the use of a male voice is relatively common, particularly in these multiple narratives. This transsexual writing is surprisingly disconcerting, raising as it does questions about gendered language use – do women and men speak differently? Can women write convincingly as men, and vice versa? The texts just mentioned by Wolf, Franck, Dückers and Lange-Müller all contain male voices. Terézia Mora's *Seltsame Materie* (Strange Materials, 1999) is a montage with two narratives with male first-person narrators. Yadé Kara chooses a Turkish-German teenage boy as the narrator of *Selam Berlin* (2003); Jeanette Lander's *Robert* (1998) is also written in a first-person, male voice – a further distancing device from this non-native writer of German. Franziska Gerstenberg claims to write in male and female voices in her collection *Wie viel Vögel* (How Many Birds, 2004), though only the merest details give clues to which, even in sexually explicit texts. One of the most acclaimed texts in recent years, Judith Hermann's *Sommerhaus, später* (Summerhouse, Later, 1998), has a male narrator in the tale 'Sonja'.[10] Moreover, the narrator of the title story, though usually taken to be a woman,[11] is in fact grammatically ambiguous; his/her sex cannot be deduced if one does not assume either heterosexuality (the narrator's group of friends have shifting homosexual and heterosexual relationships, as does Stein, with whom the narrator has had a relationship) or a correspondence of author's and narrator's sex. Cross-gender narrators are by no means particular to women writers – Schulze's text, and Marcel Beyer's, *Flughunde* (The Karnau Tapes, 1995) feature female narrators, for example, and the phenomenon is not confined to contemporary literature – but they are significant, as they undermine the assumption of authenticity (with its implicit dismissal of creativity) that has marked the reception of women writers' work.

A similar effect is achieved by unreliable narrators, whose playful or provocative stance subverts the personal narrative and, moreover, cuts across the dichotomy of ludic versus confessional writing.[12] Their relationship to the reader is also a different one from the literature of identification (*Identifikationsliteratur*) which was an earlier standard of women's writing.[13] Later in this chapter I consider how Kerstin Młynkec reclaims the picaresque in her impressive début novel, *Drachentochter* (Dragon's Daughter, 2004). The pseudo-autobiographical form of the picaresque is evident in Kerstin Hensel's earlier *Tanz am Kanal* (Dance by the Canal, 1994), which has been read as an authentic narrative by an unreliable narrator.[14] Emine Sevgi Özdamar's novel *Das Leben ist eine Karawanserai. Hat zwei Türen. Aus einer kam ich rein. Aus der anderen ging ich raus* (Life is a Caravanserai: has two doors. I came in one. I went out the other, 1992) also has elements of the picaresque, and is especially interesting in invoking the author's own autobiography, as well as creating a fictional one. Reception of writing in German by non-native speakers, like earlier reception of writing by women, has tended to assume authenticity and a biographical link with the author, however highly constructed the fiction; Özdamar's magical realist narrative counters this.[15] These narratives thematise writing as a form of self-expression, performance, or self-creation, and highlight fictionality, seen most clearly in the self-confessed liar narrators in Katja Lange-Müller's *Verfrühte Tierliebe* (Premature Animal Love, 1995), or Melanie Arns's, *Heul doch!* (Go on, Cry!, 2005). A less exaggerated but perhaps more pervasive development is that of the unsympathetic narrator, such as those in Duve's short stories in *Keine Ahnung* (No Idea, 1999) or Julia Franck's *Der neue Koch* (The New Cook, 1997) and *Liebediener* (Love on Demand, 1999), where it is uncertain whether we are supposed to believe the narrators, never mind empathise with them. Franck's work plays with this ambiguity and uncertainty, which arises from the interior monologue style of the texts: in *Der neue Koch*, the reader may find the narrator self-indulgent, petulant and possibly paranoid, but it gradually becomes apparent that she is in fact being manipulated by the cook; the revelations at the end of *Liebediener* grant credibility in retrospect to the narrator's suspicions and incessant analysis of her relationship with Albert.

Whilst these texts demonstrate that women writers and narrators have no need to represent all women, or be exemplary figures of identification,

Duve's work shows that, where such narrators verge on the delusional and pathological, this remains problematic. In Duve's *Dies ist kein Liebeslied* (This is not a Love Song, 2002), Anne Strelau narrates her eating disorder and obsession with her body and weight with some irony, both inviting empathy and challenging it, but ultimately her narrative presents a self-image which seems uncomfortably close to disordered, and the text itself runs the risk of simply confirming that women are obsessed with their weight, amongst other stereotypical notions.

Narratives of the body are conventionally a subject of women's writing, particularly in presenting an understanding of gender and its representation. In *Stimme der Medusa* (Medusa's Voice), Sigrid Weigel claims that women's presence within literature has been either as disembodied (non-gendered) voices, or voiceless bodies; women's writing reacted by linking female subjectivity to the expression of bodily experiences.[16] While bodies do not have to be limited to women's writing, themes of sexuality, eroticism and disorders of the body are still apparent in contemporary women's writing, perhaps becoming more extreme in content while moving away from connecting these to language or aesthetic strategies. Descriptions of sex as act and experience are provocative, explicit, with deliberate deviancy, expressing a complex relationship between sexuality and identity: Dückers's *Spielzone* ranges from a young girl's thoughts of sex, through lesbian mothers, threesomes, dildos and bizarre turn-ons. In Franck's *Liebediener*, sex is a transaction, neither congruent with, nor independent of, an emotional relationship; her collection *Bauchlandung* (Belly Flop, 2000) invokes incest and casual adultery. By way of contrast, the texts in Hermann's *Nichts als Gespenster* (Nothing But Ghosts, 2003) present sharing a bed as a largely platonic act, divorced of sex and relationships, while eroticism is located elsewhere. The final text I analyse is Ulrike Draesner's *Mitgift* (Legacy, 2002), which deals with the disruption of gender, sex and body image in its narratives of anorexia and hermaphroditism.

Kathrin Schmidt's 1998 début novel, *Die Gunnar-Lennefsen-Expedition* is set in the GDR in 1976. Her young protagonist, Josepha, lives with her great grandmother, Theresa, and works in a calendar factory. Josepha gets pregnant after a one-night stand with an Angolan visitor, and during the next nine months the two women reconstruct the family history by undertaking an imaginary expedition, under the name of the fictional Gunnar Lennefsen. The Schlupfburg women have magic powers, and the history, and also the text, focuses on extraordinary stories of sex and birth and is full of wilfully independent child-bearing. With her dying breath, Theresa inflates a hot air balloon made from the silk screen on which they watch the imaginary history, and Josepha and her 'black and white child' sail away from the GDR. Pertinent to considering the text's relation to women's writing are the use of fantasy, the concentration on female characters and a maternal genealogy, and Schmidt's focus on the body, sex and particularly reproduction.

This epic feminist fantasy set in the GDR recalls Irmtraud Morgner and her influential Salman-Trilogy; a comparison of the two shows how far Schmidt's text is from Morgner's earlier feminism, and illuminates the changed literary context of post-*Wende* Germany.[17] The opening sentence of Morgner's *Leben und Abenteuer der Trobadora Beatriz* (The Life and Adventures of Trobadora Beatrice, 1974) – 'Of course this country is a land where wonders happen' – was a plea; the GDR was not in fact a place for fantasy.[18] For Morgner the literary mode stood in a wider sense for utopian thinking. She brought in the fantastic, in the guise of the reincarnated *trobairitz* Beatriz de Dia, as a means of reinvigorating literature and, through it, the GDR. Her use was political and, specifically, feminist: fantasy was both counterpart and corrective to technology, the posited motor for progress in socialism, and based on masculine, rationalist thinking. Schmidt takes Morgner's opening challenge as fact and imputes magical powers to a real woman: Josepha has no counterpart as Morgner's single mother Laura has the legendary Beatriz. But her fantasy is set in the past, and is coupled with an ironic form of nostalgia that denies the form's futuristic possibilities; its ultimate manifestation is an escape from the state. In the literary context of reunified Germany in the late 1990s, Schmidt has no need to argue for the literary freedom that Morgner was advocating; using fantasy is not a political statement and thus lacks its utopian potential. Schmidt's text seems to treat the setting, the genre and the politics with the same irony and distance.

The sheer corporeality of *Die Gunnar-Lennefsen-Expedition*, I would argue, is also subject to irony, visible not least in the fantastic exaggeration. In both content and form, Schmidt's text is based on the irreducible fact of reproduction as a defining function of the female sexed body, and it raises the question of how (women) authors can write about women and their bodies without reducing them to those bodies. Does the self-consciousness of the text – the intertextuality and especially the arch narrative voice – save Schmidt from the charge of biological essentialism? Reproduction is the source of the extraordinary capabilities of the Schlupfburg women,

and a panoply of women conceive and give birth in weird and wonderful ways: Ottilie's pregnancy is either years long, or comes to full term
in an extraordinary three months, depending on which point one takes
as conception, and her son has three fathers. A more mythical example is
the creation of Adam Rippe, cut from ribs of a god by the Russian Ljusja
Andrejewna Wandrowskaja; Ljusja takes the role of creator in a despairing,
or desperate, attempt to be a mother. Morgner draws on this same biblical image in *Das heroische Testament* (Hero's Testament, 1998), the final,
unfinished instalment of the Salman trilogy, also published in 1998, and
also reverses genders: Hero cuts the male character Leander, aka Désiré,
from her own ribs as a scientific project to create the perfect lover. While
Morgner reworks the Biblical story to include female desire, creation and
creativity, Schmidt's Ljusja avoids sex out of fear of men's lust. Her version seems retrogressive and reductive compared with Morgner's revision,
though Morgner's utopian, fantastic science is also born of despair; it is
anti-erotic, and focuses both creation and imagination (the unreal) on
reproduction.

It is this physicality which divides critics and reviewers, and illustrates
the potential problems of a 'postfeminist' stance. Peter Graves criticises
the almost exclusive focus on female rather than male members of the
family, and suggests that the text 'reduces the battle of the sexes to mere
biology'.[19] If one views gender relations through the lens of a 'battle of
the sexes', the dominance of the narrative by female characters might well
appear to constitute ascendancy; however, if that is the case, it is due to
magical, therefore unreal, reproductive abilities rather than real biology.
Moreover, the text does also show the actual – historical, physical – power
of men over women; and recognises men's emotional involvement as equal
to biological paternity. But magical occurrences notwithstanding, this is
not 'mere' biology: reproduction underlines the fact that there are indeed
irreducible physical differences between the sexes – to acknowledge this is
not, however, to support sexism, or to assume that this makes the sexes
antagonistic.

Schmidt uses pregnancy as her narrative impetus: Josepha's pregnancy is
the spur to the women's imaginary expedition, a recurring theme in their
genealogical adventures, and underlies the form of the text itself, which
frames the nine months of pregnancy. Hers is a deliberately partial focus,
seen also in the insistence that this expedition is 'female' ('weiblich'), in 'the
Gunnar Lennefsen Expedition, which they hoped would take them into
the northernmost reaches of their female memories',[20] and repeated later in
the paragraph in the 'legitimisation for a female departure' (*GLE*, 19). The

tautology of the adjective suggests its use is ironic – certainly a non-ironic use would sit uncomfortably with the easy reference to the male reader in the fifth line of the text (*GLE*, 9): Schmidt not only avoids the politically correct use of the feminine form, but also appears to be assuming that male readers will read the text. Moreover, the distinctive, visible narrative voice, the sheer exuberance of the text, its irony and exaggeration, all suggest that this is an intentional – though not critical – citing of a mode of writing. In this respect, the text remains more of a literary pastiche than a parody, as does Duve's *Die entführte Prinzessin*, though it still feeds into current feminist debates. We can see Schmidt as a follower of Morgner, whose feminism and trailblazing representation of sexuality made such writing possible. In the late 1990s, Schmidt celebrates the female body and sexuality, without repressing its dark side; she takes Morgner's themes much further, and is actually able to do what Morgner's texts aimed for – and, for good measure, she projects it back into the state which had been so constrictive. However, in doing so, Schmidt seems to retreat from Morgner's universal aims; and her determined focus on the female body implies that reunified Germany still fails to give this adequate representation.

ANTI-AUTHENTICITY

Kerstin Młynkec's *Drachentochter* is the fictional autobiography of an unnamed, female narrator, born into the Sorbian minority within the GDR – all of which identities are deconstructed within the course of the novel. The narrator's outsider, critical perspective is combined with a highly poetic, yet also self-conscious narrative within the mode of the picaresque. Of interest here are the use of picaresque mode itself, which is predicated on a male protagonist, and the deconstruction of a stable identity.

Młynkec's novel displays most of the key aspects which Claudio Guillén uses to define the picaresque.[21] The *pícaro* figure is, along with the pseudo-biographical form, the main feature, and Młynkec's narrator is typical: she is an outsider and effectively an orphan – born to a poor thirteen-year-old mother in rural East Germany, she is unwanted and abused, repeatedly passed from hand to hand. Picaresque characters are often of semi-noble birth, which Młynkec amusingly updates in the narrator's belated discovery that she had been swapped at birth and was actually the daughter of a 'politically acceptable family'.[22] The episodic narration encompasses her abused childhood, time in the Walter Ulbricht children's home and other hostels, unsuccessful forays into work, and spells as horse-whisperer, photographer and gallery-owner; the narrator travels in Prenzlauer Berg and Sorbian villages, and finally to South America. Hardship and violence stress the physicality of the narrator's experience, and the materiality of the picaresque is evident in the recurring motif of potatoes with linseed oil, a traditional Sorbian dish. The first-person narrative limits our perspective to hers, which is wilfully uncomprehending and asocial, though its obscurity and unreliability arises as much through poetic devices as from her naive view.[23] It also breaks out of conventional narrative boundaries: her autobiography begins with the act of conception, in the 'Vorspiel' (foreplay/foreword), with occasional prolepsis signalling her contemporary perspective, and the text seems to end in the future, in the 'Nachspiel' (afterword), in a self-referential moment where the narrator is interrupted by her editor for the manuscript.

Where Mlynkec's text diverges from some models of the picaresque is in lacking a sense of the moral ascent of the protagonist. Her narrator is defiant, rather than regretful – her last words are 'you arseholes' (*Dt*, 288) – and she satirises the moralistic narrative: after a murderous fantasy concerning her biological parents, she adds, in parentheses, 'Dear children. Please don't try this at home. And if you do, then take to the barricades properly' (*Dt*, 285), undercutting any didactic aim with her more revolutionary alternative. Modern picaresque texts often use an unreliable, immoral or amoral narrator (such as Günter Grass's Oskar Matzerath in his *Die Blechtrommel* (The Tin Drum, 1959)) as an indirect indictment of society's morals, and while the narrator is no model, this does not, of course, preclude criticism of the GDR, the 'cage for seven million [people]' (*Dt*, 174). In this context, the anti-moralistic picaresque is also a rebuff to the variants of the *Bildungsroman* and other such exemplary texts prescribed by Socialist Realism (the narrator's mother's surname, only revealed at her funeral, is 'Kunst': Art).

The fact that the *pícaro* is continually thwarted in his ambition (the narrative necessity underlying the episodic, open text) has led critics to claim that the picaresque is reactionary rather than subversive, confirming social attitudes rather than challenging them. The question of parodic citation also applies to the gendering of the picaresque through the figure of the *pícara*: to what extent can a female character be used to appropriate a narrative form which is predicated on a male experience?[24] And what use is the mode to women writers? Like the figure of the *flâneur/flâneuse*, which has been subject to feminist revision recently to acknowledge the gendered nature of the archetype and reconsider how it may be appropriated for, or modified to, women's experience, the genre of the picaresque has hitherto been defined in relation to the possibilities of the (male) *pícaro*. The genre's setting in the 'here-and-now' dictates that the protagonist is confined to contemporary historical possibilities, or else deemed unrealistic and therefore not picaresque. Social possibilities for women have altered radically during the twentieth and twenty-first centuries, particularly within the officially (constitutionally) equal society of the GDR in which Młynkec's novel is set. If we accept that the figure of the *pícaro* (*pícara*) and the pseudo-autobiographical form are the main defining features of the mode, there seems to be no reason to discount modern texts with a female protagonist from the picaresque. It is not only the sex of the narrator that matters though: the author's sex is also significant. James Mandrell writes of early novels with *pícara* narrators (which are not always allowed as picaresque) that 'these female protagonists of picaresque novels were written by men; bypassing questions of the aims of representation, suffice it to say that these are, therefore, neither "true" nor "real life" accounts by a "woman".[25] The picaresque is thus emblematic of this association of protagonist and author which has been key in the reception of writing by women. Młynkec's text shows one of many ways in which the voice of the narrator, or protagonist, and the author can be uncoupled.

Młynkec plays with the genre of picaresque as fictional autobiography, further hinting at similarities between 'I' ('ich') and herself. The author's biographical description inside the book recalls the narrator's, and the photo on the cover – a close-up of a woman's face – is taken by the author; 'ich' also works as a photographer before turning to writing. There are two dedications, on separate pages: one to 'my daughter Katyržinka', presumably by the author; a second to Erla Mia (one of very few recurring characters), 'in the last case Patricia'. The thematising of pseudo-autobiography is also achieved in the narrator's mise-en-abyme invention of the short-lived persona ICH, who acts out ich's personality and other alternative roles, even projected into the future. It allows the expression of her self at a distance and, as a device, it represents the distance that the narrator feels from her own story, and her body.

Every aspect of the narrator's identity comes into question within the text: she rejects gendered limitations, insisting on fighting boys in the children's home, for example. When she does display a female/feminine identity, it is performed, cited from another performer, who turns out to be a transvestite sailor in character as Pippilotti Popoke. Pippilotti is referred to in the narrative as 'she'; and she rejects the narrator when the narrator begins to kiss 'delicately like a woman' (*Dt*, 162). Despite, or perhaps because of, sexual abuse in her childhood, harassment as an adult, and experimentation with sexuality and orientation, however, the narrator's

womanhood is rarely central to her identity; it is just one of many elements
of identity which are deconstructed. First her paternity, then the identity
of her mother is called into question, and though she takes on the minority
national identity of the Sorbs, learning the language and discovering the
history and culture, this, too, is thrown into uncertainty with the revelation of her birth. Born on the provincial coast, she is an outsider in Berlin,
though she does not belong in her home town either. Finally, as a child
she identifies with animals, expressed through associations and frequent
metaphors, in a further sign of her marginal perspective, subverting what
is human from its very borders.

Młynkec's vibrant, subversive novel presents a challenge to reception of
women writers in several ways. Through the genre of the picaresque she contests the notion that women's writing is a site of privileged authenticity, and
her novel treats the 'feminine' as only one among many aspects of identity.
The text shows gender as a performance or construct, within the performative mode of the pseudo-biography; the gendering of the picaresque
through a female narrator, and woman author, in turn also reflects on the
definition of the genre. The narrator's physicality is in fact more a form
of traumatised disembodiment, but highlights *ex negativo* the embodiedness of the protagonist, who can only escape her body through narrating.
This physicality which is a feature of the genre is something that the text
shares with both Schmidt and Ulrike Draesner, whose *Mitgift* engages with
narratives of bodies.

A THIRD WAY, THE THIRD SEX

Gendered bodies and narratives of physicality are at the centre of Ulrike
Draesner's 2002 novel, *Mitgift*, which explores the embodiedness of our
existence in the world, emphasising lived experience over theory, through
its tale of two sisters, one anorexic and the other hermaphrodite. Draesner's third-person narrative concentrates on elder sister Aloe, who develops
anorexia as an adult; the tale of her younger sister Anita's body is the traumatic centre of the narrative, inseparable from its implications for Aloe and
her body. Anita, born a female pseudo-hermaphrodite,[26] has surgery as a
child to normalise her genitalia and lives as a woman, even modelling, and
has a child of her own, but later decides to change (back) to a male body,
and is killed by her husband. The 'Mitgift', 'legacy', of the title is both lit-
eral and symbolic, chromosomal, legal and psychological – the 'Gift' in the
word 'Mitgift', moreover, also means poison. It links the generations; Aloe
herself, Lukas (her boyfriend) and Anita, dealing with the effects of their

upbringing and what they inherited, in the widest sense, from their parents and their wartime experiences; and Anita's son Stefan, whom Aloe adopts after her murder. Not only does the novel thematise and discuss discourses of the body, but, through its striking image of the hermaphrodite Anita, it also suggests a comparison with Jeffrey Eugenides' *Middlesex* (2002)[27] – about the hermaphrodite Calliope/Cal – which allows us to move beyond limiting assumptions of women's writing to consider how themes and narrative form, body and language, can be linked.

The narrative of Aloe's anorexia is intertwined with the other stories: through her retracing her memories, the text becomes less a clinical psychological history than a symbolic, family history. The narrativity of the condition is stressed by the structure of novel: in order to tell Anita's story, Aloe has to tell her own – or, rather, she can't tell Anita's tale without its effects on her relationship to her own body; and the unravelling of the pathology of her anorexia leads – structurally, but probably also etiologically – to childhood memories which centre on Anita. Aloe's relationship with fellow student Lukas is linked with food even at its inception: how he eats trout determines whether she will sleep with him; and at the same time she starts dieting as a response to stress. These two factors seem to lead into anorexia as her relationship with Lukas falters. Aloe's anorexia is a psychologically plausible response to pressure, and her desire to look beautiful (meaning thin) – 'the others became fat, she became beautiful'[28] – recalls references to 'Anita Aphrodita' (*M*, 71), and the paradoxically feminine beauty of the hermaphrodite body.[29] Aloe's aim is to be 'identical with the type of woman who waved from the posters, streamlined and beautiful, a dolphin, firm as a phallus, wrapped in the glow of self-control and the prevention of uncontrolled reproduction' (*M*, 133): Aloe's thoughts, in *style indirect libre*, clearly evoke the image of Anita as swimmer which recurs as a visual motif in the text. The phrasing here in the German plays on the ambiguous term 'Typ' (type, but also person or man), allowing the trick of using the male pronoun to describe a woman, a form of grammatical hermaphroditism. Significantly, and symbolically, her dieting un-genders Aloe's body. A side-effect of anorexia is to disturb androgen production; Aloe is informed by her doctor that she might develop male secondary sexual characteristics. Anita is thus linked with the goals and effects of anorexia – beauty and androgyny – on a level of narrative symbolism, as well as in the possible psychological motivation for Aloe's disorder.

Anita herself is only ever described in retrospect, both narratively (the story works backwards, and through several layers of chronology and narrative, to her and the twin traumas of her body and her death) and also physically (her body exists only in its post-operative image). Discussion of an 'original' body is deflected onto its constructions: one imposed on Anita by her parents, which represses her difference and (over-)emphasises her femininity, and Anita's own later choice to take a male form which is no less (re-)constructed:

– But it's an illusion to presume you can go back to something.
– I know, whispered Anita, I know . . . But for me, Lollo, it's simply about my everyday life. For me it's about a possibility that was put in me. I want to make it real. Otherwise I'll just be living out one half of myself, do you understand? (*M*, 359)

Anita's pragmatic, phenomenological approach stresses that authenticity and experience are not the sole property of an original body. While Anita is concerned with her daily lived experience, it is Aloe who becomes obsessed with hermaphrodites and the often mythical, mystical discourses surrounding their image.

The narrative structure removes the hermaphroditic body from the textual gaze, instead filtering it through Aloe's memory, and describing it only when it is exposed to Aloe's gaze: 'the place between Anita's legs, the small projection between the lips, around which two bloody crusts curled like tiny snakes . . . . What Aloe saw was worth a clip round the ear. A squashed, coiled worm on a white and pink leaf. With threads running through' (*M*, 171). Anita, as a girl with a penis, counters Freud's view of the female body as a visible absence of male form – what Luce Irigaray calls the 'rien á voir'. Here the penis is missing from the female body, but Anita doesn't consider her body to have a *lack*, rather she refers to her 'also male body' (*M*, 355), a simultaneity or superimposition of possibilities which does not posit an originary body to which she can return. This key memory portrays the (sight of the) uncanny body as taboo (and indescribable – note the use of similes and metaphors). As punishment, Aloe is made to stand naked on view in the living room behind a glass door; being confronted with her own body and exposed to others' gazes is her chastisement, and it seems to have consequences for Aloe's relationship to her own body, as well as linking to other recurring motifs of viewing: porn, photography and Lukas's scientific gaze in astronomy. Aloe's awareness of her own body which underlies her anorexia is a distortion of her gaze. The sisters' reconciliation is symbolised in Aloe's permitted gaze at her sister's now ambiguous form, as Anita exposes her torso to demonstrate her changing shape. And Aloe takes up photography again when she recovers from anorexia; she cuts off her long hair when Anita is killed (just as Anita had cut her hair as part of her change) and takes a photo of her own shaven head. Though she turns her gaze on herself, she externalises it through the camera and stylises herself into an image, for her own consumption. Like Spencer Tunick's nudes, the image plays with gender attributes and goes beyond them: 'Tunick's photos sucked the meaning from bodies. Male, female – even this began to dissolve' (*M*, 243). It is the precision, the detail of the gaze – and the focus on the body as it is – which frees it from conventional meaning.

Though the themes treated in Draesner's text – the body, the gaze, sexuality – are associated with women's writing, and are frequently taken up in feminist critical theory or literary criticism, they are by no means limited to this gendered context. Draesner destabilises the gender signification of bodies, not least through the striking image of Anita–Axel. To shift the focus to representation, and the interaction of themes and form, we need only compare *Mitgift* with Jeffrey Eugenides' *Middlesex*, also about a hermaphrodite. Eugenides uses a first-person narrative for his protagonist, who is brought up as a girl (Calliope) but whose male genitalia develop at puberty and who then adopts a male persona (Cal), though refuses medical intervention. The non-gender-marked first-person pronoun gives a continuity of perspective even through a radical shift in self which calls into question both sex and gender (though occasionally Cal uses the third person to refer to Calliope, to emphasise the distance, or an external viewpoint) – whereas Draesner's Anita is fixed within the feminine pronoun, taking on the masculine only in Aloe's daydreams of a possible post-operation trip to the sea. Whereas Anita's chromosomal heritage is not explored, Cal's narrative traces the genetic mutation responsible for her/his condition back to an incestuous liaison, but narratives arise around the body in both texts, set within family histories and linked to historical traumas and wars. While the central image in both texts addresses notions of gender and the sexed body, it also goes beyond this to symbolise the very stuff of fiction: the perspective and the creation of narratives.

CONCLUSION, CONTINUITIES AND CORRESPONDENCES

Striking in all three of the texts I have examined is the physicality of the narrative, but while the texts insist on the embodiedness of the characters' experience, they do not posit this as natural or authentic. This is most visible in the images of non-biological motherhood, in the fantastic occurrences in Schmidt's *Die Gunnar-Lennefsen-Expedition* and in Draesner's text when Anita wants to become Axel, and thus a father to her son, and

Aloe becomes a 'mother' to her sister's son; but it is also in the exaggerated descriptions of the effects of violence on her body that the unreliability – or fictionality – of Młynkec's narrator's story becomes apparent. The refusal of authenticity, at the same time as insisting on corporeality, represents a shift away from previous tropes of women's writing; it opens up points of comparison with other literatures. Examining these texts through their relation to women's writing also brings up fundamental questions of literary strategies: the functioning of irony and parody; the definition of genres; and the relation of content to form, perspective and narrative.

It goes without saying that writing by women does not only concern itself with women – the texts in this chapter also cover the experience of childhood or ageing, the history of the Sorbs, minority identity and language, the end of the GDR and the legacy of German history. If anything, this is perhaps the lasting development, which also implies a separation of political and literary aims: women writers do not write only as women. Does this mean that in contemporary Germany literature and self-realisation are no longer linked, or does it assume that progress in society is such that literary texts no longer need to 'represent'? It is perhaps just evidence of a generational shift among critics as well as authors, and as such indicative of contemporary thinking. Certainly, one cannot deny that much remains to be done politically, and there is still a place, and indeed a need, for texts which draw attention to the experience of women in the real world or challenge notions of gender and sexuality. What recent texts show us is that these thematic concerns can, and should, be separated from the author – but they cannot be separated from the literary strategies of the text.

NOTES

The writing of this chapter was generously supported by Leverhulme funding and a grant from the DAAD.

1. See Jo Catling, ed., *A History of Women's Writing in Germany, Austria and Switzerland* (Cambridge: Cambridge University Press, 2000).
2. Volker Hage's unfortunate term was coined in 'Literarisches Fräuleinwunder' and 'Ganz schön abgedreht', *Der Spiegel*, 12 (22 March 1999), 7, 244–6; Peter Graves takes issue with it in 'Karen Duve, Kathrin Schmidt, Judith Hermann: "Ein literarisches Fräuleinwunder"?', *German Life and Letters*, 55:2 (2002): 196–207. See also Stuart Taberner, *German Literature of the 1990s and Beyond: Normalization and the Berlin Republic* (New York: Camden House, 2005), 16–23.
3. Chris Weedon, ed., *Postwar Women's Writing in German* (Oxford: Berghahn, 1997).

4. Leslie Adelson, *Making Bodies, Making History: Feminism and German Identity* (Lincoln, NE: University of Nebraska Press, 1993); Stephanie Bird, *Women Writers and National Identity: Bachmann, Duden, Özdamar* (Cambridge: Cambridge University Press, 2003); Brigid Haines and Margaret Littler, *Contemporary German Women's Writing: Changing the Subject* (Oxford: Oxford University Press, 2004).

5. I use the term sex, rather than gender, deliberately. Toril Moi suggests that limiting gender to two categories preserves its derivation from biology rather than enabling subversive performativity, and that without this link, the term thus tends towards simply denoting identity as opposed to physicality, *What is a Woman? And Other Essays* (Oxford: Oxford University Press, 1999).

6. Elizabeth Boa looks at the blurring of generic boundaries in 'Lust or Disgust? The Blurring of Boundaries in Karen Duve's *Regenroman*' in Heike Bartel and Elizabeth Boa, eds., *Pushing at Boundaries: Approaches to Contemporary German Women Writers from Karen Duve to Jenny Erpenbeck* (Amsterdam: Rodopi, 2006), 57–72.

7. Karen Duve, *Die entführte Prinzessin* (Frankfurt: Eichborn, 2005).

8. See Alison Lewis on the romance and the quest narrative, which Irmtraud Morgner used to subvert both the genre's gendered conventions and the restrictions of the GDR, in *Subverting Patriarchy: Feminism and Fantasy in the Works of Irmtraud Morgner* (Oxford: Berg, 1995).

9. See Bird, *Women Writers and National Identity*, 1–8, and Helen Bridge, 'Christa Wolf's *Kassandra* and *Medea*: Continuity and Change', *German Life and Letters*, 57:1 (2004): 33–43.

10. Judith Hermann, *Sommerhaus, später* (Frankfurt: Fischer, 1998).

11. Both Graves, in '"Ein literarisches Fräuleinwunder"?', and Taberner, in *German Literature of the 1990s and Beyond* and in this volume, assume that the narrator is a woman.

12. See Genia Schulz, 'Kein Chorgesang: Neue Schreibweisen bei Autorinnen (aus) der DDR', in Heinz Ludwig Arnold, ed., *Bestandsaufnahme Gegenwartsliteratur* (Munich: text + kritik, 1988), 212–25.

13. See Angelika Bammer, 'Feminism, *Frauenliteratur*, and Women's Writing of the 1970s and 1980s', in Catling, ed., *A History of Women's Writing*, 216–32, esp. 226–7.

14. See Reinhild Steingröver and Jennifer Ruth Hosek's essays in Beth Linklater and Birgit Dahlke, eds., *Kerstin Hensel* (Cardiff: University of Wales Press, 2002).

15. See Margit Fröhlich, 'Reinventions of Turkey: Emine Sevgi Özdamar's *Life is a Caravanserai*' in Karen Jankowsky and Carla Love, eds., *Other Germanies: Questioning Identity in Women's Literature and Art* (Albany, New York: State University of New York Press, 1997), 56–73.

16. Sigrid Weigel, *Die Stimme der Medusa: Schreibweisen in der Gegenwartsliteratur von Frauen*, 2nd edition (Dülmen-Hiddingsel: tende, 1995), 112.

17. Schmidt admits that Morgner is an influence on the text, along with the magical realism of Günter Grass and Gabriel García Márquez: see Kathrin Schmidt,

'Im Wattenmeer der Utopie: Wie zufällig mir Günter Grass begegnete', *Freitag* (7 July 2000), http://www.freitag.de/2000/28/00281601.htm (accessed 15 February 2005).

18. Irmtraud Morgner, *Leben und Abenteuer der Trobadora Beatriz nach Zeugnissen ihrer Spielfrau Laura: Roman in dreizehn Büchern und sieben Intermezzos* (Berlin: Aufbau, 1974); available in English translation as *The Life and Adventures of Trobadora Beatrice as Chronicled by Her Minstrel Laura: A Novel in Thirteen Books and Seven Intermezzos*, trans. Jeanette Clausen (Lincoln, NE: University of Nebraska Press, 2000), translation of this first sentence modified.

19. Graves, ' "Ein literarisches Fräuleinwunder"?', 203.

20. Kathrin Schmidt, *Die Gunnar-Lennefsen-Expedition* (Cologne: Kiepenheuer & Witsch, 1998), 18. Hereafter *GLE*.

21. Claudio Guillén, 'Towards a Definition of the Picaresque' in Guillén, *Literature as System: Essays Toward The Theory of Literary History* (Princeton, NJ: Princeton University Press, 1971), 71–106.

22. Kerstin Mlynkec, *Drachentochter* (Berlin: Rowohlt, 2004). Hereafter *Dt.*

23. Compare Tanja Nause's article, 'Reduction, Regression, Silence: A Critical Look Beyond The Category of The Picaresque' in Arthur Williams, Stuart Parkes and Julian Preece, eds., *German-Language Literature Today: International and Popular?* (Oxford: Peter Lang, 2000), 173–96, which suggests that the naive perspective is a defining factor in contemporary picaresque-type narratives.

24. Judith Butler uses parody as a model of subversion of gender; see *Gender Trouble: Feminism and the Subversion of Identity* (New York: Routledge, 1999 [1990]), esp. 174–7.

25. James Mandrell, 'Questions of Genre and Gender: Contemporary American Versions of the Feminine Picaresque', *NOVEL: A Forum on Fiction*, 20:2 (Winter 1987): 149–70, here 153.

26. See Armand Marie Leroi, *Mutants* (London: HarperCollins, 2003), chapter 7, for a readable explanation of the different forms of hermaphroditism: female pseudohermaphrodites have female reproductive organs, plus male genitalia (Anita has both womb and a penis), whereas true hermaphrodites have both sets.

27. Jeffrey Eugenides, *Middlesex* (London: Bloomsbury, 2002).

28. Ulrike Draesner, *Mitgift* (Munich: Luchterhand, 2002), 77. Hereafter *M.*

29. Again, see Leroi, *Mutants*, 235.

CHAPTER II

Cultural memory and identity formation in the Berlin Republic

Margaret Littler

Doesn't immigrating to Germany also mean immigrating to the recent German past?

Zafer Şenocak[1]

The contexts for this chapter are German memory debates since the 1990s and an academic preoccupation with collective memory as a normative discourse of shared values and cultural identity.[2] Since unification, Germany has witnessed what Andreas Huyssen calls a 'hypertrophe of memory', attributable both to the need to negotiate a new sense of German identity and to anxieties about the accelerated obsolescence and space–time compression of postmodernity.[3] Although German cultural memory is seen increasingly as a site of 'memory contests'[4] rather than a consensual, culturally institutionalised heritage, and there has been a marked shift away from psychological towards performative paradigms of collective memory, it still revolves primarily around Holocaust commemoration and the Cold War. While collective memories of these events have undergone generational and political transformations, they remain grounded in a national narrative of recent German history. This perpetuates an ethno-culturalist form of German identity, quite at odds with Germany's ethnically diverse population. Nonetheless, many minority intellectuals are now intervening in debates about Holocaust and GDR memory. This chapter explores their work alongside a range of other literary texts that deterritorialise memory, loosening the links between memory and identity and rendering multiple identifications possible by means of 'affect'.

The notion of 'minor literature', derived from Gilles Deleuze and Félix Guattari,[5] is useful here, not only because some of the authors under discussion are of Turkish origin, but also because of the challenge their fictions pose to ethno-centric notions of community. These are texts that engage with and transform the familiar paradigms of Holocaust or Cold War memory, some of them importing Middle Eastern, central Asian and eastern

European memories into the German cultural consciousness. Frequently, they allude to different timescales than those shaping national histories, evoking cosmic, meteorological, or geological frameworks, which either relativise history or act as metaphors for the intimate relations between objective history and subjective recall.

Theorists from Maurice Halbwachs and Pierre Nora to the present have been concerned with the role of memory to provide a stable sense of group identity, in Deleuze and Guattari's terms, its territorialising force. This also underlies Jan Assmann's view of the normative aspects of cultural memory: 'The concept of cultural memory comprises that body of reusable texts, images, and rituals specific to each society in each epoch, whose "cultivation" serves to stabilize and convey that society's self-image.'[6] For Aleida Assmann, this coincides with the peculiarly German form of idealist individualism known as *Bildung*, although she acknowledges that this has been irrevocably ruptured by the Holocaust, no longer enjoying its 'central and centralising function'.[7]

Andreas Huyssen's *Present Pasts* (2003) begins with the premise that 'the form in which we think of the past is increasingly memory without borders rather than national history within borders',[8] suggesting a move away from the causal link between memory and national identity. He later qualifies this statement, however, warning against the globalisation of Holocaust memory, and stating 'that although memory discourses appear to be global in one register, at their core they remain tied to the histories of specific nations and states'.[9] Günter de Bruyn also cautions against the abandonment of national identifications, claiming that, 'with a lack of identity would come indifference to German history, what is past would no longer be compelling, the oppressive burden would have been shed'.[10] This emphasis on the national boundedness of cultural memory still informs recent publications on German memory debates, even though significant shifts can be detected.[11] Leslie Adelson's *The Turkish Turn in Contemporary German Literature* (2005) is the first full-length study devoted to the impact of Turkish migration on the contemporary German ethnoscape, focusing on the 1990s as a particular moment of transition towards an as yet unrealised transnationalism. This book is a milestone in acknowledging the transformative cultural potential of minority writing in German, yet when it comes to the question of 'genocide and taboo', it upholds a particularist understanding of Holocaust memory. While agreeing with Huyssen that Germany's intense preoccupation with memory and traumatic history militates against its orientation towards a shared future with its minority populations, Adelson nonetheless sees the literature of Turkish migration as 'part of an evolving national tradition of Holocaust memory in Germany'.[12]

I share Adelson's concern to bring German cultural memory into contact with the imaginative labour of Germany's minority intellectuals, but I am interested here in their contribution to a more widespread globalisation of Holocaust memory. Daniel Levy and Natan Sznaider argue that a new form of cosmopolitan memory has emerged since the 1990s, not replacing, but supplementing national memory, and forming the basis for post-national solidarities. Half a century after the Holocaust, the heirs of victims, perpetrators and bystanders alike must negotiate a shared memory: 'not shared due to some mythical desires and the belonging to some continuing community of fate, but as the product of a reflexive choice to incorporate the suffering of the "Other"'.[13] The focus here is on texts which engage with German cultural memory in new ways, which incorporate the memory of the 'Other', and which gesture towards new possibilities of community.

The philosophy of Deleuze and Guattari provides a useful framework to consider these issues, because of their dynamic view of cultures and societies in process. Minor literature aims not to reproduce existing identities (by contributing to Assmann's body of 'reusable texts'), but to imagine identities yet to come. If collective memory has so far served a territorialising, community-founding function, its literary reworkings may have deterritorialising potential, to unsettle and renegotiate the relationship of identity to memory. Moreover, the primacy which Deleuze and Guattari accord to *affect* and *intensities* can perhaps liberate us from the trauma discourse which has so dominated recent German memory debates. Affect is sensation not rooted in a subject, feeling detached from its recognised or expected origins in a familiar world of identities.[14] It is produced when language is deterritorialised, being freed from its origins in a particular identity, history, or geographical location.[15] Deterritorialised memory is here understood as a depersonalised, though not indifferent, relationship to the past. At the centre of Deleuze and Guattari's thinking is not the nation, nor even the individual human subject. The body, and individual body parts, replace the subject as the site where connections are made and affect is experienced, and embodied, often eroticised experience is an important aspect of most of the works under consideration here.

MIGRATING MEMORIES IN THE FRG AND THE FORMER GDR

Zafer Şenocak's prose depicts contemporary metropolitan experience from a perspective only occasionally marked by his non-German origins.[16] His work lends itself to a Deleuzian reading because of its resistance to conventional 'interpretation', the fluidity of identities depicted, and its depiction of eroticised experience instead of rational reflection. Yet it is still centrally concerned with issues of origins, belonging, nomadism, and is not as cast loose from his cultural origins as some critics assume. Şenocak's most recent novel, *Der Erottomane* (The Erot(t)omaniac, 1999), for all its fragmentary narrative, raises questions of historiography, of inherited guilt, of traumatic histories, but it does so in terms of the solidifying and dynamic forces in history and culture.

The title of Şenocak's novel points to one of its main themes, its protagonists' insatiable quest for sexual experience. Thus *Erottomane* equates to 'erotomaniac'. Most interest to date has been in its play on the feminisation of the orient, and its challenge to conventional ideas about masculinity; here, *Erottomane* also means 'He-Ottoman' ('Er-Ottoman').[17] Less widely acknowledged is that this is part of Şenocak's engagement with the erotic tradition in Islamic culture.[18] At the same time, erotic 'touching' is also Şenocak's alternative to notions of intercultural dialogue or understanding.[19] Erotic experience is thus part of the territorialising *and* deterritorialising structure of the narrative; it refers to a specific cultural tradition, and produces moments of intensity detached from cultural particularity, pointing to possibilities of transcultural proximity.

The novel's subtitle, *Ein Findelbuch* (A Foundling Book) points to the orphan-status, non-belonging, and nomadic nature of the book's main characters, while also signalling Şenocak's play with narrative and authorial identity. It begins as a detective story, and ends with a murder, but there the similarities with crime fiction end. The first narrator is a writer, whose lawyer friend Tom (formerly Tayfun, a naturalised Turk), sends him details of the case of the murdered R. However, it soon emerges that Tom and R.(obert) are the same person, both ambiguously related to the first narrator. What follows is a collection of episodic chapters, whose interchangeable characters are driven by desire, not intellect; identities are arbitrary, what matters is intensity.

One of these characters, Robert, describes himself as 'double-tongued',[20] indicating both his unreliable narrative stance, and his polyglot background. As in the work of Emine Sevgi Özdamar, the tongue has a metonymic relationship to language, but it also points to a sub-individual level of experience. For Deleuze, sensation, also erotic intensity, takes place at the level of body parts as well as that of the individual.[21] Erotic experience is not a matter of communication, but of pre-linguistic intensity. The narrator of 'The Second-Hand Bookseller' describes himself as 'A traveller . . . One who follows his body parts' (*E*, 35). In the erotic encounter in 'Thirst' the lovers exchange no words, only communicating with fingers, hands, tongues, the organs becoming interchangeable in the intensity of their encounter. This is a level of intimacy which is not knowledge or domination of the other, but rather palpation, which creates a zone of touch and understanding, in place of identification.[22] Elsewhere, Robert's sado-masochistic lover wields a 'seven-tongued whip', with which she intimates to him that there is always *more* the body can experience, making the mind merely 'a marginal district of the body' (*E*, 66). Intensity is the goal, to liberate the body's potential beyond the limitations of identity. Yet there are also moments of reterritorialisation in the novel's references to Ottoman, Turkish and German histories.

Locatedness is found, if not in stable subjects, then in particular geographical areas with historical, biographical and literary resonances in the Silk Road motif. The novel begins with a longing to travel the Silk Road, which traverses modern national boundaries through Romania, Ukraine, Georgia, Azerbaijan, and short, enigmatic sections entitled Odessa, Konstanza, Batumi and Baku are reminiscent of Italo Calvino's *Invisible Cities* (1974). Yet, in keeping with Calvino, the aim is not to retrace a known route, but to map a new one: 'I wasn't following in the steps of Marco Polo. I wanted to construct my own Silk Road' (*E*, 7). This journey is both an exercise in de-personalisation and one that recalls the Ottoman past of this region bordering the Black Sea and Caspian Sea. Contemporary and historical references are a reminder of how recent the current boundaries in the region are, and of the heterogeneity of modern 'Turkish' identities, which is a disavowed legacy of Ottoman times.

The mapping of a new Silk Road rather than tracing the known one is connected to the novel's distinction between ossified 'history' and fluid 'times'. The narrator of 'The Second-Hand Bookseller' takes over a chaotic bookshop, perhaps in Odessa, and tries to bring order to its contents. This is an attempt to reconcile the city with its past, entailing a distinction between 'history' and 'times: 'No place can be reconciled with its history. History is boney. But the times are fluid. They are elastic and are waiting to be put in order' (*E*, 33). When local inhabitants tell him to concentrate on the present and the future, he retorts: 'What's the good of thinking about the future if we don't properly bury our dead?' (*E*, 24). While he presents history as malleable and subject to representation, he also assumes responsibility for a past which is not dependent on identity; the exact relationship of the history collected in the shop, which includes German publications, to the identity of the bookseller remains ambiguous.

The last chapter of the novel, set in a readily recognisable Berlin, locates a ritual, sado-masochistic murder against the backdrop of the city's violent history. As the victim approaches the prostitute's house, he observes an old man looking blindly out of his window onto disused railway tracks. He muses on the relationship of memory to perception, and wonders how the man can look so dispassionately on a scene of such sinister historical associations. A knowledge of the past, it seems, is a prerequisite for the perception of today's Berlin, but this is not the prerogative of the city's indigenous inhabitants. The public prosecutor investigating R's murder consults a book on sexual murder in the Weimar Republic, to contextualise the crime: 'Berlin has always been a place of lascivious dying. A dissipated life often ends in self-destruction or in wild fantasies of order. Is it any coincidence that Hitler resided in this city? His rule combined fantasies of order *and* destruction in a unique architecture' (*E*, 116). The description of Berlin as 'a place of lascivious dying' recalls a description of the Ottomans as 'experts in slow killing' (*E*, 46), thus linking the atrocities of German and Turkish history. While the history of the Holocaust is ever-present in Berlin, genocide is not particularised to German or Jewish history alone. Instead, it is an example of the destructive potential of ritualised forms of sexual, religious and political behaviour, as contrasted with the moments of dynamic intimacy and intensity in Şenocak's work.

One such instance of positive intimacy occurs in a chapter that also points to the impact of traumatic histories on identity. 'The Tourist Guide' depicts a Turkish-speaking island community who are all 'more or less orphans' (*E*, 96), and have a rupture in their memories blocking access to the future. The tourist guide finds a 'substitute home' in the repeated ritual of taking visitors to the same ancient sites, often succumbing to the seduction of female tourists, whose proximity he soon finds oppressive. An exception is the sexual epiphany he experiences with a woman who wants a child, but makes no further demands. Their intimacy is based on a genuine affinity, not just ritual. It takes on symbolic significance, like the quarries and excavations on the island itself. These disclose ancient remains, suggesting layers of sedimented time. Elsewhere in Şenocak's work, the quarry is a metaphor for our fragmented, transnational world: 'We don't live in between cultures, but in a quarry. We must learn . . . to give up our desire for wholeness. Anyone has access to our fragmented world . . . In such a world, intimacy must be redefined. Intimacy is exchange in the smallest space, intelligibility between a few'.[23] In the absence of universal certainties and solid boundaries, we can hope to achieve only limited communities of understanding. Sexual intimacy without possessiveness or even knowledge of the other seems to be upheld as an ideal, while Şenocak refrains from envisaging the social reality which this might underpin.

Emine Sevgi Özdamar's more directly representational and autofictional novels are set in recognisable Turkish and German contexts, experienced by a female Turkish first-person narrator. Her novel *Seltsame Sterne Starren zur Erde* (Strange Stars Stare Towards Earth, 2003) offers an unexpected perspective on a moment of crisis in GDR politics, and on the divided Berlin of the mid 1970s. It does not merely insert an exotic protagonist into a familiar image of 1970s Berlin. This protagonist's idiosyncratic experience gives rise to affect, which is not just rooted in the individual subject, and which points to a much longer timescale than the diegesis itself. Moreover, there is a collective dimension of recording this history in the post-unification present of 2003 when GDR memory is rapidly being erased.

Özdamar's novel is thus a more evidently political intervention in current German memory debates, preserving for contemporary German culture the disappeared world of the GDR in the 1970s. Although the narrator is continuous, she views the divided Berlin from a detached perspective, and locates it in a trajectory reaching from the French Revolution forward to the events of unification, not depicted, but evoked by the narrative. Her Berlin, like that of Şenocak, is built on sedimented history, most immediately that of war and the Holocaust, which the narrator encounters with somatic immediacy. Thus, although the narrator expresses an Enlightenment commitment to learn from history, the way she encounters it is far less rational and more visceral, in the theatre, the Berlin streets, and the life stories she hears.

The protagonist is an aspiring actress in Turkey, who leaves her husband and country because of martial law and the hounding of left-wing intellectuals following the 1971 coup. She travels to Germany and leads a precarious existence living in a West Berlin commune with bourgeois anarchist students, while establishing herself as assistant director to Benno Besson at the East Berlin *Volksbühne* (People's Theatre). The novel details the productions on which she works, as well as the escalating political tensions in West and East Berlin, culminating in the expatriation of Wolf Biermann and arrest of Rudolf Bahro in the East, and the abduction and murder of Jürgen Ponto and Hans Martin Schleyer in the West by members of the terrorist organisation *Rote Armee Fraktion*. The predominantly diary style and reference to real historical figures (Bahro, Gysi, Heiner Müller) suggest a new level of autobiographical authenticity in Özdamar's work, and lead us to expect the tracing of a known history. But it is a highly mediated and aesthetically stylised narrative, much of its emotional impact being experienced by the reader without being processed by the narrator herself. For the reader today, names such as Gysi and Bahro resonate with more recent historical associations not available to the narrator.[24] Such resonances make all the more poignant the novel's account of the *Volksbühne* and its attempt to keep alive a revolutionary socialist theatre in the face of a clamp-down in GDR cultural policy.

The novel is a corrective to triumphalist western discourses of unification, depicting *West* Berlin as the police state, where the population is imprisoned and the narrator's own position is increasingly precarious as her visa expires and the police hunt for terrorists intensifies. The Berlin Wall, like the Bosphorus, is relativised as a porous boundary between East and West, as Gabi Gysi puts it: 'You normalise the Wall. For you, being here means an expansion of your opportunities to work and live',[25] while for millions of Germans it was an impenetrable barrier. Like the many Turkish men crossing to East Berlin for sex, the protagonist crosses the Wall with ease, joking and flirting with border guards. East Berlin is a slower, quieter, less strenuous world, the smell of coal and cheap diesel reminiscent of Istanbul. While this is no uncritically positive depiction of the GDR (telephones are tapped, Gabi's lover is a Stasi informer), it is in the East that the protagonist is able to live and work legally and finds a provisional home in the theatre community.

The history of the war and the Holocaust accompany the protagonist on the streets of Berlin. Although the bullet holes in the houses in West Berlin have been filled in, they are still visible, and those in the East remain. The holes in the house of an old East Berlin socialist, Herr Richter, represent his memories of the war and anti-fascist foundations of the GDR, and his alienation from the new bureaucratic elite. The commune in Wedding is in an old factory building, which has been witness to a century of radical politics. Everywhere in West Berlin a 'war of words' rages, of graffiti, advertising and news media. The graffiti strikes her as evidence of the young generation's rage at their parents' responsibility for the war and National Socialism. One of her flatmates explains that they had seen Berlin as an escape from the past, 'but the war is here too – all the old war widows and the old men without arms or hands. The West Berlin dogs are dogs against war loneliness. War tranquilizer tablets. The husbands are dead, the dogs have replaced them' (*SS*, 66).

The protagonist is constantly aware of the dogs' barking in West Berlin, which, as for Ingeborg Bachmann in the early 1970s, represents the repressed knowledge of violence and guilt.[26] When she overhears two old anti-Semitic widows on a park bench discussing their ignorance of the Holocaust, the narrator does not respond, but is immediately struck not just by the barking but by the dogs' excrement everywhere in West Berlin. This is an example of affect, not processed rationally by the narrator, but conveyed indirectly through her physical encounter with the city. In West Berlin the army surplus clothes in the second-hand shops are also a reminder of the war, whereas in East Berlin, history is evoked more often by absence. The Mühsamstraße, for example, recalls how brutally Erich Mühsam was killed, and that his descendants might otherwise have been among the protagonist's East German friends (*SS*, 80). For readers in the twenty-first century, who have witnessed the post-unification renaming of East Berlin streets named after prominent socialists, this takes on a proleptic poignancy, anticipating the erasure of the very history that the novel seeks to preserve.

The protagonist is repeatedly confronted with the history of the Holocaust and exile through the biographies of the people she meets. Her first lover in the GDR, the English set designer Graham, has grown up in London because his parents were Jewish exiles. Matthias Langhoff was born in Zurich, where his socialist father and Jewish mother were in exile. On a research trip to Weimar with the cast of Goethe's *Der Bürgergeneral* (The Citizen General, 1798) they pass Buchenwald, where the mother of the driver of the minibus, Hasso von Lenski, was interned. The Gysi family evokes German history, both past and future; Klaus Gysi was a member of the resistance against Hitler, his wife was from an aristocratic Jewish family who had fled the Russian Revolution, only to face anti-Semitism in Berlin in the 1930s. The mirror from St Petersburg which hangs in Gabi's flat becomes what Anne Fuchs has called an affective memory icon,[27] a repository of the family's history of migration. Like the mirrors in Özdamar's story 'Der Hof im Spiegel' (The Courtyard in the Mirror, 2001), the mirror offers a temporal and spatial extension of the protagonist's immediate environment. In it, she intuits direct access to Gabi's family and their past, to the living and the dead.

The theatre is the other site of encounter with history. In it the voices of the dead continue to speak to the present. On one return from the chaos of the West Berlin flat to the *Volksbühne* rehearsals, the narrator reflects: 'I had returned to the dead. To the dead Goethe, to Märten, Röse, Görge . . . In the theatre the dead are resurrected. They want to live on, to intervene in the future stories of the world' (*SS*, 169–70). The significance of the *Volksbühne* is its attempt to keep the tradition of revolutionary theatre alive, to produce the plays of the past for their relevance to the GDR present. The productions and debates about them which the protagonist witnesses contain much of the political insight that she lacks. Goethe's play, for example, is a satire on the Germans' inability to emulate the French Revolution.[28] The protagonist listens in to Heiner Müller's discussions with the actors, 'as if in a foreign language course' (*SS*, 202). When Gabi Gysi states that the French Revolution was more important than the October Revolution, the protagonist records this without reflecting on the significance of a French style of republicanism for migrants like herself, or indeed for Gabi's Jewish relations.

Despite such oblique political comment, and some isolated incidents of racism, Özdamar's novel avoids presenting Turks or Kurds as victims. The protagonist's charmed existence in East Berlin is in part due to her exotic singularity, but in the West, Turks are already an established part of the cityscape. Her first encounter with racism is with a Kurd, whose denigration of Armenian women makes it impossible for her to identify herself as Kurdish. Her sensitivity to anti-Armenian prejudice has its roots in a family history; her grandmother, who had witnessed almost a century of Turkish history, had taken in and cared for an Armenian woman survivor of the 1915–16 massacres. In place of a Kurdish, or even Turkish identity, the protagonist develops an indirect identification with Jewishness, mediated through the poetry of Else Lasker-Schüler. Lasker-Schüler's poem 'Sterne des Fatums' (Stars of Fate, 1902) (otherwise known as 'Liebessterne', Stars of Love),[29] the source of the novel's title, is repeatedly cited, and evoked by the actual stars shining indiscriminately down on the divided city. Lasker-Schüler's oriental conception of Jewishness, incorporating elements of Islamic, Arabic and Hebrew traditions, her many love affairs, her self-stylisation, and her exile in Zurich and Palestine all resonate with the narrator's experience. Her poetry offers access to a German heritage which can form the basis of a non-identical form of Germanness.

BORDER ZONES AND GEOLOGICAL TIME

Jan Böttcher's first novel, *Lina oder: Das kalte Moor* (Lina or: The Cold Moor, 2003), is on the face of it a story of West German childhood and adolescence, refracted through the principal narrator's passion for Mark Twain's *The Adventures of Huckleberry Finn*. Set in the drab 'territory' of the high-rise 1960s Lüneburg suburb of Kaltenmoor, and in the 'Wild West' frontier landscape on the Elbe, it evokes both the historical era of its setting (from the joys of tinned ravioli in the 1970s, to radiation anxiety after Chernobyl in 1986), and the much more ancient history of water, the river Elbe itself, its tributaries and flood plains. It is the story of two half brothers, who take refuge from their dysfunctional family in long nocturnal conversations, and of the unnamed younger brother's devotion to Lina, whose athletic promise he hopes will offer them both a way out. Each of the four laconic chapters ends with the older brother, Nico's perspective on his brother's narrative, which he is writing after Lina has left him, and his dreams of escape have been shattered.

It is an unnostalgic reflection on suburban provincial West Germany, and an indictment of the hybris of town planning of the 1960s. But this is overlaid with the awareness of other time scales altogether, from the history of National Socialism to geological time. The tower blocks of Kaltenmoor ('the cold moor, who on earth was responsible for the poetry of this name?')[30] house a community characterised by bourgeois hypocrisy and shot through with sexual scandal. This is encapsulated by the 'communal cellar', governed by endless signs and prohibitions, but from which bicycles constantly disappear. The mothers tolerate the local paedophiles who frequent the children's playground, and the narrator witnesses his father's adultery with the object of his brother Nico's desire. Italics mark quotations in the text, sometimes to highlight language use which betrays a whole world view (such as the father's mercenary cynicism), but often to illustrate a pervasive mentality, not rooted in any one individual. Hence the salacious response to a sex scandal in the village on the Elbe is rendered in dialect, quite distinct from the narrator's colloquial style (*L*, 70–1), as are the prohibitive signs which proliferate in Kaltenmoor once a group of resettlers moves in (*L*, 84).

The flats had been planned by a building concern named 'Neue Heimat' (New Home) in 1966 as a model of residential design, but their monumental solidity is a prison to the children. Built on a floodplain which had supplied Lüneburg with drinking water since the fourteenth century, the excavations had exposed fossils dating back to over two million years ago, to a sea level change known as the 'Elbe Cycle'. The brothers are impressed that the Elbe existed before humans: 'So the Elbe was always already there . . . The river is beneath us' (*L*, 30). Once Lina and the narrator begin reading about Huckleberry Finn's travels on the Mississippi, they fantasise about a similar watery escape. The opposition between the hard concrete blocks and the soft floodplain is both evoked and deconstructed, as the name of the housing scheme becomes conflated with the bog land which has been drained to build it. Moments of intimacy between the narrator and Lina usually occur in contact with the soft, undrained moor: 'Lina wallowed in the mud. I covered her with kisses. The cold moor, which had always kept its distance with its walls and abstractions, here stuck to our bodies with the smell of decomposing, of past things. In this one place . . . they hadn't closed it off, the moor. Hadn't filled it in, drained it dry' (*L*, 29–30). While rivers signify intimacy, adventure, and escape for the young characters, the 'history of the water' has other resonances in the novel.

The Elbe is both an ancient presence in the landscape and the boundary with the GDR, a country which is 'nothing but a fiction' to the young people (*L*, 69). Yet even in Kaltenmoor their lives are marked by the Cold War, with a military presence and Russian resettlers' children at their school. When the family moves to a village on the border, and the Elbe freezes, Lina and the narrator marvel at the cooperation of East and West German icebreakers, all bizarrely named after animals: 'Unification on the river, a carnival of the animals. Where on earth, if not on the Elbe, could it happen' (*L*, 69). The river also evokes the war itself, as demonstrated by a slide show for veterans of the battle for the bridgeheads on the Elbe. The slides serve as memory prompts for the old men, even evoking a collective traumatic memory of a bombing raid.

Nico, who works in the local library, tries to counter his brother's escape fantasies by instructing him about the history of National Socialism and resistance in the region. Yet water still plays a notable role in Nico's stories. Lüneburg had been a *Gauhauptstadt* (Nazi regional capital) from 1937, and the *Gauleiter* (Nazi regional governor) had wanted to divert a local river to his own farm and flood a valley. Slave labourers who had once been housed in their headmaster's house, had died within three months when given only water, and the Führer had once planned to build an immense stadium on the marshy salt flats which had been the source of Lüneburg's wealth. Nico mentions this is to impress on his brother that he cannot write about Kaltenmoor without acknowledging its recent past, while actually evoking its much more ancient origins. The younger brother begins to share this fascination with the war and the National Socialist past, which ultimately precipitates Lina's departure. He then blames Nico for filling his mind with the history of National Socialism, and asks himself: 'Why didn't I stick to the history of the water?' (*L*, 89). On the other hand, he believes that the Elbe has played a role in separating the pair, and finally accepts this.

In a surreal epilogue, the narrator lies down in the sodden moor, gradually sinking in, not bothering to shake off the slugs and snails crawling over him, returning, as it were, to the time of the river and its fertile floodplain. He begins to wonder why he had needed Lina, and to envy the self-contained life of things, which carry within them the traces of time: 'Enamel bowls and tin buckets lay around in the garden, like history books: I didn't know how far back they reached, how much weather was under the rust, under their cracked paint' (*L*, 100). His rebellion against the stasis of his provincial life ends in the desire to become part of the vast, gradual process of geological time.

The ending of *Lina* is quite different from the ending of Karen Duve's *Regenroman* (Rain Novel, 1999), where Leon also sinks into the moor, but it is a grotesquely sexualised receptacle: 'Leon sank back into the womb of his real mother. . . . Sighing, he succumbed to the damp embrace.'[31] In this novel, in which a couple from Hamburg buy up a property in the former GDR, the constant rain and sodden moor suggest a feminised landscape, albeit one which takes its revenge on the profiteering westerners who come to colonise it. The power of the fluid medium is here primarily a question of gender; Leon despises the feminine (as is revealed in his marriage to the bulimic Martina), is seduced by the voluptuous Isadora, and becomes powerless in the face of the overwhelming invertebrate life of the garden. The assault on his masculinity renders his body contours insecure, in this extended, gendered metaphor of east–west power relations since unification.

A more subtle treatment of this theme is found in Judith Hermann's understated prose, in particular the title story of the volume *Sommerhaus, später* (Summerhouse, Later, 1998), in which a west German buys a property in the east, haunted by its GDR past.[32] The metaphor of the house as a shipwreck continues the watery imagery associated with the east, as does a scene of the west Germans' hedonistic skating party on too-thin ice. The story 'Diesseits der Oder' in the same volume is set in the Oderbruch, on the border with Poland, a landscape drained under Frederick the Great, and redolent with Prussian military history. For the reclusive writer Koberling, who narrates the story, it is a welcome summer retreat, but his peace is disturbed by an unexpected visitor, who confronts him with his own past. While he resists the pressure to discuss past relationships, the landscape itself assaults him with its violent legacy. On a walk through the uncannily picturesque water meadows to the river, he had once encountered a fly-infested animal carcass, hanging in a tree: 'It looked like a vision, like a nightmare image, a gigantic and incomprehensible communication' (*S*, 182). That this message is not interpreted intensifies its impact, which is to send Koberling running and screaming back to the house.

Such moments of intensity, and unexpected intrusions of the past in the midst of ordinary lives, are characteristic of all Hermann's stories. Her characters are isolated individuals, rooted in the here and now, yet their uncanny and passionate encounters point beyond their own, limited perspectives. In 'Rote Korallen', the red coral bracelet functions as an affective memory icon (as Fuchs Calls it) linking the female protagonist to the story of her great grandmother's life in St Petersburg in pre-revolutionary Russia, her unhappy marriage and compensatory affairs. The great grandmother, an emancipated Effi Briest figure, whose husband is killed by her lover in a duel, escapes with her young daughter back to Berlin in 1905. Inge Stephan has shown how the story overturns the literary convention which links the feminine with water, desire and death.[33] The narrator, descended from her German ancestor's affair with a Russian lover, liberates herself from the family stories, from her own lover and from the aquatic imagery that pervades the text. Yet, as Stefan also shows, the great grandmother's story displaces another story, only indirectly present in Hermann's tale, that of the old Jewish family retainer Isaak Baruw, who had escaped revolutionary Russia with the great grandmother in 1905. The narrator's lover is his last remaining descendant, a grey, depressive figure who shows no interest in the 'Petersburg stories', probably because the fate of Baruw's remaining family had been infinitely more disastrous. While this is undoubtedly a reflection on the 'failure of the German-Jewish dialogue in the younger generation',[34] it is not necessary to read the story's water imagery only in terms of the 'Undine' myth. The narrator's final, defiant gesture of hurling the coral beads at her lover's therapist could also be seen as a deterritorialising one, releasing her identity from the specific coordinates of her genealogy: 'The red corals clattered on his desk, and with them clattered all of Petersburg, the large and the small Neva, great grandmother, Isaak Baruw and Nikolaij Sergejewitsch . . . the Luga, the Narova, the Black Sea and the Kaspian Sea and the Aegaean, the Gulf, the Atlantic Ocean'(S, 28).

Tanja Dückers's novel *Himmelskörper* (Heavenly Bodies, 2003) is a family saga, which, similarly to Günter Grass's *Im Krebsgang* (Crabwalk, 2002), concerns the relationship of three generations to the German flight from eastern Europe at the end of the Second World War, and to the sinking of the *Wilhelm Gustloff*. Unlike Grass's novel, however, the female narrator represents the youngest generation, and the novel focuses less on German suffering than on German complicity. Most significant in this context is the protagonist's complex negotiation of memory and identity, of elective affinities and blood ties. Freia Sandmann is an academic meteorologist, whose resistance to engagement with her family history is signalled by her androgenous appearance and professional ambition, until her own imminent motherhood makes her face up to her place in a continuous family tree. This transforms her perception of Berlin from neutral backdrop to site of historic violence, causing her to reflect: 'There was no escaping; I had to surrender to the future and to history, which, in my child's curiosity, would inextricably mix personal and collective experience.'[35]

There are three temporal layers of the narrative: Freia's adult relations with her twin brother, Paul, and parents, Peter and Renate; her childhood memories; her maternal grandparents', Jo and Mäxchen's memories of the war years. Jo had escaped from Gdynia (which she calls Gotenhafen) with the young Renate in 1945, not on the doomed *Wilhelm Gustloff*, but on a mine sweeper called the *Theodor*, from which they hear news of the sinking ship. Jo and Mäxchen both survive the war with their lives and fascist sympathies intact, even though Jo's face, like Tulla Pokriefke's white hair, bears the traces of the fear of that night. Like Tulla, also, Jo talks compulsively about the past, but hers is a stylised repertoire of war stories, about the destruction of her home, Königsberg, and the perilous flight to the West. Mäxchen's war stories focus on his suffering on the eastern front, and on the tactical blunders of the German military strategists. Renate, a distracted, melancholic, and frequently absent mother, is, as Freia only latterly understands, preoccupied with traumatic memories of the destruction of her Polish home and the fate of those who failed to escape. Although only five years old at the time of their escape, she is haunted by the guilt which her parents repress. She frequently travels to Poland to visit her cousin Kazimierz, the remaining relative in her extended German-Polish family. When Kazimierz, a successful TV presenter and communist party member, suddenly commits suicide, Freia travels to Warsaw to try to understand why.

As in *Im Krebsgang*, the transmission of collective memory is a central theme here, though while Grass seems to caution that the internet's potential to detach identity and memory will lessen responsibility for the past, Dückers's protagonist chooses to identify with her mother's Polish birthplace rather than with her compromised maternal family line. The novel abounds with reflections on the power of memory icons, such as photographs, monuments and personal mementos to preserve and transmit knowledge of the past. As in Grass's novel, photograph albums lost during the war leave a gap which cannot be filled. After the war, Jo becomes a passionate collector of photographs, the only two objects which she has managed to retain throughout her life being a mirror and an oil painting. Renate always carries photographs of her relatives with her, and obsessively collects mementos, including a lock of her daughter's plaited hair and even Jo's false teeth. Freia rebels against her mother's morbid reliquary, just as she also doubts the effectiveness of monuments to commemorate lost lives. When contemplating the monument to the Warsaw ghetto, she feels unmoved, noticing with horror how completely all traces of it have been removed, first by the Germans, then by the Poles in their rebuilding of the old town: 'in the very flawlessness of the reconstruction the pain shone through' (*H*, 172). The city of Warsaw itself fails to bring Kasimierz any closer to her, only the taste of his favourite liquorice suddenly evokes his warm presence with sensory immediacy. She realises that photographs are deceptive, but so is her grandmother's staged testimony, and only when Jo is dying of cancer does she start to reveal the truth of her status as one of the 'founder Nazi party members' (*H*, 300). This growing insight keeps Freia awake at night, 'because I didn't want to sink into this deep, soft bed, to let myself fall back into history, back to where I came from' (*H*, 220).

A further narrative strand is the almost incestuous intimacy of Freia and her brother, Paul, which at first appears a form of protection against their parents' strained marriage and their grandparents' fixation on the past. Their bond is only intensified by their simultaneous attachment to the enigmatic Wieland, who is first Freia's lover, and then transfers his desire to her brother. Wieland's response to his own unhappy home life is a 'zero theory', a passionate determination to live in the present, which becomes increasingly untenable for Freia in the light of her growing attachment to her family's Polish past. Wieland associates Freia's name with Richard Wagner's *Rheingold*, and challenges her with its politically tainted connotations. However, her brother Paul had chosen the name of this norse weather goddess for her, in preference to the Biblical Eva Maria as she was baptised. Thus a different set of associations for the deity is asserted, which evoke also Freia's academic discipline. She is compiling an atlas of cloud formations for the twenty-first century, and has only to find one final rare specimen, the barely perceptible Cirrus Perlucidus. She finally photographs it in Gdynia, at the site of her mother's flight in 1945. It seems to embody the imperceptible boundary between communicative memory and collective memory, between subjective stories and objective history, a boundary which the novel itself palpates, while holding open the possibility of identifications other than those based on blood ties.

CONCLUSION

This selection of prose from the past decade demonstrates a continuing preoccupation with collective memories of National Socialism, the Holocaust, and the Cold War, but also a variety of perspectives on their consequences for German identities. As Şenocak has pointed out, his father experienced 1945 as neither liberation nor collapse, he was neither victim nor perpetrator.[36] The Holocaust has no direct consequences for his identity, but he is passionately concerned that its political lessons for the present be learned. This recalls Levy and Sznaider's cosmopolitan memory, underwriting a transnational discourse of human rights. Şenocak's fiction presents a challenge to all ethnically fixed notions of identity, while still retaining a sense of responsibility to the past. For Özdamar also, there is no escaping entirely from nationally bounded memory, but the German Cold War divide is transformed by the gaze of one whose identity it has not shaped. All of the authors invoke the memory of 'Others' of the national cultures in which they participate, be it that of the Armenians, the Jews, the Poles, the former GDR, or indeed the geological time of the earth itself, which decentres national and human agency. In many of the texts, moments of intensity have deterritorialising force, and intimacy takes on new and unfamiliar forms. Collective memory may have lost none of its imaginary power, but the global concerns of the present are proliferating the kinds of identity and community to which it may give rise.

NOTES

1. Zafer Şenocak, *Atlas des tropischen Deutschland* (Berlin: Babel, 1993), 16.
2. See Aleida Assmann, *Arbeit am nationalen Gedächtnis: Eine kurze Geschichte der deutschen Bildungsidee* (Frankfurt: Campus Verlag, 1993), Aleida Assmann and Heidrun Friese, eds., *Identitäten: Erinnerung, Geschichte, Identität 3* (Frankfurt: Suhrkamp, 1998).
3. Andreas Huyssen, *Present Pasts: Urban Palimpsests and the Politics of Memory* (Stanford CA: Stanford University Press, 2003), 3, 23.
4. See Mary Cosgrove and Anne Fuchs, eds., *Memory Contests*, special number of *German Life and Letters*, 59/2 (2006). See also Anne Fuchs, Mary Cosgrove and Georg Grote, eds., *German Memory Contests: The Quest for Identity in Literature, Film and Discourse since 1990* (Rochester: Camden House, 2006).
5. Gilles Deleuze and Félix Guattari, *Kafka: Toward a Minor Literature* [French 1975, German 1976], trans. Dana Polan (Minneapolis: University of Minnesota Press, 1986).
6. Jan Assmann, 'Collective Memory and Cultural Identity', *New German Critique*, 65 (1995): 125–33, here 132.
7. Aleida Assmann, *Arbeit am nationalen Gedächtnis*, 111.
8. Huyssen, *Present Pasts*, 4.
9. Ibid., 16.
10. Günter de Bruyn, *Unzeitgemäßes: Betrachtungen über Vergangenheit und Gegenwart* (Frankfurt: Fischer, 2003 [2001]), 20.

11. In Silke Arnold-de Simine's volume *Memory Traces: 1989 and the Question of German Cultural Identity*, only Friederike Eigler's essay broadens the debates beyond national parameters. Friederike Eigler, 'Memory, Moralism, and Coming to Terms with the Present: Martin Walser and Zafer Şenocak' in Silke Arnold-de Simine, ed., *Memory Traces: 1989 and the Question of German Cultural Identity* (Bern: Lang, 2005), 55–78. Friederike Eigler's *Gedächtnis und Geschichte in Generationenromanen seit der Wende* (Berlin: Erich Schmidt, 2005) is also notable for including a chapter on Zafer Şenocak. Cosgrove and Fuchs's title *Memory Contests* points to the performative nature of memory debates, but only Monika Shafi's essay addresses the ethno-centrism of German constructions of 1968. Monika Shafi, 'Talkin' 'Bout my Generation: Memories of 1968 in Recent German Novels' in Cosgrove and Fuchs, eds., *Memory Contests*, 201–16.

12. Leslie A. Adelson, *The Turkish Turn in Contemporary German Literature: Toward a New Critical Grammar of Migration* (New York: Palgrave Macmillan, 2005), 81, 84.

13. Daniel Levy and Natan Sznaider, 'Memory Unbound: The Holocaust and the Formation of Cosmopolitan Memory', *European Journal of Social Theory*, 5:1 (2002): 87–106, here 103.

14. See Claire Colebrook, *Gilles Deleuze* (London: Routledge, 2002) for a discussion of affect.

15. See Deleuze and Guattari, *Kafka: Toward a Minor Literature*, trans. Polan, 19.

16. The exception is *Gefährliche Verwandtschaft* (1998), which addresses the impact of traumatic histories for German and Turkish identity formation. See Margaret Littler, 'Guilt, Victimhood, and Identity in Zafer Şenocak's *Gefährliche Verwandtschaft*', *The German Quarterly*, 78:3 (2005): 357–73.

17. See Moray McGowan, 'Odysseus on the Ottoman, or "The Man in Skirts": Exploratory Masculinities in the Prose Texts of Zafer Şenocak' in Tom Cheesman and Karin Yeşilada, eds., *Zafer Şenocak* (Cardiff: University of Wales Press, 2003), 61–79.

18. See Zafer Şenocak, 'Das Schweigen der muslimischen Kultur' in *Zungenentfernung: Bericht aus der Quarantänestation* (Munich: Babel, 2001), 75–8.

19. See Leslie A. Adelson, 'Touching Tales of Turks, Germans and Jews: Cultural Alterity, Historical Narrative, and Literary Riddles for the 1990s', *New German Critique*, 80 (2000): 93–124.

20. Zafer Şenocak, *Der Erottomane* (Munich: Babel, 1999), 15. Hereafter *E*.

21. See Todd May, *Gilles Deleuze: An Introduction* (Cambridge: Cambridge University Press, 2005), 167–9 on erotics of love in Deleuze.

22. May, *Gilles Deleuze*, 20.

23. Zafer Şenocak, 'Orte zum Kennenlernen und Genießen', *Zungenentfernung*, 35–44, here 42.

24. Rudolf Bahro (1935–1997), social scientist and philosopher of the green movement, was arrested in 1977 and served two years in prison before being deported from the GDR in 1979 for publication of *Die Alternative: Zur Kritik des real existierenden Sozialismus* (1977). Gregor Gysi (b. 1948), a lawyer and activist

for political reform, defended Bahro in the 1970s, then went on to become a prominent SED/PDS politician, 1989–1993.

25. Emine Sevgi Özdamar, *Seltsame Sterne starren zur Erde* (Cologne: Kiepenheuer & Witsch, 2003), 182. Hereafter *SS*.

26. Ingeborg Bachmann, 'Das Gebell' in *Simultan* (Munich: Piper, 1991 [1972]), 97–117.

27. 'A . . . characteristic of post-Wende memory contests consists in the employment of affective memory icons that aid or trigger the narrator's investigations of a historical event that is perceived as a disturbance. Memory icons are objects such as photographs, diaries or letters which serve to enshrine a particular version of family history. Although enshrined, such memory icons are invested with the affective imprints of a traumatic historical experience.' See Anne Fuchs, 'From "Vergangenheitsbewältigung" to Generational Memory Contests in Günter Grass, Monika Maron and Uwe Timm', *German Life and Letters*, 59/2 (2006), 169–86, here 184.

28. See Moray McGowan, '"Sie kucken beide an Milch Topf": Goethe's *Bürgergeneral* in double refraction' in Andreas Stuhlmann and Patrick Studer, eds., *Language-Text-Bildung. Sprache-Text-Bildung: Essays in Honour of Beate Dreike* (Frankfurt: Lang, 2005), 79–88.

29. Else Lasker-Schüler, *Gesammelte Werke,* vol. 1, ed. Friedhelm Kemp (Frankfurt: Suhrkamp), 1998.

30. Jan Böttcher, *Lina oder: Das kalte Moor* (Idstein: kookbooks, 2005 [2003]), 9. Hereafter *L*.

31. Karen Duve, *Regenroman* (Frankfurt: Eichborn, 2002), 297.

32. Judith Hermann, *Sommerhaus, später* (Frankfurt: Fischer, 2000 [1998]), 139–56. Hereafter *S*.

33. Inge Stephan, 'Undine an der Newa und am Suzhou River: Wasserfrauen-Phantasien im interkulturellen und intermedialen Vergleich', *Zeitschrift für Germanistik*, 12 (2002): 547–63.

34. Stephan, 'Undine an der Newa', 554.

35. Tanja Dückers, *Himmelskörper* (Berlin: Aufbau, 2003), 255. Hereafter *H*.

36. Zafer Şenocak, 'Gedanken zum 8. Mai 1995', *Zungenentfernung*, 25–8, here 26.

CHAPTER 12

Turkish-German fiction since the mid 1990s

Moray McGowan

By the mid 1990s, Turkish-German fiction, always more than the unsophisticated literature of labour migration in which guise it first appeared
on the German literary scene, had become thematically and aesthetically
at least as diverse and irreducible to ethnic generalisations as the Turkish-
German population at large.[1] At the inevitable risk of ethnic essentialism,
'Turkish-German literature' is taken here to mean texts by writers of Turkish origin significantly associated with Germany by birth, residence or citizenship, and published in German. This does not prescribe a given text's
themes, techniques, registers or literary ambitions: some have clearly ethnic
perspectives, others apparently avoid them completely; some are as easily
consumed as the most lightweight popular reading, others are as stubbornly
anti-hermeneutic as any in German literature. By the mid-1990s, this writing had left the 'Pappkoffer', the cardboard suitcase, emblem of the migrant
worker's social exclusion and transitory status, firmly behind in favour of a
striking plurality of themes and forms and a polyphony of narrative voices,
only some of which can be examined here. It is a literature, too, which lends
itself to being viewed through the lenses of a wide range of contemporary
theories, which this chapter can only touch on.

The very ambiguity of Turkish-German writing, at once inside the (German) nation, 'outside the nation'[2] and superseding the nation, is its potential strength. For one leading scholar, the consequence is no less than a
Turkish Turn in German Literature, a paradigm shift in the range of view-
points, figures and forms through which modern Germany can be narrated.[3]
Certainly, Turkish-German writing offers alternative views of what it means
to be German in the changing Germany in which, for example, by 2005
in Berlin, 26 per cent of schoolchildren and 33 per cent of new entrants
to primary school were not native speakers of German. But this is not just
a point about demography. Turkish-German writing reflects on Germany
from a perspective that may constitute a reverse ethnography ('the other
speaks back'[4]), or, more subtly, engage with 'emerging forms of Turkish

identification *with* the host country'.[5] German identity was increasingly being rethought in the old Federal Republic, as mono-ethnic conceptions of the nation became ever less tenable; but this was obscured by the national question defined as unresolved east/west division. Now that unification has ended the rigid bipolarity of Cold War oppositions (though not, of course, east–west *differences*), Turkish-German culture, including imaginative writing, can contribute signally to united Germany's self-redefinition. Such contributions include not just alternative views of the German present, but also new manners of access to German history. The same applies to the distinctive Turkish-German perspective on ideas of Europe.[6] Moreover, precisely because Turkey is *not* typically Islamic and Turkish-Germans are *not* representatives of Turkey, Turkish-German writing can provide invaluable insights into how forms of Islamic culture develop not just in contact with, but actually within, western modernity.

In terms of Turkish-German writing's impact on the wider literary market, there were two key turning points in the 1990s. The first was the publication of Emine Sevgi Özdamar's *Mutterzunge* (Mother Tongue) in 1990 and the award of the Bachmann Prize in 1991 for extracts from her novel *Das Leben ist eine Karawanserai. Hat zwei Türen. Aus einer kam ich rein. Aus der anderen ging ich raus* (Life is a Carawanserai: has two doors, I came in one, I went out the other, 1992). Though German reviewers often emphasised Özdamar's supposedly defective German, her texts in fact began to challenge the conception of migrants caught, or buffeted, between languages, demonstrating the empowering rather than disempowering effect of multilinguality.

The second turning point was the publication of Feridun Zaimoğlu's *Kanak Sprak: 24 Mißtöne vom Rande der Gesellschaft* (Kanak Speak: 24 Discordant Notes from the Margins of Society) in 1995, which together with the author's media presence brought Turkish-German writing to an entirely new audience. Ironically, given *Kanak Sprak*'s own often startling address of taboos, its success promoted a 'normalisation', arguably even a commodification, of Turkish-German writing. Satirical prose now appears with mainstream publishers, such as the novel *Kanaken-Gandhi* (1998) by Osman Engin, whose hero, a Turk disguised as an Indian to escape a deportation order, staggers from one crazy situation to another through a Germany rendered ridiculous by its own multiple prejudices, those of the Turkish population included. There is too a significant amount of so-called pop literature by Turkish-German authors: writing by, for and about young people, concerned with lifestyle, life chances, consumption, sex and disenchantment with organised politics.[7] This writing underlines the participation by, especially, third-generation Turkish-Germans (those born in Germany) in a post-national, multi-media, metropolitan culture where writers such as Imran Ayata move more confidently than do most ethnic German writers of earlier generations. Ayata, born in Ulm to Anatolian immigrant parents, contributor to radical left journal *Die Beute* and alternative magazines such as *Jungle World*, PR consultant, DJ and co-founder with Feridun Zaimoğlu and others of *Kanak Attak* (see below), writes 'Polaroids' (his own term): mood snapshots rather than strictly stories. The protagonists of *Hürriyet Love Express* (2005: the title story concerns contact ads in the newspaper *Hürriyet*), if identifiable as Turks at all, are mostly young men sampling the urban cool of both Berlin and Istanbul and searching, as young men irrespective of their ethnicity do, both for the meaning of contemporary life and for reasonably priced sunglasses.

Beginning with the novel *Es ist so einsam in Sattel, seit das Pferd tot ist* (It's so Lonely in the Saddle since the Horse died, 1995), Selim Özdogan has published numerous texts of adolescent, mostly male, pursuit of experience and purpose in the mode of Salinger's *Catcher in the Rye*: 'somehow everything just made me sick – books, sex, drugs, music, films, dancing, writing, sweating – I wanted more, or to chuck it all in'.[8] The stories in *Trinkgeld vom Schicksal* (Fate's Gratuity, 2003) show his skill at evoking the moment of romantic or sexual attraction, the spark ignited by music or lifestyle, in a world of rapidly forged and broken yet not necessarily 'casual' relationships, where ethnic markers are mostly secondary factors. Özdogan's *Die Tochter des Schmieds* (The Blacksmith's Daughter, 2005) is thus a significant departure, his first major work to address migration explicitly. His heroine, Gül, experiences domestic oppression and limited horizons in Anatolia in the late 1940s, but the novel avoids a fatalist representation of underdevelopment: Turkey's own increasing prosperity is the push factor that prompts the migration process. The material oppression of Anatolian women is a central motif, but this is not a lachrymose victim novel; rather, it is a differentiated, though certainly often melancholy exploration of the dialectics of migration.

The oppression of Muslim women in their countries of origin, and its assumed continuation in Germany, are themes rarely absent from German bookshops, kept topical by much publicised instances of forced marriages or 'honour killings', underpinned by populist, often anonymous, works whose happy end, when present, consists of escape from the backwardness of Islam via integration into western modernity, such as 'Ayse', *Mich hat keiner gefragt* (No-one consulted Me, 2005) or Inci Y., *Erstickt an euren Lügen* (Suffocated by your Lies, 2005). As Mark

Terkessidis comments: 'The media re-liberate the Muslim woman every few years'.[9]

While popular literature is beginning also to embrace counter-voices to this persistent tradition of representing Muslim woman as victim, such as *Einmal Hans mit scharfer Soße* (One Hans with Hot Sauce, 2005) by Hatice Akyün, the most emphatic rejection of the tradition remains the work of Emine Sevgi Özdamar. Her texts celebrate female solidarity, uninhibited sexuality and physicality, subversive humour and direct or indirect challenges to a patriarchy whose power is, however, not underestimated. Since these aspects of Özdamar's work have been widely studied, the section on her work below explores other facets, in particular the bridge motif. Like the image of the divided tongue as an emblem of migrant discomfort engendered by enforced multilinguality, the bridge (between continents, cultures, languages) has been a central metaphor of Turkish-German writing and in particular of its reception, and a noticeable feature of Turkish-German writing is its critical and self-critical engagement with just such constituent metaphors and stereotypes.

Related to Özdamar's questionings of the bridge motif are her portrayals of transitions within divided Berlin and between it and Turkey, especially Istanbul. Berlin's Turkish population of 130,000 is the largest in Germany (and the largest in a single city outside Turkey itself) and contains the whole spectrum of Turkish-German life in microcosm. But beyond the reflection of contemporary ethnic experience, Turkish writers are well placed to articulate Berlin as a place of suture, now less between the two sides in the Cold War than between national and global, mono- and multi-ethnic realities and mentalities. Turkish-German engagements with Berlin are often expressed in the narrating self's complex experiences of time and place.[10] Aras Ören's *Unerwarteter Besuch* (Unexpected Visit, 1997) deploys multiple narrators and an intricate temporal structure ranging from the early 1960s to the immediate post-1989 period. In his afterword to *Sehnsucht nach Hollywood* (Longing for Hollywood, 1999, first published in Turkish 1991), Ören symptomatically refers to a self-aware 'artificial language', generated by 'the new sensations which I continuously experience here', which he re-forges 'at my laboratory bench, in every text I write. My linguistic homeland is Turkish, yes, but as a Turk I speak and write the language of Europe. Perhaps that is what is disconcerting and at the same time normal.'[11]

In the 1970s, Ören's Berlin trilogy of narrative poems set migrant labour experience into a wider context both of international class struggle and of a Europe being transformed by migration. Latterly, he and other writers have begun to develop Turkish-German perspectives on Berlin's earlier history. Ören's *Berlin Savignyplatz* (1995) alludes to Alfred Döblin's *Berlin Alexanderplatz*, a milieu that plays a role too in *Sehnsucht nach Hollywood*, though in a double refraction, since the novel concerns a film located in Berlin in the 1920s, but being made in the post-war rubble of 1947. In Güney Dal's *Teestunden am Ring* (Teatime at the Ring, 1999) Turkish philosopher, painter and boxing promoter Sabri Mahir has followed a trajectory of artistic migration – comparable to that of several of Özdamar's narrators – from Istanbul via Paris to the 1920s Berlin of Brecht and Dietrich. Zafer Şenocak's *Der Mann im Unterhemd*, considered below, explores the traces of a traumatic history in post-unification Berlin.

In Yadé Kara's *Selam Berlin* (2003), nineteen-year old Hasan feels impelled to return from Istanbul to his native Berlin when the Wall falls. The Wall's pathos-free normality for Hasan as a child echoes Peter Schneider's *Mauerspringer* (Wall-Jumper, 1982), its relationship to a hormonal teenager's erections in Thomas Brüssig's *Helden wie wir* (Heroes Like Us, 1995); Hasan's father Baba's ability to travel visa-free between West and East Berlin (facilitating an illicit affair) recycles a central motif in Özdamar's work. A Turkish version of the aging 68er, Baba contrasts with his East Berlin girlfriend, Rosa Marx (the comically allusive name a reminder that this novel does not expect to be taken literally), whom forty years of socialism have turned into a gung-ho entrepreneur. But precisely as a derivative novel which, entertainingly if somewhat mechanically, rehearses sociological or ethnographic facts about Turkish culture in Germany, *Selam Berlin* exemplifies Turkish-German writing's establishment as a marketable commodity.

The examples of recent Turkish-German fiction examined below, by Feridun Zaimoğlu, Emine Sevgi Özdamar and Zafer Şenocak, do not purport to be a cross-section of the range of writing that has appeared since the mid-1990s. Rather, they are noteworthy for sharing a questioning and refusal of representation, as a response to a reception which is often still only able to recognise collective biographies, the migrant labourer in the Turk, the unsophisticated *Gastarbeiterliteratur* (guest-worker literature) in the text by a writer with a Turkish name. They do not go as far as the meta-fictional novel *Ja, sagt Molly* (Yes, says Molly, 1998) by Kemal Kurt, which subtly embeds migrant, especially Turkish-German, experience in a sweeping imaginative history of modernity and its self-inflicted catastrophes, and is probably the most forceful antidote to literalist readings of Turkish-German writing. But in their different ways the works of Zaimoğlu, Özdamar and Şenocak each belong to that more innovative Turkish-German writing which develops 'a persona of migration as historical formation, not of ethnicity as anthropological inscription'.[12] That is, figures in literary texts

who are designated as 'Turkish' are not necessarily ethnic, let alone ethni-
cised characters; they are points of view, subject positions from which to
engage with German narratives, histories and memory cultures with which
they are not embroiled or compromised, unlike those positions from which
these histories and memories are usually viewed and explored. Or rather, as
Şenocak's novel *Gefährliche Verwandtschaft* (Perilous Kinship, 1998) shows
by bringing the repressed *Turkish* history of the Armenian genocide into
contact with a German-Jewish narrative, Turkish-German subject positions
have their own embroilments, whose similarities and differences to more
familiar ones in German culture establish common ground whilst gener-
ating productive friction, opportunities to narrate German, European and
global concerns in new ways.

FERIDUN ZAIMOĞLU

One consequence of the revived consciousness of the German nation at
a time of socio-economic uncertainty in the early 1990s was outbreaks of
xenophobic violence, much of it against Turks. In 1993, the year in which
five members of one family died in an arson attack in Solingen, Zafer
Şenocak with Claus Leggewie published the bilingual manifesto *Deutsche
Türken/Türk Almanlar: Das Ende der Geduld/Sabrn sonu* (German Turks:
The End of Patience), rejecting the patience with which migrants accepted
present mistreatment in the hope of a better future.

In his writing and public appearances, Feridun Zaimoğlu embodies this
new impatience, savaging passive victimhood, deference and the patron-
ising rhetoric of multiculturalism alike. He was, moreover, effectively the
first writer to demonstrate in the forms of his texts that the post-migrant
generations (those born in Germany) could not be, and would not let
themselves be, understood in the terms that applied to their migrant parents. The impact of this work and its author was a key factor in a quan-
tum leap in awareness of Turkish-German themes in German culture at
large from the mid-1990s (though Zaimoğlu would insist that he is not
Turkish-German but a German citizen with a Turkish name). When his
Kanak Sprak: 24 Mißtöne vom Rande der Gesellschaft appeared in 1995, the
interview format provoked disputes about its authenticity. But as in the
sampling culture to which his work as writer, performer and publicist has
numerous links (indeed it can be read as pop literature[13]), authenticity
is essentially irrelevant, both to the recognition factor for young audi-
ences and to the literary quality of these skilfully distilled and linguistically
inventive texts that share none of the limitations of the registers off which
they feed. *Kanak Sprak* is a textual turntable on which Zaimoğlu mixes a

polyphony of the demotic speech of Turkish, German and international youth, the registers, rhythms, syntax and attitudes of rap and hip-hop and the slang of petty crime. That the world it references is necessarily much more low-life than that of most of its readership is part of its appeal.

The young Turkish male voices of *Kanak Sprak* bristle with virility and self-empowering transgression, adopting a performative delivery style which Zaimoğlu in his introduction to the exterior and interior worlds of the second and third generation of Turks in Germany calls the 'anchor position': 'arms wide, the left leg firmly grounded and taking the weight, and the right leg scraping the ground with the toe of the shoe'. From this position, half soapbox orator, half raging bull, the twenty-four monologues pugnaciously reject every externally imposed identity, though especially that of the 'poor, but good-hearted Turk Ali' and the 'garbage-man prose' of *Gastarbeiter* literature.[14] Treated as 'dreck' ('scum'), Zaimoğlu's narrators – sex workers, petty criminals, addicts, unemployed men, an asylum seeker, a break dancer, a transsexual, a psychiatric patient, but also a poet or a sociologist – celebrate their denigration in comic exaggeration of racial stereotypes and Rabelaisian verbal excess. Like Jean Genet inverting his stigmatisation as a criminal and pervert into a celebration, they defiantly affirm that they are 'Kanakstas' (combining rap-influenced 'gangsta' poses with 'Kanake', a Polynesian word for human being, now German racist slang for foreigner) and intensify this role into its own exaggerated parody, a 'pseudo-ethnicity' performed in order to attack the reduction of complex identities to ethnic ones.[15]

The cumulative effect of the polyphony within each monologue is as important as individual psychologies, biographies or stories as such. Notably, though, Zaimoğlu closes with a reminder of where, if too long frustrated, the energies *Kanak Sprak* articulates may lead: the angry indictments of German society's corrupt godlessness by the Islamic fundamentalist Yücel, which have a prophetic force when reread in the knowledge of the involvement of Muslims from Europe in terrorist attacks since 2001.

Through its first-person narratives, authentic or not, *Kanak Sprak* inverts the ethnographic gaze usually directed onto migrant youth. It is a text about the Germans and the Germany the 'Kanakstas' engage with, glimpsed in the swirling narrative streams of facts, hypotheses and fantasies. Among a number of provocative references to the Holocaust, for example, are the speculations of a Turkish gigolo on the state of mind of a German 'christ lady' that prompts her to project onto him an identity as 'my beautiful jew' during their sexual encounters, and as 'my bad jew-diddle' when they part. Punning the ambiguous endearment of 'Judenschniddel' ('schniddel' denoting penis, dimunition and things severed), the affronted gigolo reflects on the Nazi past when 'the ol' *alemanne* was top-dog barbarian in cutting up jews for filets' (*judenschnitzeln*) (*KS*, 69–71). The gigolo's pun, typical of both Zaimoğlu's Joycean association technique and his startling directness, highlights both the eroticisation of guilt and a classic process of repression, displacement and re-emergence.[16] At such moments, *Kanak Sprak* makes it clear that Turkish-German texts have things to say about memory traces in the contemporary German psyche that a German text might not be able to say or a German ear to hear.

Zaimoğlu built on *Kanak Sprak*'s success with the monologue of a Turkish-German petty criminal, *Abschaum* (Scum, 1997; filmed as *Kanak Attack!* in 2000), the similarly combative Turkish female monologues in *Koppstoff: Kanaka Sprak vom Rande der Gesellschaft* (Headstuff: Kanaka Speak from the Margins of Society, 1998), and the 'Kanak compendium' *Kopf und Kragen* (Risking your Neck, 2001). His street credibility, impatience with sacred cows and improvisational verve rapidly made him a folk hero amongst multi-ethnic youth, a talk-show regular and newspaper columnist.[17] Prizes, writer residencies and guest professorships followed. He used this prominence to indict the state, media and other practices of exclusion, and victim mentalities within the Turkish population itself, and to help launch 'Kanak Attak' (not to be confused with the mass of derivative 'Kanaksta' comedy spawned by his success), a multi-media network of performance artists in the late 1990s. In adopting the majority's pejorative label as a weapon and a badge of pride, 'Kanak Attak' and its multi-ethnic consciousness-raising about minority rights and the impact of globalisation on migrants echoed, with considerably more media access and sophistication, the *Südwind Gastarbeiterdeutsch* (Southwind Guest-worker-German) project of the early 1980s, whose instigators explicitly deployed the term *Gastarbeiter* (guest worker), since precisely as a threadbare euphemism it drew attention to cross-ethnic exploitation and outsider status.

Zaimoğlu has been accused of facilitating the hate speech which his texts rework by lowering thresholds for public use of terms such as 'Kanake', and of practising new forms of exclusion, in that the broad mass of Turks in Germany have little access to the world he invokes or the language he deploys. Such criticism partly misses the point: Zaimoğlu stresses that he is a critical citizen of a Germany where the 'Kanaksta' can be of any ethnicity, the determining factor being the socio-economic marginalisation against which the 'Kanaksta' takes arms. But it is hard not to hear, in his attacks on 'garbage-man prose', a sneer at the garbage man himself.

In formally more conventional fiction such as the artist-novel satire *German Amok* (2002) or the crime novel *Leinwand* (Canvas, 2003), Zaimoğlu has honed his aggressive creativity into a technique capable of sustaining a major piece of historical narrative. With parallels to Özdogan's *Die Tochter des Schmieds*, Zaimoğlu's *Leyla* (2006) is the novel of a young woman's upbringing between a loving but powerless mother and a brutally dominant father, and her eventually successful quest for freedom. It moves from her near-medieval Anatolian village in the 1930s via Istanbul to her arrival as a migrant at Munich station, in a Germany she perceives as her opportunity to escape patriarchal oppression. As such it echoes but challenges the best-selling victim narratives of Muslim women. Zaimoğlu's turn to a classic tale, and classic trail, of migration, might surprise; but he has always insisted that his rejection of conventional equations of Turkish-German identity with particular patterns or experiences of migration is not a denial of the material factors, primarily socio-economic, that generate oppression. Anatolia is in any case far from schematically portrayed, beginning with the ethnic diversity in Leyla's own family: her father is Chechen, her mother Armenian. While her mother's repressed past as an Armenian rape victim with no surviving relatives haunts the novel, its main temporal focus is the 1950s, when Turkey bought NATO membership by sending troops to Korea, dragging a still largely pre-industrial country into the Cold War, an anti-Communism and pro-Americanism which cut Turkey off from its own history.

In 2004 Zaimoğlu, the iconoclast *par excellence*, admitted practising elements of Muslim ritual. But he did so as a German, he insisted: 'I don't suddenly become Turkish when I sacrifice a sheep.'[18] (Even in the mid 2000s, a challenging image for the German public sphere.) With his ability to intervene in public discourse firmly established, Zaimoğlu can afford to turn in *Leyla* to a potentially highly traditional theme without forfeiting his reputation as a writer who has broken emphatically, though not unproblematically, with that tradition and its reception in German culture.

EMINE SEVGI ÖZDAMAR

Following the publication of the four stories in *Mutterzunge* in 1990 and the award of the Bachmann Prize in 1991 for extracts from her *Karawanserai* novel, Emine Sevgi Özdamar became the most widely read and discussed Turkish-German writer. In January 2002, she was one of only three writers, with Christa Wolf and Günter Grass, invited to read at a literary event in the Federal Chancellery. Özdamar's work has been widely understood as one in which a Turkish-German female subject 'finds her voice', asserts her identity, engages with multilinguality and multiculturality, and confronts German culture with otherness through her use in her German texts not only of fragments of original Turkish, but also near-literal renderings of Turkish syntax or idioms.[19] Reception of her work now takes more account too of the elements of playful, even parodistic performance of gender, ethnicity and national history.

However, her work also explores critically topographical and spatial metaphors for issues of national identity and cultural mobility: the 'Germany-door' as migrant threshold in her play *Karagöz in Alamania* (premiered 1986: Black-Eye in Germany); the divided rooms in a divided city in the story 'Großvaterzunge' (Grandfather's Tongue, in the collection *Mutterzunge*); the title motifs of *Das Leben ist eine Karawanserai* and *Die Brücke vom Goldenen Horn* (The Bridge of the Golden Horn, 1998) and their reflection in the form of the narrative; the courtyard and the reflected gaze on it in the title story of *Der Hof im Spiegel* (The Courtyard in the Mirror, 2001);[20] the East–West traverses and (literally) bird's eye view of Berlin in *Seltsame Sterne starren zur Erde* (Strange Stars Stare Towards Earth, 2003).

Özdamar's *Die Brücke vom Goldenen Horn* (1998) deploys Istanbul's ironic, shifting identity at the juncture of two continents to expose, by taking them literally, the widespread, well-meaning yet simplistic metaphors of Turkish-Germans, or their literature, or Turks, or Turkey, as 'bridges between cultures', metaphors that trap their objects like specimens between glass.[21] The novel opens in 1966 with a motif that awakens expectations of a conventional tale of labour migration: its eighteen-year-old narrator's train journey to be a *Gastarbeiterin* (female guest worker) in Berlin. But it then follows her to Paris, back to Istanbul and to Anatolia, and closes with her on another train to Berlin in 1975, this time to work in the theatre. The narrative ranges through the political and intellectual scenes of three European metropoli in the heyday of left-wing activism. It links Turkish student protest with labour and other political struggles – industrial accidents, strikes, anti-union brutalities, right-wing terror – and links both in turn to US imperialism.

The novel's representations of place resist binary models of European/Asian difference. Istanbul and Turkey are shown neither as simply part of Europe, nor as outside it, but as participating, in specifically Turkish ways, in what is conventionally seen in the west as the essentially western phenomenon of '68. Intellectual life in Istanbul is portrayed as relatively

liberal yet shot through with the same sexism whose presence in the German student movement provoked the upsurge of German feminism. A
starker polarity is that between urban modernity and the brutalities of the
rural patriarchy the narrator encounters in Anatolia. Turkey's dismal human
rights record too, often cited in the west as disqualifying it for membership of 'Europe', is reflected in chronicles of torture and political murder,
though contrasted with another fascist regime in a country whose result-
ing right to belong to 'Europe' was rarely questioned: Spain in the Franco
era.

Expectations, in Turkey as in the west, of a linear hierarchy of development between Asia and Europe are invoked, only to be undermined.
Returning from her first visit to Berlin, the narrator asks: 'Mother, has
Istanbul got darker?' 'No, my daughter . . . your eyes have got used to
German light.'[22] Even Istanbul, Turkey's most western city, lags behind the
west's technology and Enlightenment rationality. But the over-explicitness
of the illumination allegory suggests these passages are self-mocking. The
novel shows how cultural perception and cultural learning depend on
complex exchange processes that are rarely one-directional. In Berlin as
a *Gastarbeiterin*, segregated in a hostel and speaking no German, the narrator primarily experiences reinforcement of her separate Turkish identity,
her contacts with the German host culture being largely restricted to comic
misunderstandings. Much of her experience of 'Europe' in fact takes place
in Istanbul. This is not just a matter of encounters with cultural artefacts
such as Mozart, Brecht or Soviet film. The intellectual circles portrayed
in the novel, for all their Marxist-informed social criticism, harbour views
of what characterises the 'European' that are both spurious and snobbish.
Thus the narrator's Anatolian appearance assigns her a lowly place in a Euro-
pean/Asian, urban/rural hierarchy endorsed by Istanbul Turks themselves,
despite the status she gains from her 'European' experience in Germany:
'One could number you amongst the Europeans, but that's not possible
with your thick eyebrows like a peasant woman's' (*B*, 180).

The Golden Horn and the Bosphorus, the two distinct but mingling
stretches of water that both divide Istanbul and join it together, play key
roles, spatially, symbolically and in narrative structure, for the novel's over-
turning of schematic dualisms. The act of crossing the Bosphorus 'between
Europe and Asia' (*B*, 206), is represented as a transition from the narrator's
family on the Asian side to the greater freedoms of the European side, where
the drama school, left-wing bohemian circles, and indeed the doctor willing to carry out the abortion she undergoes to achieve her independence,
are to be found. Her key experience, the decision to reject domesticity

for an acting career, is taken on the Bosphorus ferry, midway between continents.

Özdamar endows this in itself conventional dichotomy of Asia and Europe with several important ambiguities. Istanbul's bridges commonly symbolise the link between two continents, two worlds; but the bridges in question are the Bosphorus bridges and emphatically not the Golden Horn Bridge of Özdamar's title. For the Golden Horn reaches westwards from the Bosphorus into the European continent, and thus does not link Europe and Asia at all, but two parts of Europe.

In doing so, though, it connects 'Europe' in Europe and 'Asia' in Europe: That is, on the northern side are Galata and Beyoğlu, the traditional 'western' quarters. On the southern side are Sultanahmet and Beyazit, crowded with Islamic monuments and home of the bazaar, which for many west Europeans epitomises the orient. However, just as the most famous of these monuments on the Ottoman, 'Asian' southern side, the Aya Sofya mosque, was in fact originally a Christian church, so too during the Ottoman empire the medieval Genoese settlement of Galata on the 'European' northern side developed into an enclave of bustling multi-ethnicity, which was, demographically speaking, very largely European, yet fulfilled every European expectation of oriental, or at least Levantine exoticism.

Here, on the European 'Bridge on the Golden Horn' between the Christian-Ottoman, Asiatic southern quarter and the European-Levantine northern quarter of a geographically speaking wholly European half-city, Özdamar situates the exotic bustle which in Europe is often perceived as 'Asiatic' or 'oriental': tumult, feral dogs, water-sellers, blind grain-hawkers decked in plundering pigeons (*B*, 187–8). This Istanbul, which seethes on and around the bridge, is not only the synapse of Asia and Europe, but also a European city. From the novel's title through its structural and thematic piling up of semiotic possibilities, the bridge metaphor is charged and recharged with meaning until it collapses under its own contradictions.[23]

In Özdamar's *Seltsame Sterne starren zur Erde*, the bridge motif initially appears absent but is in fact replaced by the real and imaginary traversings of political and psychological borders the Turkish narrator undertakes in Germany and especially in Berlin: 'Zwischen', 'between', now describes not an exclusion ordained by others, but a capacity and a freedom to bridge the German divide which is denied her German friends. Stripped of its national pathos by the reverse ethnographic gaze of a Turkish-German writer at ease in German cultural discourse yet not caught in its determinations, the German–German border is a minor hurdle above which the narrator rises with barely an effort: 'When I returned to the Friedrichstraße border crossing, I felt myself grow ever lighter; I was a bird flying over East Berlin, which would gaze on all the streets Brecht and Besson ever walked and laugh with delight. Cock-a-doodle-doo, cock-a-doodle-doo.'[24]

The example of Özdamar shows that bridge motifs have not lost their fundamental relevance, but that the tendency of the bridge motif deterministically to fix Turkish-German subject positions as victim positions has provoked critical engagement with these experiences and with their metaphoric description, and as a result generated new subject positions within the German-language cultural landscape. This reflexive engagement with its own traditions and reception has characterised much Turkish-German writing since the mid 1990s.

ZAFER ŞENOCAK

In Zafer Şenocak's tetralogy of interlinked prose *Der Mann im Unterhemd* (The Man in the Undershirt, 1995), *Die Prärie* (The Prairie, 1997), *Gefährliche Verwandtschaft* and *Der Erottomane* (The Erot(t)omaniac, 1999), the protagonists roam through textual landscapes shaped by the suspension and subversion of fixed notions of time, space, gender, ethnicity or character. They move, too, in and out of representation itself: the boundaries between figures as experiencing subjects and as symbolic or other textual markers are open and shifting. The sense of selves, especially male selves, in flux in Şenocak's fiction is interwoven with his pursuit, in his essays, of a new consciousness of 'what it means to be German [in which he clearly includes German Turks such as himself] in an ethnically and culturally heterogeneous German society'.[25] By the middle of the first decade of the twenty-first century, Şenocak was much studied outside Germany,[26] and translated into at least eleven languages, yet notably undervalued in Germany itself.

The male body plays a central role in the tetralogy, but it is not the male body as casualty of migrant labour,[27] since for most of the male protagonists work is absent, peripheral or, typically, that of the writer. Şenocak's male figures display traits often associated with an 'effeminate' Orient: lassitude, passivity, ambiguous sexual orientation. Read literally, the polymorphous, sometimes sado-masochistic sexual practices frequently invoked in the texts can appear pornographic, but they are also poetic metaphors for the dissolution of boundaries not only of gender, but also of ethnicity, nation, spatial and temporal logic. *Die Prärie*, for example, is a text of male and narratorial as much as migrant self-exploration. Sascha is inconstant, elusive, spendthrift, three times divorced, loses his 'orientation' whilst writer-in-residence at a US college,[28] repeatedly delegates his narrator role, and focuses all his limited energies on the pursuit of sex. Indeed he is more interested in sex than in his Islamic roots, something the German media in the novel, with their blinkered view of legitimate themes for migrant authors, cannot grasp.

Ironically, given its allusion to the 'virility fiction' of Ernest Hemingway, *Der Mann im Unterhemd* is the one text in the tetralogy where a female figure is more than a shadowy bit player to the male principals. A series of 'Lisa' texts link a grandmother, mother and daughter. The grandmother, a prostitute serving top Nazis in Berlin in the Weimar Republic's final phase, commits suicide after her poet lover is probably – the text is characteristically imprecise – murdered by the SA (Nazi storm troopers). Her granddaughter in reunified Berlin uses the same profession as a means of empowerment, kidnapping and torturing half-willing men in ritual orgies. Taking revenge by emasculating the grandsons of her grandmother's equally male tormentors, she enacts a transformation both private and (somewhat obviously) symbolic. *Der Mann im Unterhemd* is an intense, poetic engagement with post-wall Berlin as 'the navel of no man's land', a city suddenly freed of its historical shackles, yet still haunted by its historical determinations, a place of radical, but guilt-ridden opportunity.[29]

In *Gefährliche Verwandtschaft*, Şenocak enmeshes his narrator, writer Sascha Muhteschem, in a Jewish-Turkish-German-Armenian family history that is a dense pattern of interrelated circumstances he never fully knows or understands.[30] The result is not a historical novel but a provocative and perspectively distinctive contribution to the debates about cultural memory in the 1990s, exploring the paradoxes of seeking to secure a sense of belonging to a society of which one is a part but whose collective historical traumas one has not shared.

Sascha grew up a German, largely unconscious of his ethnic background as son of a European-educated bourgeois Turkish father and Jewish German mother. But when he returns to post-*Wende* (after the fall of the Wall) Berlin from the USA, he discovers that he no longer belongs. He has missed participation in the historic events that revitalised German national sentiment, and he finds himself involuntarily identified as an ethnic interloper. Disoriented (or, perhaps, re-oriented), he begins to investigate a family past previously withheld and of little interest to him. His mother survived Nazism by fleeing to Turkey, where Sascha was later conceived; thus, absurdly, Sascha would not exist without the Holocaust. But in her efforts to secure his assimilation in the Germany where he was then born, his mother has created a lacuna in his sense of self by suppressing all memory of the Holocaust. His Turkish grandfather fought on the German side in World War I, then against the Allied occupation alongside Mustafa Kemal, later known as Atatürk, founder of modern Turkey, and was responsible for deportations of Armenians in 1921. He committed suicide in Berlin in 1936. Thus Sascha's previously unconsidered Turkish and Jewish descent links him, potentially, to collective memories of both perpetration and victimhood. Confronted with scattered hints such as his grandfather's relationship to an Armenian woman at the time of the Turkish massacres of Armenians in 1915–16, Sascha invents an autobiographical text supposedly by his grandfather that implicates the latter in the massacres, and provides a link from them to his suicide.

Though the novel is studded with references to twentieth-century European history, it provides a narrative neither of the massacres nor of the complex background to their contested historiography, in which patriotic Armenian historians and German revisionists promote them as an anticipation of the Holocaust and Turkish historians drastically downplay their magnitude. Rather, Sascha further instrumentalises the massacres for his own purposes. He would prefer, he says, not to be part of 'a community bound together by fateful history [*Schicksalsgemeinschaft*]'. But 'to be taken seriously as a complete person', he needs origins.[31] In post-Holocaust Germany, the offspring of victims and of perpetrators are linked, across the divide of their ancestors' role in it or their contemporary assessment of it, by a common past whose contested status only increases its phenomenological significance. If this is what a reconstituted, 'normalised' German identity will be based on, Germans without this past, such as Sascha, can only participate through bizarre counterfeits.

So, faking a war-criminal grandfather, he straps on 'a prosthesis-like identity' (*GV*, 121). Now he can speak the 'lingua franca' (*GV*, 60) of contemporary Germany, the language of contrition, alongside his German fellows-in-guilt. 'Suddenly I was no longer a stranger in Berlin. I was no longer just at home here. I belonged here' (*GV*, 47). Sascha is excluded from the imagined community of perpetrator offspring until his fictionalised addition to his grandfather's biography provides his passport to integration. Thus the historical genocide is invoked to solve Sascha's identity crisis.

One should not, of course, confuse narrator with author. It is possible to read *Gefährliche Verwandtschaft* as a critique precisely of Sascha's practice of buying belonging with the counterfeit coinage of an invented culpability. Critics have also admonished the flat, lifeless figures in Şenocak's work generally, and the unemotional vagueness of Sascha's engagement with the history he uncovers in particular. One could see this laconic lassitude in the face of a genocidal legacy as a defence mechanism or, as he himself implies (*GV*, 61), a principled refusal to mime the forced affectedness of rituals and monuments of Holocaust commemoration in Germany.

However, analyses such as this, which posit Sascha as a consistent psychological entity, though they cannot wholly be dispensed with, soon reach their limits. Sascha is also an example of the narrating 'I' producing 'an illusion of reference' that is repeatedly interrupted.[32] He is not a consistent moral subject or a representative of an ethnic or even socio-economic group, certainly not a 'Turk' or 'Turkish-German'. Rather, he is a construct, a textual ganglion where transnational historical processes intersect, from which Şenocak can develop new perspectives on central questions in modern German culture, unsettle and challenge German and Turkish myths of self and other, explore the implications of a commingled Turkish and German remembrance, and introduce new terms to topple the syllogisms of ethnicity rather than remaining trapped in their false-premise logic.

Şenocak's *Der Erottomane* (1999) extensively and intensively explores masculinities and the male body's cultural, psychological, sexual signifying possibilities.[33] The title, punning 'erotomaniac' and 'He-Ottoman,' blends the author's gender awareness and the orientalist image of the sensual Turk. The subtitle, *Ein Findelbuch*, playing on 'Findelkind', the abandoned child of unknown parents, reflects the text's complex games with authorship. The focus shifts between first the main narrator, secondly his friend Tom, who had been the Turk Tayfun before undergoing the 'cosmetic operation'[34] of acquiring German citizenship (the unnatural undertaken in order to become naturalised), and thirdly the texts of the writer R. (Robert), whose murder it is Tom's task as public prosecutor to investigate. But it is always probable that all three are one person, or rather that the text's anti-literality extends to its protagonists, who are figures less in the sense of psychological characters than in the sense of tropes: of migration, transition and ambivalence.

Repeated motifs of aborted or inconclusive journeys challenge linear purposefulness and the discrete self. R. has no goals, uses an outdated map, and in each new city discards both his clothing and his past. His nickname, the 'Erottoman', combining his sexual reputation with an orientalist projection onto his ethnic origins, emphasises the fact that the body R. inhabits is partly constructed in the perceptions of others, a process which feminises the migrant body and inverts gender practices. One of his sexual partners, indeed, 'wrote her ideas on his body' (*E*, 63), subjecting it to female signification as well as the female gaze. R. arouses not women's femininity but 'their masculinity', expressed, for example, in penetrations by various phallic women.

In the 'seven-tongued whip' ('siebenzüngige Peitsche', the German equivalent of 'cat-o'-nine-tails'), which one of these women wields, the tongue, organ of speech, and therefore both of domination and revolt, manifests itself as an instrument whose capacity to deliver punishment and pleasure is a consequence of its multiplicity (*E*, 63–5). This recalls Şenocak's early poem 'Doppelmann' with its image of the 'border' running 'down the middle of my tongue', which was widely interpreted when it appeared in 1984 as encapsulating the linguistic as well as material alienation of migrants, but where in fact Şenocak already evokes the ludic potential in discomfort, 'the game on a wound'.[35] Thus from the beginning his work went beyond the motif of the tongue as site of migrant suffering. In *Zungenentfernung* (Removal of the Tongue(s), 2001), the essay 'Jenseits der Landessprache' (Beyond the Language of the Country) also questions the motif of the tongue as site of self-assertion, common in migrant literature, by insisting on the non-congruity of self and language and arguing the superiority of Paul Celan's relentlessly counter-hermeneutic poetry over Enzensberger's socially engaged rationality,[36] while the volume's title gives notice of an act of removal of and from the tongue as a refusal to perpetuate familiar tropes, whether of migrant inarticulacy or garrulity. Şenocak's work is one of the most strikingly original examples of a dialectic whereby, out of a process set in train by Turkish migration to Germany, writing is emerging which has long liberated itself from the determining influence of these origins.

CONCLUSION

Contemporary Germany would be unthinkable without the contribution of migration, including labour migration, to its economy, society and culture, though it has taken the mainstream culture many decades to acknowledge this, for example with the two major exhibitions 'Zuwanderungsland Deutschland' (Germany: A Country of Immigration) and 'Migrationen 1500–2005' (Migrations 1500–2005) at the Deutsches Historisches Museum in Berlin in 2005. Meanwhile, Turkish-German writing, which would not exist in its contemporary variety and aesthetic sophistication without the history of labour migration, has moved well beyond these origins: as this chapter has shown, there is no excuse for hearing only the dull throb of a *Gastarbeiter* beating on a cardboard suitcase in the rich polyphony of contemporary Turkish-German writing.

NOTES

1. See Sabine Fischer and Moray McGowan, 'From Pappkoffer to Pluralism: Migrant Writing in the Federal Republic of Germany' in Russell King, John Connell and Paul White, eds., *Writing Across Worlds: Literature and Migration* (London and New York: Routledge, 1995), 39–56; Sargut Şölçün, 'Literatur der türkischen Migration' in Carmine Chiellino, ed., *Interkulturelle Literatur in Deutschland: Ein Handbuch* (Stuttgart: Metzler, 2000), 135–53.

2. Azade Seyhan, *Writing Outside the Nation* (Princeton University Press, 2001).

3. Leslie A. Adelson, *The Turkish Turn in Contemporary German Literature: Towards a Critical Grammar of Migration* (New York and Basingstoke: Palgrave Macmillan, 2005).

4. Alene A. Teraoka, '*Gastarbeiterliteratur*: The Other Speaks Back', *Cultural Critique* 7 (Fall 1987): 77–101.

5. Joyce Mushaben, quoted by Adelson, *The Turkish Turn*, 14.

6. See Moray McGowan, 'Some Turkish-German Views and Visions of "Europa" ' in Barrie Axford, Daniela Berghahn and Nick Hewlett, eds., *Unity and Diversity in the New Europe* (Oxford: Peter Lang, 2000), 339–54.

7. Tom Cheesman, 'Talking "*Kanak*": Zaimoğlu contra *Leitkultur*', *New German Critique* 92 (2004): 82–100, here 93.

8. Selim Özdogan, *Es ist so einsam in Sattel, seit das Pferd tot ist* (Berlin: Aufbau 1997), 7.

9. Mark Terkessidis, 'Nicht ohne meine Klage', *Welt am Sonntag* (3 July 2005).

10. See Karin E. Yeşilada, 'Topographien im "tropischen Deutschland" – türkisch-deutsche Literatur nach der Wiedervereinigung' in Ursula Beitter, ed., *Literatur und Identität: Deutsch–deutsche Befindlichkeiten und die multikulturelle Gesellschaft* (New York: Peter Lang, 2000), 325–6.

11. Aras Ören, *Sehnsucht nach Hollywood* (Berlin: Elefanten Press, 1999), 139.

12. Adelson, *The Turkish Turn*, 169.

13. Cheesman, 'Talking "*Kanak*"', 93.

14. *Kanak Sprak: 24 Mißtöne vom Rande der Gesellschaft* (Hamburg: Rotbuch, 1995), 11–12. Hereafter *KS*.

15. Cheesman, 'Talking "*Kanak*"', 83.

16. See Adelson, *The Turkish Turn*, 95–104.

17. See Cheesman, 'Talking "*Kanak*"'.

18. 'Deutsch muß man lernen', *Die Zeit* (30 September 2004), 47.

19. Marilya Veteto-Conrad, *Finding a Voice: Identity and the Works of German-Language Turkish Writers in the Federal Republic of Germany to 1990* (Berne: Lang, 1996); Annete Wierschke, *Schreiben als Selbstbehauptung: Kulturkonflikt und Identität in den Werken von Aysel Özakin, Alev Tekinay und Emine Sevgi Özdamar* (Frankfurt: Iko, 1996).

20. See Adelson, *The Turkish Turn*, 40–77.

21. See Leslie A. Adelson, 'Against Between: A Manifesto' in Salah Hassan and Iftikhar Dadi, eds., *Unpacking Europe: Towards a Critical Reading* (Rotterdam: Nai Publishers, 2001), 244–55; Moray McGowan, 'Brücken und

Brücken-Köpfe: Wandlungen einer Metapher in der türkisch-deutschen Literatur' in Manfred Durzak and Nilüfer Kuruyazici, eds., *Die andere deutsche Literatur* (Würzburg: Königshausen & Neumann 2004), 31–40.

22. Emine Sevgi Özdamar, *Die Brücke vom Goldenen Horn* (Cologne: Kiepenheuer & Witsch, 1998), 107. Hereafter *B*.

23. See Moray McGowan, '"The Bridge of the Golden Horn": Istanbul, Europe and the "Fractured Gaze from the West" in Turkish Writing in Germany', *Yearbook of European Studies* 15 (2000): 53–69.

24. *Seltsame Sterne starren zur Erde* (Cologne: Kiepenheuer & Witsch, 2003), 34.

25. Zafer Şenocak, *Atlas of a Tropical Germany*, trans. Leslie A. Adelson (Lincoln, NE: University of Nebraska Press, 2000), xl-xli.

26. See Tom Cheesman and Karin E. Yeşilada, eds., *Zafer Şenocak* (Cardiff: University of Wales Press, 2003).

27. See Moray McGowan: 'Multiple Masculinities in Turkish-German Men's Writing' in Roy Jerome, ed., *Conceptions of Postwar German Masculinity* (Albany: SUNY Press, 2001), 289–312.

28. Zafer Şenocak, *Die Prärie* (Hamburg: Rotbuch, 1997), 69.

29. *Der Mann im Unterhemd* (Munich: Babel, 1995), 36. See Yeşilada, 'Topographien', 317.

30. See Margaret Littler, 'Guilt, Victimhood, and Identity in Zafer Şenocak's *Gefährliche Verwandtschaft*', *German Quarterly* 78:3 (2005): 357–73, and Adelson, *The Turkish Turn*, 104–22.

31. Zafer Şenocak, *Gefährliche Verwandtschaft* (Munich: Babel 1998), 121. Hereafter *GV*.

32. Adelson, *The Turkish Turn*, 112 (paraphrasing Paul de Man) and 118.

33. See Moray McGowan, 'Odysseus on the Ottoman, or "The Man in Skirts": Exploratory Masculinities in the Prose Texts of Zafer Şenocak' in Cheesman and Yeşilada, eds., *Zafer Şenocak*, 61–79.

34. Zafer Şenocak, *Der Erottomane* (Munich: Babel, 1999), 8. Hereafter *E*.

35. Anthologised in Irmgard Ackermann, ed., *Türken deutscher Sprache* (Munich: dtv, 1984); republished in Şenocak, *Übergang* (Munich: Babel, 2005), 147.

36. Zafer Şenocak, *Zungenentfernung* (Munich: Babel, 2001), 81–103.

CHAPTER 13

German-language writing from eastern and central Europe

Brigid Haines

Germany's Turkish-German writers have attracted much critical attention, particularly in the UK and the USA, and its German-Jewish writers are beginning to do the same, yet the treatment of writers from, or whose parents were from, former eastern bloc countries other than the GDR has been patchy. While several prize-winning authors fall into this category, their works remain underresearched. This chapter argues that in recent years these writers have made not only a distinguished but also a distinctive contribution to German literature and that, despite the varied nature of their writing, there is a strong case, at present at least, for considering their works collectively.

The reasons why this body of writing exists at all have to do firstly with the presence of large numbers of Germans in the countries of eastern and central Europe from the middle ages until the mid to late twentieth century. This was a result of successive waves of colonisation from the twelfth to the eighteenth centuries. Germans tended to dominate the region economically and the German minorities were privileged under Habsburg rule up to the collapse of Austria-Hungary in 1918. Secondly, the fall of communism and the economic success of the Federal Republic of Germany have led to a wave of migration *to* Germany of ethnic Germans but also of many others from eastern and central Europe since 1990. This migration largely completed the task of 'bringing Germans home', which was begun with the mass deportations of Germans from countries such as Czechoslovakia after the Second World War (Germans from the east who happened also to be Jewish having been either exterminated in the Holocaust or having mostly emigrated elsewhere).[1] These factors have led to the emergence of a new generation of writers, some of whom are native speakers of German and some of whom have learned it as a second language, but all of whom have direct or indirect (via their parents) experience of life in such countries as Bulgaria, Hungary, Romania, Russia and Poland, both pre- and post-communism, and view Germany through, or partially through, the perspective of an outsider. Their texts are a reminder that a Germany without imperial ambitions and with agreed and fixed borders in which the vast majority of ethnic Germans reside is a relatively recent phenomenon; one only has to note the birthplace of 'canonical' twentieth-century German-language writers such as Franz Kafka (Prague, the Czech Republic), Paul Celan (Czernovitz, Romania) and Günter Grass (Gdansk, Poland) to appreciate the truth of this statement.

Among ethnic Germans from abroad, the most voluble group in terms of literary output has long been the Romanian-Germans, notably Richard Wagner and Herta Müller. Before the *Wende* (the fall of the Berlin Wall), the Romanian-Germans were already recognised as a distinct sub-group of German literature and have even been called the 'fifth' German literature (after the literatures of East and West Germany, Austria and Switzerland). Earlier works by Wagner, in particular *Ausreiseantrag* (Application to Leave, 1988) and *Begrüßungsgeld* (Welcome Money, 1989), and by Müller, in particular *Niederungen* (Flat Lands, 1984), *Reisende auf einem Bein* (Travelling on one Leg, 1989) and *Der Fuchs war damals schon der Jäger* (The Fox was even then the Hunter, 1992), described life in the Romanian Banat and the alienating experience of ethnic German immigrants arriving in the 'homeland' to find themselves subtly excluded from day-to-day life there. Immigrants of other ethnicities include Libuše Moníková (first language: Czech), Carmen-Francesca Banciu (first language: Romanian) and Terézia Mora (brought up bilingual: Hungarian and German). Among the children of immigrants, the writer Zsuzsa Bánk (whose parents are from Hungary) stands out. More marginal to the present chapter because of the volume's focus on the Berlin Republic, are the works of writers from eastern and central Europe who, sometimes by chance, have gravitated towards German-speaking countries other than Germany. Into this group fall, for example, Irena Brežná and Florian Catalin Florescu, who were born in Czechoslovakia and Romania respectively but moved to Switzerland, and Radek Knapp, born in Poland but now living in Austria. The literature discussed in this chapter thus resists containment and easy categorisation, crossing as it does linguistic and political borders, but, as I hope to show, this is a major source of its significance: these texts demand to be read in multiple contexts, not just in relation to national literatures such as German but also to such categories as European literature, literature of trauma, post-Holocaust literature, and post-communist literature. Incidentally, the four novels which will be the main focus of my analysis, Libuše Moníková's *Verklärte Nacht* (Transfigured Night, 1996), Herta Müller's *Herztier* (Heart Beast, 1994), Zsuzsa Bánk's *Der Schwimmer* (The Swimmer, 2002) and Terézia Mora's *Alle Tage* (Every

Day, 2004), happen to be by women, who all have interesting things to say about gender, but gender is not my primary line of enquiry here. Neither is it the dominant theme in any of the novels, a fact which perhaps reflects the suspicion with which women from eastern bloc countries have typically regarded western feminism.[2]

The complex history of central and eastern Europe is inevitably reflected in the texts under discussion. It is a mistake to regard the area as a homogenous bloc even during the period of Soviet domination, for the individual national histories of the many peoples of the region, each rooted in its own foundation myths and particular combination of geographical, religious and ethnic factors, continued to be played out at that time. It is also a mistake to overlook the many historical and cultural commonalities between some of these nations, particularly those northern countries with a long tradition of belonging to Catholic Christendom, and the nations of western Europe: Czechs are fond of pointing out, for example, that Prague lies to the west of Vienna, and both Poland and Hungary can look back on long periods of sovereign statehood. Any generalising statements about the region must therefore be regarded with caution. Nevertheless, it is also the case that the countries of eastern and central Europe share a certain common history which distinguishes them from the countries of western Europe and which predates communism by many centuries.[3] While it is commonplace, for example, to think of the term 'eastern Europe' as being a Cold-War, and therefore relatively recent term, it is instructive to remember that the Iron Curtain essentially reproduced the border of Charlemagne's Holy Roman Empire. Common to these countries is not just the Soviet domination from the late 1940s to 1990 but the experience of domination per se: before 1918 they were dominated by the Habsburg Empire, Russia and Ottoman Turkey, later by the Nazis. Since the nineteenth century the aspirations to nationhood of the various peoples in the region have often been thwarted by larger powers and their attempts at democracy undermined, most notoriously when the western powers refused to defend Czechoslovakia against Hitler in 1938. They also have in common a tradition of multiculturalism and multilingualism, but also of ethnic tensions. Despite the differing course taken by these countries during the period of communist rule and the differing results (for example the relative prosperity of Czechoslovakia and Hungary in the 1980s in relation to Romania), certain dates had resonance throughout the Soviet bloc, most notably 1953 (the death of Stalin and the uprising in the GDR), 1956 (the Hungarian uprising), 1968 (the crushing of the Prague Spring) and 1989/90 (the fall of communism). These dates also had significance in the west but did not bind the populations in the same way (and some, particularly 1968, had extra and quite other meanings for westerners). The countries of central and eastern Europe also share a variety of experiences arising from the fall of communism, most typically an initial period of euphoria, quickly fol-lowed by instability caused by the fast pace of reform and the unleashing of market economics, frequently accompanied by the rise of nationalism and xenophobia. In comparison with the current relative political and eco-nomic stagnation of, say, Germany and France, the prevailing mood with regard to the European Union could currently be described as one of opti-mism, although, as in the new *Bundesländer* (federal states), some in the population hark back with nostalgia to the securities of the past.

WHERE IS MY HOMELAND?

One of the commonest tropes of recent years has been the return of the exile from western Europe after the *Wende* to the land of their birth, in search of an authentic sense of belonging, a quest which inevitably fails. In Richard Wagner's *Habseligkeiten* (Belongings, 2004), the first-person narrator's return to the Romanian Banat leads to reflections on his fam-ily's history, including the unsuccessful attempt by his great-grandparents to settle in the USA, and on his own double alienation as a Romanian-German in the Federal Republic. Carmen-Francesca Banciu's *Vaterflucht* (Flight from the Father, 1998) uses the occasion of the female narrator's return to Romania to explore the damage inflicted on her by growing up in a family where the parents were hard-line communists. Though sometimes veering towards self-pity, Banciu's autobiographically-based narrator recalls the excitement engendered during the early days of Ceauşescu's rule, espe-cially when he stood up to the Soviet Union over the Prague Spring, and successfully conveys the sense of frustration that Romania has always been on the losing side in history. The figure of her great-grandmother holds a particular fascination: affectionate and spontaneous, unlike the narra-tor's cold and dutiful parents, she was neverthless a dangerous role model because she was not a comrade but a devout Catholic, a supporter of the Kaiser who saw herself not as a Romanian but a European and citizen of the world.

Both of these works end on a note of reconciliation: Wagner's protago-nist marries a prostitute from Budapest, and Banciu's narrator is able to feel sorry for her father whose utopian dreams have come to nothing. Catalin Dorian Florescu's *Der kurze Weg nach Hause* (The Short Way Home, 2002) adopts a more complex narrative strategy to convey both a wider sense of damage in contemporary Europe and the incommensurability of experience. Ovidiu, a twenty-three-year-old who left Romania nine years previously, is accompanied on his return home in the spring of 1990, three months after the death of Ceauşescu, by his Italian friend Luca, the son of a *Gastarbeiter* (guest worker in the Federal Republic of Germany). While Ovidiu's father, happy to be in prosperous Switzerland, urges him not to go, Switzerland's young people are shown to be alienated: the young men's friend Toma is a drug addict, and Luca, traumatised by his childhood separation from his family for reasons of economic necessity, is on the run from the present. Return brings disorientation for Ovidiu: his clothes and gestures mark him as a westerner, yet he feels an expatriate Romanian's shame at the poverty and depression he witnesses. Crucially, he has missed the period of transition, and when these dramatic events are narrated to him by witnesses, he evades translating the full account for Luca; instead he sanitises, simplifies or embellishes in order not to mediate the full horror of events. He cannot relay the brutal truth, for example, that an old man cheated his wife when he found some meat. There is a love story with a Hungarian here too, but it is used to explore the traditional hatred between the Hungarians and the Romanians and also the new economic exploitation by Germans and Swiss of Hungarian women.

The protagonist who returns to Prague from the Federal Republic in Libuše Moníková's *Verklärte Nacht* is not young but middle-aged and world-weary; indeed she identifies strongly with Emilia Marty, the three-hundred-year-old heroine of Janáček's opera, *The Makropulos Case*, and even shares her surname.[4] Emilia Marty's longevity was due to a potion which her father, on the orders of Rudolf II, tried out on her. Lonely, tired of life, and ageing at last, she returned to Prague to die. Leonora Marty is similarly isolated and misanthropic, railing against the guilt of obedient fathers everywhere; she too takes a long view of history. The moment at which she returns is highly significant for the fate of her country: it is 1992, just before Czechoslovakia, that artificial state set up in 1918 and interrupted by the Nazis, then dominated by the Soviet Union until the 'Velvet Revolution' of 1989, was finally to split into its component parts, and the novel contains a reckoning with Czech history in general and the history of Prague in particular.[5] Marty's declaration that 'the delusion of the powerful is reality for the weak' (*VN*, 69) provides one model for her understanding of history. Identifying with those over the ages in besieged towns such as Troy and Masada, she reads, with not a little satisfaction, newspaper stories revealing details of the recent crumbling of the Soviet empire: about the dolphins trained for military purposes now redeployed to swim with children, about the shocking case of a Russian soldier on duty who died of starvation, and about the extent of environmental damage in the Soviet Union.

She feels pride at the speed with which the Soviet troops were made to leave her country, and relief that they are finally gone, but in the country that remains there is much to feel uncomfortable about. There are the unwelcome revelations about those who collaborated with the state security under communism, shame at the practice of open prostitution on the E55 road to Germany – 'that is also my country' (VN, 63–4) – and irritation at the mass of tourists in Prague, the ugliness of the new suburbs and the flood of trashy, mass-produced imported goods on sale in the shops. Marty even notes newspaper criticism of Václav Havel, the playwright turned president, embodiment of resistance under communism, for allowing himself to be courted on the world stage while serious domestic tensions were building up at home.

Marty's critique is personal and spontaneous, and partly inspired by her western outlook, but is also the result of a poststructuralist conception of history and subjectivity which acknowledges difference, allows space for celebration of the particular, yet resists essentialist thinking. Janáček's music provides the model: 'No composer combined so closely the dissonant on the edge of tonality with melody, with passion' (VN, 89). Although Marty mourns the passing of the country called 'Czechoslovakia' and is occasionally tempted to imagine that it had a sense of integrity, she is aware, even as it unravels before her eyes, that it was always shot through with difference. Though herself a Czech, she feels nostalgia for Slovakia, for example, yet is aware intellectually that the grievances of the Slovaks within the state Czechoslovakia were not unfounded. Any consideration of Czechoslovakia must also address the German question, and this Marty does honestly, and on two levels. First, she acknowledges the German influence on the architecture and culture of Prague: 'The history of the city is a history of the reciprocal answers between Czechs and Germans, without one side ever having asked a question' (VN, 39). Culture, particularly in central Europe, can be cosmopolitan, or can fall on deaf ears: Prague is the city where Mozart, misunderstood in Vienna, was understood, but where, a hundred years later, Janáček, loved in provincial Brno, was reviled.

Secondly, Marty is forced to confront the expulsion of the Sudeten Germans from Czechoslovakia after the Second World War and consider their claim also to belong to 'Czechoslovakia'. When she meets and reluctantly falls in love with Thomas Asperger, a German, members of whose family came from the Sudetenland, together they work through aspects of Czech and German identity, a painful task which involves confronting their own prejudices and preconceptions. These are transcended through the erotic moment prefigured in the reference to atonal composer Schoenberg's musical piece *Verklärte Nacht*. The novel suggests finally that the question 'where is my homeland?', which is the title of the Czech national anthem, is more important than any answers it might produce.

SPEAKING THE UNSPEAKABLE

A second category of texts attempts to bear witness to the horrors of life under communist rule. In her memoirs, *Alle Farben der Sonne und der Nacht* (All Colours of the Sun and the Night, 2003), for example, the German-Jewish writer Lenka Reinerová, who is still resident in Prague where she was born in 1916 and who has often been compared with Anna Seghers, recalls her arrest and imprisonment by her former comrades in the early 1950s. Most texts in this category dispense with hindsight altogether: Aglaja Veteranyi's novel *Warum das Kind in der Polenta kocht* (Why the Child is Cooking in the Polenta, 1999) invokes the inhumanity, violence and abjection of daily life in Romania, a country reduced to Third World conditions, where some resorted to eating their dogs and selling their children, through the naive perspective of a girl growing up in a circus family.[6] On leaving for the west the fragile family unit implodes. The lack of the historical understanding found in Banciu's text is more than compensated for by the immediacy attained through a spare, poetic prose in which less is more. To quieten the girl's fear when her beloved mother performs dangerous feats on the high wire, for example, her older sister tells her the story of the child who falls into the polenta; on being asked why God allows this, she replies 'GOD IS ALWAYS VERY HUNGRY' (*WKP*, 75, upper case in the original). Other examples of childlike formulations resonating with philosophical or theological profundity or unsentimental pathos include 'IN EVERY LANGUAGE THE SAME IS CALLED DIFFERENT' (*WKP*, 87); 'PEOPLE ARE GOOD BECAUSE THEY ARE AFRAID OF THE DEVIL' (*WKP*, 95), and 'MY SISTER HAS BECOME MY MOTHER' (*WKP*, 98).

Herta Müller's *Herztier* also employs language economically; the technique here, however, is not naive but surrealist.[7] A dreamlike style, in which certain words are symbolically overdetermined, is used to convey the damage done to friendship and to individual consciousness by extreme political terror, for, as Müller maintained in interview, 'you can't write a woodenly realistic book about a dictatorship'.[8] Four friends, all ethnic Germans, students and intellectuals, are persecuted by the Securitate, Ceauşescu's secret service. They undergo interrogations before being forcibly dispersed to various spots around the country, only managing to keep in touch by writing to each other in code. Two of the group are driven to suicide, while another girl, Lola, also commits suicide near the beginning of the text, and the narrator's greatest friend Tereza, a member of the Romanian communist elite, betrays her. The text is clearly decodable in terms of Müller's own biography: after a period of persecution she and her then husband, Richard Wagner, left for the Federal Republic together; their friends and fellow writers Rolf Bossert and Roland Kirch died. As members of the German community in Romania, the narrator and her friends are heirs to a particular tradition of double dictatorship. The German community preserved its sense of identity through rigidly codified values and overwhelmingly supported Hitler, the men volunteering in droves for the SS. The narrator and her friends reject this heritage, though the emotional blackmail practised by their mothers, ill with stress, and the Securitate's clever tactic of involving the families in the persecution of the students, ensure maximum feelings of personal guilt. They are privileged in relation to their Romanian compatriots in that they have a right to leave if they wish (Ceauşescu effectively sold Germans to the Federal Republic, which welcomed them), yet none of the friends wants to leave the country, having no sense of belonging anywhere else. But they are nearly all forced to do so when the state makes life impossible for them.

Müller fictionalises and depersonalises in order to connect with other literature of trauma and to make unexpected connections within the text. The expression 'making graveyards',[9] for example, is used to link the crimes of the narrator's father, an ex-member of the SS and still an unreconstructed Nazi, with those of the dictator, that is, Ceauşescu (*Ht*, 8). The narrator and her friend Edgar, the survivors, look back on the series of tragedies from the relative safety of the west and find themselves in a bind with regard to the task of bearing witness: '"When we don't speak", said Edgar, "we become unbearable, and when we do, we make fools of ourselves . . . The words in our mouths do as much damage as our feet on the grass. But so do our silences"' (*Ht*, 7). As the phrase 'making graveyards' illustrates, the solution Müller finds is to speak indirectly, investing objects with meaning and juxtaposing them to surreal effect. Thus when the narrator writes enigmatically at the opening of the novel, 'To this day, I can't really picture a grave. Only a belt, a window, a nut, and a rope' (*Ht*, 7), she is referrring indirectly to the four deaths and the associated trauma: Lola, pregnant with a Party official's unwanted child, hanged herself with the narrator's belt and was posthumously expelled from the Party by a unanimous popular vote in which the narrator herself took part; Georg, the first of the friends to succumb to pressure and leave the country, only to find himself still within the reach of the Securitate, throws himself (or is pushed) out of the window of a Frankfurt hostel to his death; Tereza dies of a cancer which first manifests itself in a nut-like growth under her arm; and Kurt, too depressed to emigrate after witnessing scenes in a slaughterhouse where the hungry workers drink fresh cows' blood, hangs himself with a rope.

Other metonymic symbols are less easy to decode or require more local knowledge. By analysing the formulation 'the proletariat of tin sheep and wooden melons' (*Ht*, 37), Valentina Glajar, for example, demonstrates that Müller is mounting a critique of the expropriation and nationalisation which tried but failed to turn peasants into proletarians and the country from an agricultural into an industrial one overnight.[10] In its focus on details invested with meaning and its avoidance of universalising statements, Müller's open style is a deliberate reversal of the utopian visions and prescriptive formulas of Socialist Realism with which she grew up. These lead, in her view, to terror. Indeed the narrator's interrogation by Captain Pjele centres on their differing conceptions of literature: he insists that a poem by Gellu Naum which merely expresses a yearning for freedom from fear,

> Everyone had a friend in every wisp of cloud
> that's how it is where the world is full of fear
> even my mother said, that's how it is
> friends are out of the question
> think of more serious things   (*Ht*, 89)

is a direct and therefore treasonous incitement to flee the country, a charge she rejects.

SWIMMING AGAINST THE COLD WAR

Zsuzsa Bánk's *Der Schwimmer* is an elegiac story of loss. It is perhaps significant that the most melancholy text and the one which grieves most intensely over the fracture of Europe caused by the Iron Curtain is the one written by the child of immigrants who grew up in the Federal Republic. The novel is narrated from the perspective of Kata, a young girl, whose mother, also called Kata, flees to the west after the Hungarian uprising of 1956. The young Kata's depressed father, Verencei Kálmán, takes his daughter and her younger brother Isti travelling the length and breadth of

Hungary, staying with relatives along the way. The children are enormously hurt by the loss of their mother and their inability to reach her although she is not so far away: their grandmother is able to visit her in Austria. They live in fear that their itinerant, distant and womanising father, their only carer, will also leave them. Kata focuses her pain onto looking after her more vulnerable and unusually sensitive younger brother, who never comes to terms with the loss of his mother. The family's only moments of happiness occur in the waters of Lake Balaton where swimming gives all of them, especially Kálmán and Isti, a temporary release from tension. But Isti later dies as a result of falling into a frozen river (in his delirium he says he was following his mother), leaving daughter and father alone.

The novel is a meditation on loss in the widest sense: familial, political, existential. It becomes clear that many absent people haunt the present: not just the mother, but also Miklos, Kálmán's father, a wealthy farmer who committed suicide when his land was expropriated, leaving his wife and son destitute. Others whose physical absence is powerfully felt are Jenö, the children's cousin who flees to the west for a better life, their other cousin Virag's unnamed sister, from whose death in infancy her family never recovers, and, finally, Isti, whose loss is the end point and structuring principle of the novel. But still others are absent in their presence, and this can be more terrible. Zoltán, for example, Kálmán's cousin and the dead child's father, is suffering from a form of dementia. Largely unaware of his surroundings, he occasionally, unwittingly or not, makes telling and poignant remarks. When he sees the dying Isti in bed, for example, he says, 'that boy, I know him, what's the matter with him?'.[11] But above all it is the brooding presence of Kálmán that dominates the novel, despite the fact that none of his words are recorded and the children have no access to his inner life, though they frequently witness him 'diving' (S, 8) into his thoughts. The reader can guess that the damage done to him when he had to cut down his hanged father led to his later restlessness, but is also called on to empathise with the insecurity of the children forced to endure his scorn and indifference and the constant fear of abandonment.

The family tragedies are intimately bound up with political events. The mother apparently leaves for personal reasons – she cannot bear the poverty of village life or the drudgery of factory work, and her unlikely love match with Kálmán suddenly turns sour – yet, leaving in 1956, she joins a flood of refugees who, though they only intend to stay in the west for a short while, are unable to return. The name given to her in jest when she has to hand over her wedding ring to the trafficker who helps her leave, Kata Ringlos (Kata Ringless), signifies for the children the cruelty of her freedom which, because of the political situation, imprisons them. Just as the children feel abandoned, so the common feeling is that Hungary was abandoned to its fate by the west: 'someone had called the world, via the radio, but the world had refused, as though no one had heard, as though they had invented the radio but not for us' (*S*, 130). The backwater that Hungary represents, with its lakes and rivers, its timeless rituals and rural traditions, in which only the trains symbolise speed, communications and modernity, cannot compete with the attraction of the west, which lures first Kata and then Jenö away. Two moments do create a link between Hungary and the outside world, but only with the Warsaw Pact countries. The first comes when Kálmán and his cousin Zsófi are in Budapest when the news of Stalin's death is announced. The passage is worth quoting in full as an example of Bánk's elegiac, flowing style:

Everyone stood and was silent, not just here, but in the whole country, even in the countries roundabout, in the north, east and south, in factories, on streets, in the town, in the country, and then they had stood silently, Zsófi and Kálmán, like all the others. Something had finished, a life was over and with it a time, a calendar, and Zsófi and our father had felt something that was like sadness, that had almost been sadness, and only later, years later, when they knew more, when everyone knew more, had they felt ashamed that they had been able to feel such a thing. (*S*, 252)

The second comes right at the end of the novel when the news of Jan Palach's self-immolation after the Prague Spring reaches the population of Hungary. The generations react differently: cousin Ági finds it absurd that someone should do such a thing, but her daughter, Virág, and her friend, Mihály, believe it.

PRACTISING PEACE AMID WAR

The Slovak writer Irena Brežná's powerful essays in the volumes *Falsche Mythen* (False Myths, 1999) and *Die Sammlerin der Seelen* (The Collector of Souls, 2003) contain reportage from many areas of Europe, a region to which, she resolutely insists, Russia also belongs, since the fall of communism. Brežná, who describes herself as a bridge builder,[12] catalogues in particular the effects of recent violence in such places as Chechnya and Kosovo. Here, nationalist conflict has produced damaged souls and restless, rootless individuals of the type also found in Terézia Mora's *Alle Tage*. Mora's much feted, ambitious and extraordinary novel is set probably in Germany in the 1990s, although the geographical coordinates and local colour which Brežná is so attentive to are deliberately omitted. Indeed, the novel highlights its playful fictionality, opening with the words 'Let's call the time *now*, the place *here*.'[13] Its uncanny protagonist is apparently from former Yugoslavia, though the country is not named. Traumatised by the loss of his father, who walked out on the family when he was twelve, by the loss of his childhood friend and object of his unrequited love, Ilia, and by the loss of his country, which has imploded bloodily since he left, he lives an aimless existence in the west. Even after things settle down he cannot return, because he fled military service. He also has an unusual gift: after an accident he wakes with an amazing ability to absorb languages, so he learns ten and thereafter earns his living as a translator and teacher. He enters into a sham marriage, travels, encounters a huge cast of itinerant, dispossessed characters – drug dealers, refugees, musicians, street children – then, after a final act of violence, recovers his normality.

From the outside, Abel Nema is an enigma. His name is suggestive of his role as perpetual stranger: 'Nema' means mute, from the Slavic 'Nemec', but also German, or barbarian (*AT*, 14), while Abel, a Hebrew name, means breath or emptiness. Abel Nema's persona is paradoxical: hailed as a genius for his ability to speak ten languages like a native, he has nothing of his own to say; he cannot communicate, never asks questions and has no accent in any language. He looks like Christ without a beard (the Christ analogy is further underlined by the fact that he spends three days unconscious after his mind-altering accident, and is thirty-three years old in the narrative present) – or Rasputin. He barely needs sleep, has no sense of taste, drinks, but cannot get drunk. He appears both young and old, tragic and ridiculous. His birthday falls on 29 February, allowing him to joke that he is six and a half years old (*AT*, 198). People of both sexes feel drawn to him: on the road they notice him and want to tell him their stories, yet he has no interest in anyone else. His friend Kinga calls him a 'Fata Morgana' after the fairy enchantress who can change shape. His sexuality appears equally ambiguous. Most puzzling is his relationship with Mercedes, the wife who loves him despite their marriage being a sham.

The highly unstable narrative perspective, shifting between first and third person sometimes within the same sentence, further undermines the stability of the reading experience. One whole chapter is consistently narrated from Nema's perspective, but here he is in a drug-induced delirium. In this chapter he explores the causes of his hurt, imagines confronting his father and returning home and, finally, recounts the facts of his beloved Ilia's death. At the height of the delirium he undergoes a trial where he pleads his innocence of all charges until his humanity is challenged with the questions, 'Were you clever? Were you just? Were you courageous? Did you show moderation?', to which he can only reply in the negative (*AT*, 392). He also speaks here about his gift, which is also a burden. He reveals that he can understand not just ten but, like God, all languages, and that, unlike his father and friend Ilia, he had no ambition to travel, wanting nothing more than to live his life as 'a secretly gay teacher in the provinces' (*AT*, 402). His childhood questions about God and the cosmos have been replaced by an existence in which he lives 'like an amoeba' (*AT*, 403), sometimes – continuing the Christ analogy – filled with love and devotion, sometimes with disgust (*AT*, 405–6). He was able to practise peace every day in his new fatherland, but only at the cost of denying his past and diverting all his energy into shame, 'humiliating, despairing shame. That I come from where I come from. That what happened happened' (*AT*, 406).

To Verena Auffermann, reviewing the novel for *Die Zeit*, Abel Nema is reminiscent of the haunting figure of Bartleby in Herman Melville's *Bartleby, the Scrivener* (1853), an office drone, productive and servile, supporting the American economy which exploits workers, but one who begins to reject the system and becomes a threat.[14] Melville offers a social critique of nineteenth-century capitalism; Mora, by contrast, tests how far the roots binding late twentieth-century people to traditional ways of belonging have been cut. She also measures the depth of the damage thereby inflicted but also celebrates the new freedoms thus conferred. Abel Nema's description of his everyday peace and the shame it is built on reminds the reader that Mora's title is borrowed from Ingeborg Bachmann's eponymous poem in which war 'is no longer declared, but continued', and 'the extraordinary has become commonplace'.[15] Abel Nema is profoundly affected by war and exists in an extraordinary, though increasingly typical state: without the need for possessions, papers, keys, language, other people, a sense of sexual identity, emotion, language, or maturity, in other words, the things taken for granted in the past. In successive, farcical scenes – where he, for example, successfully plays the perfect husband and father for the benefit of the officials who come to check up on the validity of his marriage – he also makes a mockery of the institutions on which all but the dispossessed still depend: the family, the law, education, medicine.

CONCLUSION

The settings of three of the four main novels considered here are precisely evoked in terms of place and time: *Verklärte Nacht* is the most specific, being set in Prague in 1992, while *Herztier* evokes several locations in

Romania in the 1980s, and *Der Schwimmer* does the same in Hungary in the late 1950s and 1960s. *Alle Tage* is set in the very recent past, after the ethnic conflicts arising from the dissolution of Yugoslavia, and differs from the other texts in that it invokes no single country, but the 'good old Babylon' (*AT*, 5) that is Europe. National borders have ceased to be important for Abel Nema since war has made a return home impossible; what matters instead is language. The texts could be said to belong in a certain sense within the national literatures of the Czech Republic, Romania and Hungary respectively, except for the fact that they are written in German by writers resident in Germany; they thus also assert a place within the rapidly expanding field of German literature. These novels have some features in common with east German literature, not least the tasks of evaluating the lasting legacy of communism, cataloguing a rapidly disappearing world without sentimentalising it, and critiquing the rapidity of change since the *Wende*. In common with Turkish-German literature they also challenge what it is to be German.

The aesthetic strategies employed in the four texts are very different. Moníková adopts dissonance and difference in order to explore the rapidity of historical change and the inherent hybridity of culture, even national culture; Müller uses the openness of the surreal in order to bear witness to inexpressible suffering and terror; Bánk's flowing prose attempts almost the reverse, seeking to soothe pain through beauty and to shore up the tragedy which always threatens to break through and inevitably does in the end. Finally, Mora's chaotic, allusive, labyrinthine text reflects the unboundedness, fun and tragedy of late twentieth-century life. The German writing discussed in this chapter above all reminds the reader that the Berlin Republic cannot be divorced from the history of Germany within Europe, particularly its relations with its eastern neighbours. These novels bear witness to the turbulence, trauma and migrations which characterised the twentieth century and testify to the fact that Europe is a continent in which borders shift and empires come and go, leaving their traces in the psyches of the peoples.

NOTES

1. Further details of the reverse migration can be found in the appropriately named *Coming Home to Germany? The Integration of Ethnic Germans from Central and Eastern Europe in the Federal Republic*, edited by David Rock and Stefan Wolff (New York and Oxford: Berghahn, 2002). See also Stefan Wolff, ed., *German Minorities in Europe: Ethnic Identity and Cultural Belonging* (New York and Oxford: Berghahn, 2000).

2. For a study of gender in German women's writing from eastern Europe, including two of the authors treated in this chapter, see Lyn Marven, *Body and Narrative in Contemporary Literatures in German: Herta Müller, Libuše Moníková and Kerstin Hensel* (Oxford: Clarendon Press, 2005).

3. See Philip Longworth, *The Making of Eastern Europe* (Basingstoke: Macmillan, 1992), 1–9.

4. Libuše Moníková, *Verklärte Nacht* (Munich: Hanser, 1996). Hereafter *VN*.

5. For a fuller analysis of Moníková's treatment of history, see Brigid Haines, '"Barren Territory for Grand Narratives"? Czech History in the Works of Libuše Moníková' in Brigid Haines and Lyn Marven, eds., *Libuše Moníková in Memoriam* (Amsterdam: Rodopi, 2005), 179–200.

6. Aglaja Veteranyi, *Warum das Kind in der Polenta kocht* (Munich: dtv, 2001). Hereafter *WKP*.

7. George Steiner identified Müller's technique as in part surrealist in 'You're ruled by hooligans. Your friends spy on you. Hellish, isn't it? Review of *The Land of Green Plums*', *The Observer*, 30 August 1998.

8. Brigid Haines and Margaret Littler, 'Gespräch mit Herta Müller' in Brigid Haines, ed., *Herta Müller* (Cardiff: Cardiff University Press, 1998), 14–24, p. 19.

9. Quotations from *Herztier* are taken from the prize-winning translation by Michael Hofmann, *The Land of Green Plums* (London: Granta, 1996); page numbers refer to the German text. Herta Müller, *Herztier* (Reinbek bei Hamburg: Rowohlt, 1994), 21. Hereafter *Ht*.

10. Valentina Glajar, *The German Legacy in East Central Europe as Recorded in Recent German-Language Literature* (Columbia: Camden House, 2004), 133–4.

11. Zsuzsa Bánk, *Der Schwimmer* (Frankfurt: Fischer, 2004), 278. Hereafter *S*.

12. See Brežná's personal website, http://www.brezna.ch/ (accessed 18 December 2006).

13. Terézia Mora, *Alle Tage* (Munich: Luchterhand, 2004), 9. Hereafter *AT*.

14. Verena Auffermann, *Die Zeit*, 2 September 2004.

15. Ingeborg Bachmann, 'Alle Tage' in Christine Koschel, Inge von Weidenbaum and Clemens Münster, eds., *Ingeborg Bachmann: Werke*, 2nd edn (Munich and Zurich: Piper, 1982), vol. 1, 46.

CHAPTER 14

Writing by Germany's Jewish minority

Erin McGlothlin

Since the late 1980s, and especially continuing after German unification in 1990, there has been a veritable renaissance in German-Jewish literature by writers born after the Holocaust.[1] This flowering of literature by Jews who either live in Germany or write in German has prompted some critics to posit the question as to whether one can view these developments as the resurrection of the old dream of a 'German–Jewish symbiosis'. The notion of a symbiosis, which dominated discourse on Germans and Jews in the first half of the twentieth century, holds that the interaction betweens Jews and the greater German society in which they lived might result in mutual improvement: German culture might be enriched by its Jewish minority, while Jews in Germany might participate fully in German society and at the same time express their Jewish identity. After the Holocaust, Jewish intellectuals took a hard look at this old dream and declared it to be largely mythical; Gershom Scholem claimed that the notion of a symbiosis was a self-deceptive monologue among Jews never attended to by a German audience, while Dan Diner characterised the post-war relations between Germans and Jews as a 'negative symbiosis' in which the two groups were joined together in 'a kind of communality of opposites'.[2] But the new wave of German-Jewish writing that emerged in the 1980s and 1990s, led by writers such as Barbara Honigmann, Esther Dischereit, Maxim Biller, Katja Behrens and Rafael Seligmann, seemed to indicate a sea change in the participation of Jews in German culture, giving rise to the hope for a reestablishment of a symbiotic connection and, with that, the normalisation of relations between Germans and Jews in the Berlin Republic.

Despite the emergence of a productive, versatile and sophisticated body of contemporary German-Jewish literature, however, two factors belie the reconstruction of a symbiosis. The first concerns the German reception of the literature (and Jewish culture in general), which is marked by contradiction. On the one hand, there has been a surge in interest in all things Jewish. Part of this interest is directed towards German-Jewish writing, especially narratives about the Holocaust such as Ruth Klüger's *weiter leben* (Still Alive, 1992) and Victor Klemperer's *Tagebücher* (Diaries, 1995), but a great deal of the enthusiasm concerns not the conventional products of classical or modern German-Jewish 'high' culture, but rather a more folk-oriented notion of Jewish culture imported from the pre-Holocaust communities of eastern Europe. This includes a growing fascination for Yiddish language, literature and theatre, and especially, an explosive passion for klezmer music.[3] In the case of the latter, the music is often performed and recorded by non-Jewish Germans, as many German Jews distance themselves from an artistic form that was not a part of the pre-Holocaust German-Jewish cultural canon. Jewish culture is thus, as Leslie Morris and Karen Remmler argue, 'exoticized, fetishized and commodified'[4] as popular nostalgia that has often very little to do with either German-Jewish history or contemporary Jewish life in Germany. On the other hand, the German public's fascination with Jewish culture, whether literary or folk, is not matched by a corresponding interest on the part of the German literary media or German scholars. To be sure, German-Jewish fiction has been written about extensively by Anglo-American Germanists, but their German counterparts, apart from those in Jewish Studies, have taken almost no notice of modern-day German-Jewish texts. Few studies produced in Germany of post-1990 German literature, whether scholarly or popular, mention either Jewish authors or the resurgence of diverse and productive German-Jewish narratives.[5] Although German-Jewish texts *are* being read in Germany, one can conclude from this near absence that they are not read as belonging to German literature.

A second factor that complicates any declaration of a renewed German–Jewish symbiosis comes from German-Jewish writers themselves, who throughout the 1980s and 1990s explicitly rejected the idea that their texts are evidence of a reconstructed German–Jewish dialogue. Rather, texts from this period reflect the problematics of Jewish identity in contemporary society and the impossibility of participating in the cultural sphere as both Germans and Jews. As Esther Dischereit writes in her essay 'Kein Ausgang aus diesem Judentum' (No Exit from this Jewry, 1998), the full and easy inclusion of Jews in German society is continually thwarted by narrow definitions of what it means to be German: 'For we seem to be able to be neither German Jews nor Jewish Germans; rather, we remain both simultaneously – alongside and against each other. Jews and Germans. Whether we regard ourselves as such or are so designated by the majority makes a definite difference. Thus German public life stands in need of a regular enlightenment about the fact that Jews were and are Germans.'[6] For

Dischereit, Jews in Germany do not experience the hyphenated identities common in multicultural societies, and thus they are unable to balance the competing claims of what society considers as two mutually exclusive qualities: the Jewish and the German. Either their Jewishness is invisible or downplayed by non-Jewish Germans as merely 'a sociopolitical theme' (*KA*, 18) or private religious confession, or it is hyper-emphasised and commodified as exotic by a public that, according to Liliane Weissberg, explores its own German identity 'via the study of an Other'.[7] Jews in contemporary Germany are caught between contradictory, competing claims, for they are accepted in German culture only provisionally and always as outsiders, a predicament Katja Behrens characterises as 'the rift, the gulf, the dichotomy, and not the symbiosis'.[8]

German-Jewish writing from the mid 1990s continues the inquiry of German-Jewish texts from the late 1980s and early 1990s in that it problematises the notion of a German–Jewish symbiosis, exposes the multiple contradictions inherent in the construction of Jewish life in contemporary Germany, and reflects on the impossibility of a literature that is both German and Jewish. At the same time, however, as I demonstrate with readings of three texts written by established German-Jewish writers, Barbara Honigmann's *Soharas Reise* (Zohara's Journey, 1996), Rafael Seligmann's *Der Milchmann* (The Milkman, 1999) and Maxim Biller's *Bernsteintage* (Amber Days, 2004), German-Jewish fiction of the last ten years has attempted to move beyond some of these contradictions and oppositions to find a way out of its 'either-or' dilemma. Significantly, this endeavour to work through the tensions is not a synthetic resolution, nor an ironing out of critical difference, nor the capitulation of a minority to the interests of a majority. Rather, it involves finding a way of existing within the tension between the two poles of the German and the Jewish. The writers of these narratives envision how things *might* be, not in an ideal, utopian world, but in their own world as Jews in Germany. Their texts comprise a blueprint for how German–Jewish relations might progress and for how Jews might realistically expect to become an integral part of German society. German-Jewish literature in the Berlin Republic does not seek to resurrect a supposed German–Jewish symbiosis, but it does gesture towards a normalisation of relations between Germans and Jews.

OVERVIEW OF GERMAN-JEWISH LITERATURE IN THE BERLIN REPUBLIC

Before moving on to specific texts, it is useful to outline some of the more pertinent aspects of present-day German-Jewish writing, especially as they relate to the contradictions and tensions mentioned above. One of the most obvious contradictions is the relationship between contemporary German-Jewish literature and the actual Jewish population in Germany. In the 1990s, Germany saw a precipitous increase in its Jewish population. Before unification, there were about 30,000 Jews in the Federal Republic; beginning in the mid 1990s, this number increased dramatically, when Germany accepted more than 190,000 immigrants it deemed to be Jewish from the former Soviet Union (many of these immigrants do not consider themselves Jewish, and many are not defined as such by the Central Council of Jews in Germany, which numbers those officially recognised as Jews at about 105,000).[9] The composition of the German-Jewish community was thus transformed drastically, yet German-Jewish fiction of this period does not reflect these changes. Except for Wladimir Kaminer, who came to Berlin shortly after the fall of the Berlin Wall and, with texts such as *Russendisko* (Russian Disco, 2000), is generally considered a Russian author who writes in German and not a German-Jewish writer, no writers have emerged from the new Jewish immigrant community and its situation has remained largely unevoked in recent German-Jewish fiction.

A critical feature of German-Jewish writing of the last ten years is its international character, which further contributes to a number of tensions and contradictions. German-Jewish literature is not only, or even primarily, tied to Germany, but, as Andreas Kilcher argues, maintains an 'extraterritorial relationship . . . on the edge or even outside Germany in an imaginary and symbolic space of a sublimated German culture'.[10] This perhaps accounts for some of the German critical unease with these works and a reluctance to include them in the German canon. Part of this international and extraterritorial quality comes from the writers themselves, who come from widely divergent backgrounds and have varying relationships to both Judaism and Jewish culture as well as to Germany and German society. Relatively few authors commonly considered German-Jewish were born in Germany; of the group discussed in this chapter, only Katja Behrens and Esther Dischereit were born in the Federal Republic, and only Barbara Honigmann, Chaim Noll and Matthias Hermann hail from the German Democratic Republic (all three left the GDR before the fall of the Berlin Wall). Many writers, such as Maxim Biller, Wladimir Kaminer, Rafael Seligmann, Ronnith Neumann, and Jeannette Lander, were not born in Germany, but migrated there as children or young adults from Czechoslovakia, the Soviet Union, Israel and the USA. German is not the native language of Biller, Kaminer and Lander, yet they choose to write and publish in German. Practically all of the German-Jewish writers who live in Germany have strong ties to other places, in particular Israel, the

USA and eastern Europe. Several prominent authors choose not to live in Germany at all, but they continue to write in German for a German audience. This group includes Barbara Honigmann, who lives in Strasbourg, Laura Waco, who emigrated to the USA, Lea Fleischmann and Chaim Noll, who live in Israel, and Gila Lustiger, who lives in Paris. In addition, the category 'German-Jewish literature' generally includes Jewish writers, such as Ruth Beckermann, Daniel Ganzfried, Peter Stephan Jungk, Eva Menasse, Robert Menasse, Anna Mitgutsch, Doron Rabinovici, Robert Schindel and Vladimir Vertlib, who live in Austria or Switzerland and write in German. However, although their prolific output (especially that of the Austrian Jews) is very important to the overall picture of Jewish writing in the German language, because of the limited focus of the present chapter on the Berlin Republic, it will suffice to merely mention them. Furthermore, there are authors who are generally not considered Jewish, such as Elfriede Jelinek and Monika Maron, but who have discovered their Jewish ancestry and explored it in their writing. Others from this group, such as Anna Mitgutsch, have converted to Judaism. And finally, Irene Dische, an American who lives in Berlin, is often seen as belonging to German-Jewish literary culture, despite the fact that she writes all of her manuscripts in English and then has them subsequently translated for the German book market.[11]

This very diverse group of writers participates in German-Jewish literary culture in a number of different ways. Many of them, including Biller, Behrens, Dischereit and Seligmann, take on the role of public intellectual, representing Jews in Germany in debates over Holocaust memory and multiculturalism. Of this group, Biller, Fleischmann and Seligmann, along with other German-Jewish non-literary writers such as Henryk Broder, produce journalistic writing as well, and, in such publications as *Die Zeit* and *Der Spiegel*, attempt to inform the German public of various concerns that relate to Germany's Jewish minority. Several writers have published essays or collections of essays on their relationships to Jewishness and Jewish identity, including Maxim Biller's *Deutschbuch* (German Book, 2001), Esther Dischereit's *Übungen, jüdisch zu sein* (Exercises in being Jewish, 1998) and *Mit Eichmann an der Börse* (With Eichmann on the Stock Market, 2001), and Robert Schindel's *Mein liebster Feind* (My Dearest Enemy, 2004). While most of the writers discussed here produce fictional texts, much of their writing, particularly that of Behrens, Biller, Dischereit, Honigmann, Kaminer, Lander, Lustiger, Seligmann and Waco, is autobiographical and semi-autobiographical as well; Barbara Honigmann creates a series of auto-biographical family portraits in *Damals, dann und danach* (At That Time,

Then and Afterwards, 1999) and *Ein Kapitel aus meinem Leben* (A Chapter from My Life, 2004); Gila Lustiger pieces together a family chronicle from facts, legends, memory and fantasy in *So sind wir* (That's the Way We Are, 2005); Jeannette Lander explores the different cultures in which she has lived as reflected in their various cuisines in *Überbleibsel: Eine kleine Erotik der Küche* (Leftovers: A Petite Erotics of Cuisine, 1995), and Laura Waco traces her childhood among Polish-Jewish Holocaust survivors in Munich in the 1950s and 1960s in *Von Zuhause wird nichts erzählt: Eine jüdische Geschichte aus Deutschland* (Don't Talk About Home: A Jewish Story from Germany, 1996). Finally, several writers of prose, including Esther Dischereit, Robert Schindel and Matthias Hermann, are also known for their lyric poetry.

Despite the diversity of contemporary German-Jewish writing, several common themes appear in many of the texts associated with this body of work. As one might expect, the Holocaust is a prominent, if often oblique, subject in many works, indicating a subtle shift in focus beginning in the mid 1990s. Whereas texts by Holocaust survivors such as Jurek Becker, Edgar Hilsenrath, Ruth Klüger and Fred Wander continued to be published in the first years after unification, by the latter part of the decade, first-hand literary testimonies of the Holocaust began to appear less frequently. Since the mid 1990s, German-Jewish literature about the Holocaust has been written largely from the mediated perspective of the second and third generations, which generally do not attempt to depict the experience of the Holocaust itself (notable exceptions include Gila Lustiger's *Die Bestandsaufnahme* (The Inventory, 1995) and Irene Dische's youth narrative *Zwischen zwei Scheiben Glück* (Between Two Seasons of Happiness, 1997), both of which are set in the Nazi era). Rather, they address how the Holocaust continues to shape the present for both Germans and Jews and explore but also question the notion of the Holocaust as foundational part of German-Jewish identity. Many of the narratives that concern the legacy of the Holocaust, particularly those by Maxim Biller and Rafael Seligmann, provoke both their Jewish and non-Jewish readership by transgressing against dominant conventions of representing and addressing the Holocaust past, especially the notion that, according to Morris and Remmler, 'stories by Jews about the Shoah should remain pious, respectful, and, above all, devoid of references to sex'.[12] With narratives such as Biller's collections of stories *Wenn ich einmal reich und tot bin* (Once I'm Rich and Dead, 1990), *Land der Väter und Verräter* (Land of the Fathers and Traitors, 1994) and *Moralische Geschichten* (Moral Stories, 2005) and Seligmann's novels *Der Musterjude* (The Model Jew, 1997) and *Der Milchmann*, these

writers puncture the sanctified aura that surrounds Holocaust discourse in
Germany by presenting satirical and shocking images of corrupt and self-
serving Holocaust survivors, weak and narcissistic children of survivors,
Jews and non-Jews who wish to divert some of the aura of Holocaust
victimhood to themselves, and a German mass culture that is obsessed
with stories of the Holocaust. Such narratives also share a related theme
common in contemporary German-Jewish literature, namely the presence
in German society of anti-Semitism and its almost equally problematic
flip side, philo-Semitism. In Biller's and Seligmann's texts (in particular,
Der Musterjude, which parodies contemporary German media and their
desire for a 'model Jew' who is allowed to speak 'truths' that Germans are
unable to express themselves), but also in the fictional and non-fictional
writings of Dischereit, Broder, and Behrens, the German fascination with
what Germans see as the exoticism of Jewish life, in both its negative and
positive manifestations, is shown to be one of the greatest hindrances to
the construction of Jewish identity in Germany and to the development of
a substantive and mutual German–Jewish discourse.

In addition to a concentration on the legacy of the Holocaust, contemporary German-Jewish writers explore issues of Jewish identity that have
little to do with the Holocaust. The place of religion in contemporary
German-Jewish life, for example, is a theme that occupies the writing of
Seligmann, Dischereit and Honigmann, the latter of whom attempts to
find a Jewish identity that transcends German definitions of Jewishness:
'When my first son was born, I wanted him not only to be of "Jewish
ancestry", but to be able to lead together with me a Jewish life. My decision
is often interpreted as a flight into orthodoxy. In reality, I was searching
for a minimum of Jewish identity in my life, for a natural development of
the year not according to the Christian calendar, but the Jewish calendar,
and a discussion about Jewishness beyond that of the perpetual discourse
of anti-Semitism. A minimum, I would also still say today, something that
suits me exactly for a life between worlds, but which for German standards
is already too much.'[13] (Other writers, such as Biller, insist on a definition of
Jewishness that does not rely on religious affiliation.) A related concern that
occupies not only Honigmann, but other German-Jewish women writers
as well, such as Lander, Dischereit and Behrens, is the issue of gender and
female identity in relation to both German society and Jewish theology and
tradition. Another theme, especially for writers who grew up in East Germany, such as Honigmann and Noll, concerns the problematic legacy of
the GDR's treatment of its Jewish citizens and the difficulty of determining
Jewish identity in a state that declared every sign of Jewishness 'Zionist' and

thus hostile to the socialist project. Works like Jeannette Lander's *Robert* (1998) take this inquiry further by examining the tensions between east and west in post-unification Germany.

A final aspect of contemporary German-Jewish fiction, related to the above discussion of the diversity of its writers, is the international focus of its texts. Whereas contemporary non-Jewish German literature concentrates primarily, if not exclusively, on German characters and settings, its Jewish counterpart expands its narrative perspective to include a number of other countries and cultures. This heterogeneity is not simply a result of twenty-first-century globalism, however; rather, it reflects the diasporic nature of post-Holocaust Jewish life and the decentred, extraterritorial character of German-Jewish culture. Just as most of the writers of this literature ground their identities not only in Germany, but in the other countries in which they have lived, their writing locates its initial focus in Germany, but establishes further spatial points in the Jewish cultures of Israel, North America and eastern Europe. Israel plays a large role in the writing of several of the authors mentioned in this chapter – not as a self-understood homeland, but as a place to which the writers maintain an ambivalent connection. In Biller's stories and his novel *Die Tochter* (The Daughter, 2000), Seligmann's *Schalom meine Liebe* (Shalom, My Love, 1998) and *Der Milchmann*, and Behrens's stories, the characters, whether German-Jewish or Israeli (or a combination of both), live out their lives between Germany and Israel. In Biller's novel, the Israeli protagonist is caught between his life in Israel, where he is traumatised by his violent past as a soldier in the invasion of Lebanon, and his existence in Germany, where he becomes the exotic Other. Seligmann's protagonists feel divided between Germany and Israel, even if they eventually realise that their home is in Germany, where they remain perpetual outsiders. Anna Mitgutsch's *Abschied von Jerusalem* (Farewell to Jerusalem, 1995) tells the tale of a young Austrian woman who goes to Jerusalem to find a Jewish identity. The USA, in particular New York, also plays a role in several contemporary German-Jewish narratives, including several of Biller's stories, Mitgutsch's *Haus der Kindheit* (House of Childhood, 2000) and Daniel Ganzfried's *Der Absender* (The Sender, 1995). America functions in here as both a concrete space of post-Holocaust Jewish culture (especially a literary culture) and the symbol of successful assimilation. As Todd Herzog argues, 'this fantasy America is a space of all possibilities, a place where one is not forced to choose a fixed identity'.[14] Finally, Maxim Biller's and Wladimir Kaminer's texts often look back to the eastern Europe they left behind. In some of Biller's stories, the protagonists vacillate between the memory of their childhood in Czechoslovakia, where they were unaware of their otherness as Jews, and their present existence in Germany. This narrative glance towards eastern Europe is not a nostalgic longing for traditional Ashkenazi culture, but rather indicates how twentieth-century history – not just the traumatic history of the Holocaust, but the upheavals in the eastern bloc as well – has displaced European Jewish culture in all its manifestations from its moorings.

As I outline above, the tensions and contradictions that attend Jewish life in Germany are reflected in and thematised by contemporary German-Jewish writing, which expresses evocatively the 'either-or' dilemma particular to the position of Jews in German culture. In the final sections of this chapter, I demonstrate how some German-Jewish writers have moved beyond the representation of this problem to posit possible ways of working through it.

JUST OVER THE BORDER

Issues of German and Jewish identity occupy much of the work of Barbara Honigmann, one of the most prolific of modern-day German-Jewish writers. Honigmann's connection to German culture is complicated; she writes that, although it is difficult for her to claim a German identity, she identifies with the German literary tradition in which she was raised: 'it sounds paradoxical, but I am a German writer, even though I don't feel like a German'.[15] Honigmann's complex relationship to Germany is intensified by her decision to live in France. With regard to German culture, Honigmann writes from a doubly displaced perspective – physically, from her position over the border looking towards Germany and writing in German, and culturally, as a Jew writing for a German audience.

Displacement is the theme of Honigmann's acclaimed 1997 novella, *Soharas Reise*. Sohara, a religious Sephardic Jew and the text's narrator, lives in Strasbourg in a Jewish community largely composed of Ashkenazim, but she was born in Algeria, where her family had lived for sixty generations. Her family's forced ejection at the end of the Algerian war for independence, when she was a young girl, constitutes the first of two significant ruptures in her life. The second trauma, the event that precipitates the action in the novella, is the kidnapping of her six children by her husband, an itinerant rabbi who claims to travel to collect charity for a yeshiva but who, as Sohara learns even before the kidnapping, is a con man. Sohara chronicles her experiences after the kidnapping, beginning with depression, isolation and alienation, which begin to abate when she reaches out to Frau Kahn, an assimilated German Jew who survived the Holocaust and has not returned to Germany in over fifty years, preferring to remain just over the border in Strasbourg. In the end, with Frau Kahn's help and that of the larger Jewish community in which she lives, which organises an international 'Torah connection'[16] that goes into action to trap her husband, Sohara is able to recover her children.

As a text written by a German-Jewish writer for a German readership, *Soharas Reise* is anomalous in two ways. First, it presents Germany and German-Jewish history from Sohara's distanced perspective. For Sohara, the Holocaust, which is seen by the culture in which she lives as the defining aspect of Jewishness, is an event that has little significance in her own history and culture – as she says, it's 'just a story' (*SR*, 24) – and thus it remains irrelevant to her identity as a Jew. Honigmann informs her readers through Sohara that the Holocaust is not the primary narrative for all Jews and that Germany is not the ultimate reference point for Jewish self-understanding; rather, for Sohara and her fellow Algerian Jews, their expulsion from Algeria is the historical event that dominates their lives. Second, Honigmann's depiction of the vibrant culture in which Sohara lives contrasts sharply with the way in which Jews are often represented in Germany, which generally assigns them strictly memorial functions and often views them as signifiers for those who perished in the Holocaust. Moreover, the novella denies the idea of a monolithic Jewish culture by hinting at the broad spectrum of Jewish identity and religious practice. As William Collins Donahue argues, it provides a 'corrective to the jaundiced view many Germans may have of Jews': 'Contrary to what most Germans could observe firsthand, this novella depicts Jews as a richly diverse group of people, often divided, as we have seen in the novella's depiction of the Ashkenazim–Sephardim antagonism, by serious cultural and religious differences.'[17]

With Sohara's story, Honigmann sets aside the problems of the German–Jewish negative symbiosis for a moment to show her readers a world – in particular, a Jewish world – in which the Holocaust and the post-Holocaust problems between Germans and Jews are not paramount to Jewish self-understanding. By presenting a story that exists apart from this problematic, *Soharas Reise* thus argues against both a conception of Jewish identity that is essentially fixed to the Holocaust and a notion of German–Jewish relations that has them tied together eternally in a mutual impasse of guilt, blame and helplessness. Honigmann accomplishes this not by chronicling once again the failed symbiosis, but by bypassing this problem altogether. Her alternative, however remote from German-Jewish life, provides a model for conducting contemporary German–Jewish relations outside a fixed cycle of denial and despair.

LIVING IN HITLERLAND

Rafael Seligmann's novel *Rubinsteins Versteigerung* (Rubinstein's Auction, 1989) is generally considered to have ushered in the present period of contemporary German-Jewish fiction.[18] This text, as well as his subsequent novels, which include *Die jiddische Mamme* (The Yiddish Mama, 1990), *Der Musterjude* and *Schalom meine Liebe*, all take as their subject Jews in Germany. As previously noted, they violate taboos on the representation of Jews and challenge philo-Semitic stereotypes by presenting unsympathetic images of Jews, particularly Holocaust survivors. Seligmann's *Der Milchmann* continues the project of his previous works, but whereas the earlier texts object to German denial of the Holocaust and its Jewish minority, the later book responds to debates throughout the 1990s about the Holocaust and German culpability. Moreover, in contrast to the previous novels, whose protagonists are all the children of survivors, the main character is a Holocaust survivor, Jakob Weinberg, a Polish Jew who settled in Munich after the war. With this alteration in perspective, Seligmann attempts to accomplish something different. As Stuart Taberner points out, in *Der Milchmann* 'we begin to perceive a subtle but still important shift', suggesting that 'Jews can have faith in the new German "normality" – and finally feel at home'.[19]

The events in *Der Milchmann* take place in November 1995 during the week in which Yitzchak Rabin, the prime minister of Israel, was assassinated, and it is this event that provides the historical context for the private exchanges between Jakob and the other characters in the novel. Jakob is seen by the Munich Jewish community as a hero who gave precious milk to his fellow prisoners in Auschwitz, but we as readers are apprised of a scene in the prologue that contradicts the hero narrative and shows the ethically ambiguous actions he performed to stay alive. After the war, Jakob came to believe his own lie about being a hero, and his entire life in the present is built on this fiction.[20] Seligmann's text demonstrates the psychic cost of maintaining the public image of the Holocaust hero: Jakob is unable to connect with or have empathy for either his grown children or his fellow survivors, one of whom is going blind, yet he himself is a hypochondriac who obsesses about his health.

Focalised through Jakob's consciousness, the novel presents his contradictory responses to his residence in Germany, the people in his life, and his own troubled history. Jakob reveres Israel and is proud of the grandson who will soon be a soldier in the Israeli army, but for reasons he himself is unable to fathom, he prefers to stay in Germany: 'Most likely there isn't one, but rather sixty thousand answers. Sixty thousand Jews in Germany ask the same question every day: How can I live in Hitlerland? No one has an answer. No one forces us to remain here. In Israel they would greet us with open arms, and nevertheless we stick here.'[21] He sees the Germans around him as disguised Nazis – or the descendants of Nazis – and has contempt for them, but at the same time he is in love with a younger, non-Jewish German woman with whom he is very tender physically and verbally but to whom he refers in his mind as the 'Shickse', a derogatory Yiddish term for a non-Jewish woman. His two grown children also maintain genuine love relationships with non-Jewish Germans, yet all three reproach one another for what they see as shameful acts of tribal and filial betrayal. Each member of the Weinberg family, especially Jakob himself, expects the others to live up to an unattainable ideal and to remain apart from German society in a Jewish sphere that is uncontaminated, as it were, by the Germans around it, yet at the same time they all struggle individually with their own desire for self-determination and connection to the greater non-Jewish world in which they live.

By the end of the novel, all three Weinbergs realise that they have inadvertently made Germany their home: 'Jakob Weinberg, his family and friends had become German Jews without wanting to' (*DM*, 326). As Taberner notes, 'Seligmann's solution to the problem of German-Jewish identity – or at least the solution by his protagonists – may often appear simplistic.'[22] At the same time, however, the text provides no anagnorisis, happy ending or resolution to the conflicts between the characters. What emerges in the course of the novel is a sense that the problems between Germans and Jews are perhaps best worked out on the level of individual relationships and not through grand memorial projects or discursive gestures. In the German-Jewish future forecast by *Der Milchmann*, the Jews will remain Jews and the Germans will have trouble understanding how they fit into German society; yet even so, Seligmann suggests that the forward march of time will ultimately dissolve some of the differences between the descendants of the perpetrators and those of the victims.

A THIRD VIEW

After writing the novels *Die Tochter* and *Esra* (2003),[23] Maxim Biller returned to the genre of which he is a master, the short story, with his 2004 collection *Bernsteintage*. Here, Biller continues the project of his short fiction from the late 1980s and early 1990s with a penetrating scrutiny of post-Holocaust European Jewish life. However, with its subtle and introspective tone, this book differs greatly from the author's earlier work, much of which, such as his acclaimed story 'Harlem Holocaust' (1990), is provocative, aggressive and sardonic. Critics have responded with praise to this new view of Biller, remarking on his previously unrevealed 'butter-soft' side.[24]

In all of the stories of *Bernsteintage*, time and space are paramount. Biller reintroduces the spatial nexus points typical of his earlier work; in almost every story the protagonist's life is played out between Germany and the memory of either Israel or Czechoslovakia, a place from which the character is in exile, physically or emotionally. In each story the protagonist is preoccupied with a singular event in his past, usually connected with a traumatic period (the Holocaust, the Prague Spring, the first Intifada). The theme of memory connects the stories together; the narratives of the past, which the characters are compelled to review, are embedded in a present that seems to have very little to do with what happened before but which is eventually revealed to be inextricably yoked to the previous experience. In the first story, which bears the same title as the volume and chronicles the experiences of a small boy who spends the summer of 1968 in a Bohemian health spa just before the Soviet army marches into Czechoslovakia, Biller introduces the leitmotif for the book, the metaphor of an object contained in amber: 'His Czech childhood was as firmly contained in his memory as a tiny insect in a block of amber – he himself was the insect, but he was also the one who looked at it from the outside, and perhaps that distorted his gaze.'[25] The double perspective, by which the narrator's orientation alternates between the point of view of the protagonist of the present and that of the protagonist of the past, produces a story that inevitably changes both present and past, but at the same time allows for a third view that is neither fixated on repetitive retellings of the past nor severed from it in a forgetful present.

One story in particular, 'Elsbeth liebt Ernst' (Elsbeth loves Ernst), depicts the post-war relations between Germans and Jews from this new perspective. Based loosely on the relationship between the writers Günter Eich and Ilse Aichinger, the story presents the characters of Ernst and Elsbeth, a long-time married couple. Elsbeth is a German-Jewish writer known for her books about her experience as a half-Jew in wartime Vienna, while Ernst writes radio plays in the post-war period. Into their happy marriage history suddenly intrudes: an article appears in *Der Spiegel*, written by Ernst's best friend, that exposes Ernst's 'skeletons in the closet' (*B*, 23) – during the war, he wrote an anti-Semitic radio play. As the story opens, Ernst waits for his wife to return home from a day out, knowing that she must have learned about his past, since the story has been taken up by all the newspapers. He anticipates the worst: that she will leave him. But when Elsbeth arrives, the altercation both Ernst and the reader have come to expect does not take place. When the two finally discuss the past, their confrontation is vague and almost anticlimactic: she claims that she was his personal Anne Frank, he raises his voice and asks if he was her Hitler, and the fight is over. The expected break does not happen; at the end of the story, the two go to bed and continue their life together.

'Elsbeth liebt Ernst' differs from the conflict-ridden, almost grotesque relations between Germans and Jews in Biller's earlier work; in this story the Holocaust past suddenly appears and threatens to destroy the present, but the couple's thirty years together are strong enough to overcome this rupture. With this new ending, Biller does not propose that Jews should forget the Holocaust and absolve Germans of responsibility for it; rather he insists that the past will remain between them. However, the story suggests that, even though Jews and Germans are locked at times in a 'negative symbiosis' in which each group symbolises aspects of the past for the other – the one group plays Anne Frank to the other's Hitler – this does not preclude interaction, even love, between them, as the title of the story signifies. The answer lies not in the erasure of their differences, but in the acknowledgement of them, as recognised by Ernst: 'Yes, he noted the difference between her and himself, and he would have found it naive not to do so. How can two people be the same, two peoples, two races? Are two leaves the same? Two fingerprints? One has to learn not to interpret the difference to the disadvantage of the other. Not to her disadvantage, but also not to his' (*B*, 130).

CONCLUSION

Barbara Honigmann, Rafael Seligmann and Maxim Biller, all of whom have been integral for the establishment of German-Jewish literature since the 1980s and who have now entered into a mature phase of their work, have made in their fictional texts from the mid 1990s onwards tentative gestures towards a kind of rapprochement with German society. Their writings should not be interpreted as a move towards forgetting the Holocaust past or conforming to a German society that does not accept difference, nor do they posit a resolution to the problem of German–Jewish relations. Rather, these texts grapple with how individuals might work at reducing the inner and outer contradictions of German-Jewish identity and become a more integral part of German culture. This impulse towards normalising the position of Jews in German society (and, likewise, Jewish authors in German fiction) is far from a well-developed aesthetic programme; on the contrary, it is still in the visionary stage, as evidenced by the three texts analysed above, which can only hint at possible methods for realising an open dialogue between Germans and Jews. However, in these narratives one can clearly discern an attempt in the twenty-first century to move past the rigid conflicts and paralysing contradictions of the twentieth. Questions remain as to whether these attempts will be successful: will the German reading public take notice of these gestures and respond to them, and will German-Jewish literature finally be accepted into the popular and critical canon?

NOTES

1. For the purposes of this chapter, 'German-Jewish literature' is defined as texts written in German by writers who identify themselves as Jewish and often, though by no means necessarily, contain aspects of Jewishness and Jewish life. Such authors are referred to as 'German-Jewish writers', even if they were not born in Germany or do not consider themselves primarily German. For discussion of the term 'German-Jewish literature', see the introductions to Sander L. Gilman and Jack Zipes, eds., *Yale Companion to Jewish Writing and Thought in German Culture, 1096–1996* (New Haven: Yale University Press, 1997), xvii–xxxiv and Andreas B. Kilcher, ed., *Metzler Lexikon der deutsch-jüdischen Literatur* (Stuttgart: Verlag J. B. Metzler, 2000), v–xx.

2. Gershom Scholem, 'Wider den Mythos vom deutsch-jüdischen Gespräch' in *Judaica II* (Frankfurt: Suhrkamp, 1970), 7–11; Dan Diner, 'Negative Symbiose: Deutsche und Juden nach Auschwitz' in Dan Diner, ed., *Ist der Nationalismus Geschichte? Zu Historisierung und Historikerstreit* (Frankfurt: Fischer, 1987), 185–97, 185. For more recent discussion of the German–Jewish symbiosis, see Leslie Morris and Jack Zipes, eds., *Unlikely History: The Changing German–Jewish Symbiosis, 1945–2000* (New York: Palgrave, 2002) and Sander L. Gilman and Karen Remmler, eds., *Reemerging Jewish Culture in Germany: Life and Literature Since 1989* (New York: New York University Press, 1994).

3. See Thomas Groß, 'Der auserwählte Folk', *Die Zeit* 31 (24 July 2003).

4. Leslie Morris and Karen Remmler, introduction to *Contemporary Jewish Writing in Germany: An Anthology* (Lincoln, Nebraska: University of Nebraska Press, 2002), 1–31, 3.

5. See Volker Hage, *Propheten im eigenen Land: Auf der Suche nach der deutschen Literatur* (Munich: Deutscher Taschenbuch Verlag, 1999); Volker Wehedeking and Anne-Marie Corbin, *Deutschsprachige Erzählprosa seit 1990 im europäischen Kontext* (Trier: Wissenschaftlicher Verlag Trier, 2003); Clemens Kammler and Torsten Pflugmacher, eds., *Deutschsprachige Gegenwartsliteratur seit 1989: Zwischenbilanzen – Analysen – Vermittlungsperspektiven* (Heidelberg:

Synchron, 2004); Clemens Kammler, Jost Keller and Renhard Wilczek, eds., *Deutschsprachige Gegenwartsliteratur seit 1989: Gattungen– Themen – Autoren. Eine Auswahlbibliographie* (Heidelberg: Synchron, 2003); Hubert Winkel, *Gute Zeichen: Deutsche Literatur 1995–2005* (Cologne: Kiepenheuer & Witsch, 2005). Of the five works, only the two volumes edited by Kammler discuss texts by German-Jewish authors written after 1995. None of the volumes addresses the phenomenon of contemporary German-Jewish literature.

6. Esther Dischereit, 'Kein Ausgang aus diesem Judentum' in *Übungen, jüdisch zu sein* (Frankfurt: Suhrkamp, 1998), 16–35, 29–30. Hereafter *KA*.

7. Liliane Weissberg, 'Reflecting on the Past, Envisioning the Future: Perspectives for German-Jewish Studies', *GHI Bulletin* 35 (2004): 11–32, 13.

8. Katja Behrens, 'The Rift and Not the Symbiosis' in Leslie Morris and Jack Zipes, eds., *Unlikely History*, 31–45, 39.

9. See *Tatsachen über Deutschland*, (http://www.tatsachen-ueber-deutschland.de/.

10. Andreas Kilcher, 'Extraterritorialitäten: Zur kulturellen Selbstreflexion der aktuellen deutsch-jüdischen Literatur' in Sander L. Gilman and Hartmut Steinecke, eds., *Deutsch-jüdische Literatur der neunziger Jahre: Die Generation nach der Shoah* (Berlin: Erich Schmidt Verlag, 2002), 131–146, 137.

11. The online version of the *Kritisches Lexikon zur deutschsprachigen Gegenwartsliteratur* (www.klgonline.de) includes Dische in its lexicon of German-language writers.

12. Morris and Remmler, introduction to *Contemporary Jewish Writing in Germany*, 5.

13. Barbara Honigmann, *Damals, dann und danach* (Munich: Carl Hanser Verlag, 1999), 15.

14. Todd Herzog, '"New York is More Fun": Amerika in der zeitgenössischen deutsch-jüdischen Literatur: Die zeitgenössische deutsch-jüdische Literatur in Amerika' in Gilman and Steinecke, eds., *Deutsch-jüdische Literatur der neunziger Jahre*, 204–213, 205.

15. Honigmann, *Damals, dann und danach*, 17.

16. Barbara Honigmann, *Soharas Reise* (Berlin: Rowohlt, 1996), 96. Hereafter *SR*.

17. Williams Collins Donahue, 'The real "Tora Connection" in Barbara Honigmann's *Soharas Reise*' in Ursula E. Beitter, ed., *Literatur und Identität: Deutsch–deutsche Befindlichkeiten und die multikulturelle Gesellschaft* (New York: Peter Lang, 2000), 69–79, 78.

18. See Rita Bashaw, 'Comic Vision and "Negative Symbiosis" in Maxim Biller's *Harlem Holocaust* and Rafael Seligmann's *Der Musterjude*' in Leslie Morris and Jack Zipes, eds., *Unlikely History*, 263–76, 270. Despite Seligmann's significance for the reemergence of German-Jewish literature, his work has been mainly ignored by German scholars. The online *Kritisches Lexikon zur deutschsprachigen Gegenwartsliteratur*, which has entries on most of the other major German-Jewish writers discussed in this chapter, does not furnish an entry for him.

19. Stuart Taberner, *German Literature of the 1990s and Beyond* (Rochester: Camden House, 2005), 180, 181.

20. Jakob's confidence in his hero status contrasts with that of his literary Holocaust predecessor Jakob Heym in Jurek Becker's *Jakob der Lügner*, yet both Jakobs are thrust inadvertently into that role. The title of Seligmann's novel makes reference to a further unwitting hero of Jewish literature, Scholem Aleichem's classic character, Tevye the Milkman.

21. Rafael Seligmann, *Der Milchmann* (Munich: Deutscher Taschenbuch Verlag, 1999), 203. Hereafter *DM*.

22. Taberner, *German Literature of the 1990s and Beyond*, 182.

23. Shortly after publication, *Esra* was removed from the market and barred from being read aloud in public by the state court in Munich because characters in the novel were found to resemble Biller's ex-girlfriend and her mother too closely.

24. Andreas Isenschmid, 'Luzenbader Elegie: Ein fast neuer Maxim Biller' in *Die Zeit* 12 (11 February 2004).

25. Maxim Biller, *Bernsteintage* (Cologne: Kiepenheuer & Witsch, 2004), 24. Hereafter *B*.

Index